Margaret Fuller: Visionary of the New Age

DOUBLE TRIANGLE, SERPENT AND RAYS

Patient serpent, circle round,
Till in death thy life is found;
Double form of godly prime
Holding the whole thought of time,
When the perfect two embrace,
Male & female, black & white,
Soul is justified in space,
Dark made fruitful by the light;
And, centred in the diamond Sun,
Time & Eternity are one.

Margaret Fuller:
Visionary of the New Age

Edited by Marie Mitchell Olesen Urbanski

Northern Lights • Orono, Maine •1994

Published by
Northern Lights
493 College Avenue
Orono, Maine 04473

ISBN 1-880811-14-6
Library of Congress Catalog Card Number: 93-087696

Contents

Margaret Fuller: Visionary of the New Age

R. Buckminster Fuller

Letter to Marie Urbanski

May 18, 1980

DEAR MARIE:

Your daughter writes me that she has already told you about my exultation over your magnificent treatment of Margaret and *Woman in the Nineteenth Century*.

I am sending you a set of items in view of your probable second printing or even a second edition. I would like to see some of this highly relevant and supporting information included by you. I think you have done masterful work in successfully ridding Margaret of the false image of her that had been evolved by her contemporaries.

You must read the Emerson-Carlyle letter with the same care that you have applied to your other research work. You will note the change in the tone of words of Emerson-to-Carlyle prior to Margaret's meeting Carlyle, and those which follow. You will notice the change in viewpoint of Carlyle. Towards the end of the whole series, Carlyle's appreciation of Margaret is magnificent. Most importantly, you will note that Carlyle interrogates Emerson several times and gets no reply regarding the biographies written about her; one by Mazzini, one by Robert, and one by Elizabeth Browning. These were sent to America, apparently by ships that were not lost, for Carlyle and the three authors would have been aware of such a fact, and said so. That none of these three extraordinarily important and favorable biographies were ever acknowledged or published makes the behavior of her contemporaries in American (sic) even more shockingly suspect.

You will notice that Charles Eliot Norton found only one letter to be missing in the two-way series of exchanges between Emerson and Carlyle—that being the one immediately following her first meeting with Carlyle. The latter refers to his very favorable impression of her in his following letters. Apparently Emerson destroyed that letter as he deliberately destroyed other items which did not agree with the "image" he was building of Margaret. I do not put it beyond Emerson to have invented in its stead the story about Margaret's "I accept the Universe" and Carlyle's retort, "Egad, she'd better." In view of Carlyle's own written remarks about and to her, I doubt you found any supporting evidence for that "Perry Miller emphasized" anecdote. I doubt its having been said by Carlyle. I suspect it was invented by Emerson.

The successive discoveries of Copernicus, Kepler and Galileo made possible Newton's discovery of the only mathematically expressible interattraction existing between any two celestial bodies, which varies inversely as the second power of the arithmetical distances intervening. Sumtotally, these four scientists had discovered several constant interrelationships existing between parts of a system not discoverable by the separate consideration of any one part of the system. Such a phenomenon is called synergy.

Nothing in the behavior of an atom, considered only by itself, predicts atoms compounding to form a molecule. Nothing in a molecule per se predicts biological protoplasm. Nothing in proto-plasm per se predicts camels and palm trees, as well as both of their lives being dependent upon the respiratory gas discharges of one serving as the other's sustaining respiratory gas and vice-versa.

It is evident that the whole Universe operates only synergetically in its only non-simultaneously occurring, overlapping complexity of omnieverywhere and everywhen non-simultaneous intertransform-ings. Considered only altogether do these non-simultaneous intertransformings manifest the eternal regenerativity of Universe. The 100% efficiency of the cosmic system is manifest only by the totality of the energy involved, which never increases or decreases.

Our whole educational system operates in reverse of synergetic persuasion. We take the innately curious child, comprehending only synergetically and asking its parents questions about logical interrela-tionships of both macro and micro phenomena, and getting the answer, "Wait until you get to school, dear." At school they say, "Never mind what you think, pay attention! We are trying to teach you. Never mind the Universe. We are going to give you an A, a B and a C. When you can handle that, we will get to D, E, and F. If you acquire enough A's, B's and C's, and 1's, 2's and 3's, you may sometime come to the 'Universe' and may find your own answers about it."

We block cosmic understanding. We fractionate the child's Uni-verse into what we call "elementary" education, which deals only in separate parts.

This fractionation came about thousands of years ago when the greatest muscle-and-cunning constituted the power structure. The power structure's grand strategy was "divide to conquer and keep conquered the education of the "intellectuals" into ever more finely angled compartments, occupied by ever more sharply specialized "bright ones." Today, the power structure says to the specialist, "Don't fool around with that undignified applied science. Stick to your pure science—I may give you a Nobel Prize. You *lay* the eggs. I will decide what to do with them."

The foregoing being the world's operating system explains why the intellectuals laughed at the idea of Margaret's always employing the Universe as the starting point of her thinking and coping.

The many quotations appreciative of Margaret made by Carlyle will greatly enhance your book.

You may use this whole letter if you wish in your new edition. You may also wish to use the two additional informations presented by Deiss in the two items I am sending you which were published after his "Roman Years". These latter items completely verify her marriage.

I have another important piece of information for you regarding the Ossoli family. On several occasions, I have visited the island of Rhodes, where there still exists in fine condition, as restored by Mussolini-era Italians, the hospital of the Crusaders which, built in the 13th century was, and as yet is, a vast and luxurious stone castle. Many, if not most, of the Crusaders had grown too old and weary to return to their native lands. These committed and pooled their campaigning resources to provide and protect them for the balance of their lives. All of them had vast home-land properties and as yet operative home-land organized political and military power to operate and protect their respective home properties throughout Europe. They still held high prerogative over European affairs. As a consequence, all the great nations of Europe sent ambassadors to them. Running alongside one long side of the castle is a street called "Street of the Embassies." Here all the ambassadors to the Crusaders lived. At the head of the street is the number one embassy of those times— that of Rome and the Pope. Its first ambassador was an Ossoli, as is declared by a carved announcement over the embassy's massive door. This takes the Ossoli family back to a 13th century role of highest distinction. I think you should mention that in your next edition.

I hope you will like the particular piece on prediction-made-by-Margaret that I extracted from my book, *Ideas and Integrities*. It was from this piece that I took the quote I used in my official comment about your book—for use on its dust cover.

I hope you will like the piece written by Guerin, of Southwestern Methodist University, which finds a similarity between Margaret's and my own viewpoints, and their written expositions.

Because my father was the first merchant in seven generations of Fullers, the others having been ministers and lawyers, there was much talk in my boyhood about current events and little about Margaret. All I knew was that I had a great aunt named "Margaret" of whom a few people spoke as being famous.

My father died when I was young. My mother and my school teachers said "Never mind what you think, listen, we are trying to teach you." The older people misassumed that the cerebral faculties of the young were utterly unreliable and, like unjelled Jello or clay, had to be preferentially "formed". I knew that my mother loved me very much and that my teachers liked me. Because my thoughts often differed regarding the significance of that which I was experiencing and that which I was being taught, I had to assume that my own "different" thinking was freakish and that I would have to learn to live with that freak. I did everything I could to learn *not* to pay attention to my own thinking.

My rich uncle said, "If your father had lived, he would have told you that our Planet Earth has nowhere nearly enough of the essentials of life support to take care of the world's population. That is why there are so many poor people in evidence. If you want to be economically and socially successful, you are going to have to get over your sensitivity. You are going to have to get wisely and farsightedly tough and selfish—if you want to look after your family."

Because my uncle was telling me this in terms of his declared affection for my father, I assumed that he must know what he was talking about. My uncle himself was rich. I didn't like it when he told me that if I were to look out effectively for my family, I would have to deprive many other families of the chance of not only prospering but of existing. Paying attention to my mother, my school teachers and my uncle, I did everything I could to get over my sensitivity—particularly my distaste for what I had been told.

I tried my best to learn the game of life as those who loved me were trying to teach me to play it. By the age of 32, I found I was not good at the game and never would be. It was counter to my heart's and mind's intuiting. When it came to the critical moment, I always said to myself, "Let the other fellow have it, I can get along somehow. I am healthier and more resourceful than he is."

I was an inherent business failure. In 1927, at the age of 32, I decided to do away with myself or to start doing my own thinking, and doing it only on behalf of everybody on our Planet and never for self, or for "my side." It was then that I unleashed an enormous stream of thought and started writing feverishly. I came to ponder the phenomenon "time" as a scientific entity. I found that Goethe had written regarding *time* per se. Searching the books by and about Goethe in the Chicago library, I came upon a book titled "Margaret Fuller and Goethe". It was written by a man called Braun who was the head of the German Philosophy Department at Harvard. It was there and then that I began to discover the real Margaret. I had inherited some of her books and the "Memoirs". I had never before thought to read them. I acquired and am still acquiring everything that I can find that is published about her. I was amazed to find that my thinking and writing frequently coincided with her ways of thinking and writing.

I am enclosing a copy of my frequently re-written "Lord's Prayer". this particular version of it is the way I read it when I was asked to take the pulpit of the Cathedral of St. John the Divine in New York a year ago, and it is also the way it was written when I read it in the Temple

Emmanu-El in New York six months ago, which I'm told is the largest Jewish house-of-worship in the world. It was enthusiastically received on both occasions.

You might try writing a magazine article embracing the powerful information that I am sending you as a sequel to your book, with the intent that you thereafter incorporate the information where appropriate in a second edition of your book.

I think that you might also print in a second edition of your book that, despite the very favorable statements by Poe about Margaret and her writing, his subsequent negative attitude towards her was engendered not by any change in his viewpoint regarding her intellect and writing capability but only because of his annoyance over her interference in one of his personal love affairs. This is mentioned only in a divided manner in your book. For those who knew that Poe had a latter-day antipathy towards Margaret but are unfamiliar with his affirmative intellectual assessment of her, it is necessary that you include and interrelate the total evidence.

As her now oldest living relative, I thank you with all my heart and mind for the beautiful work you have done, and I thank God for inspiring you to do so.

Faithfully,
Buckminster Fuller

Joan von Mehren

Figuring out Fuller

U PON RESETTLING in America in the late 60s after living in Rome, my longing to return there took the form of reading accounts of Americans who had chosen the expatriate life in Italy. Of all the people who had been "incurably bitten," as Henry James wrote, by the Roman wolf (1: 129), Margaret Fuller was the most problematic. By chance, the first Fuller biography I read was Emma Detti's *Margaret Fuller Ossoli e i Suoi Corrispondenti*; this led to Joseph Deiss's *The Roman Years of Margaret Fuller*, a narrative of interesting results, but it left unanswered many causes and beginnings. All the standard biographies, marvelous and rich as some of them are "in their leadings," as Fuller would say, still left too much unanswered. There was clearly more to the story, more than meets the eye.

The next step, as many others realized, was to no longer sidestep the problem of the desecrated sources, and to try to get the facts in order. By the late 70s and early 80s, as Fuller biography and scholarship began to burgeon into a minor industry, it became difficult to keep up, but by then I was haunting libraries in Warsaw, London, Rome, New York and Newark, New Jersey. Figuring out Fuller had become a compulsion.

In the 80s, I was targeting Fuller's political activism and socialism. What did socialism mean to an American intellectual elitist in the late 1840s? What did Elizabeth Barrett Browning mean when she called Fuller "one of the out and out Reds" when they first met in 1849? (Later, Browning came to admire Fuller for being "truthful, spiritual in her habitual mode of mind, . .not only exalted, but "exalted in her opinions . . . ." (3: 285,297). Throughout the 80s I was involved in a form of late twentieth-century feminist social activism and hoped to be able to pinpoint a Fuller conversion in 1845 New York City, but instead, I was forced to see that the distance between Novalis and Fourier was not a leap into my century at all.

Another challenge was to analyze the portraits Fuller's friends drew of her. Patriarchal prejudice, feminine loyalty, justified pique and praise, as well as chivalry, and decency to the dead continually confused the image. In the late 80s, partly to find out if I could make sense of her, I began to write a biography of Fuller. It is difficult to compress her paradoxes into a linear narrative form. In her search for ways to express what she called "the many turning Ulyssean culture" of America (Emerson, "Journals 11: 425), she herself experimented continually with conventional literary structures, as well as unconventional ways of dealing with her restless inner life. The word, experiment, was one of her favorites. She used it as we in this century use the word experience. She saw the American experience and the American experiment as one and the same, just as she saw her life as a continual chain of linked experiments, be it an enterprise like her Boston Conversations, a book like *Summer on the Lakes*, a relationship like her adoration of Anna Barker, her love affair with James Nathan, or her fascination with extrasensory perception. To follow through on Fuller becomes thus, in its way, another American experiment.

Joan von Mehren

Margaret Fuller: Woman Of Letters

WHEN A FRIEND of Margaret Fuller told her in 1832 that she was destined to become an author and, in spite of herself, "the founder of American literature" (Clarke 35), she replied that she was not exactly flattered. From what she knew about the "mental history" of women authors, writing was a vocation of mixed blessings. She felt divided about her future. "I have often told you that I had two souls, and they seem to roll over one another in the most incomprehensible way. Tastes and wishes point one way and I seem forced the other" (Margaret Fuller Papers [1832?]). This early response is an epigraph for her life story. As she grew older, the divisions multiplied and compounded. She became an expert at negotiating multiple positions.

Fuller judged that a national literature was a task for a later generation; yet she became a distinguished author—our first dark lady of letters, a strong-minded, mature, literary personality, who "with all her passionate sensibility"—as George Eliot described Fuller, would not have been satisfied "without intellectual production" (Eliot 201). She became a recognized literary figure in a career that was remarkably successful in accommodating her turbulent inner life.

When she first considered her vocation, Fuller thought of herself as an idealist, but one with a "bias towards the living and practical" (Margaret Fuller Papers [1832?]). Though ambitious for a wide experience of life, she was not yet ready to sacrifice the possibility of a conventional marriage and family, nor sure that serious authorship would not preclude the latter.

In her mid-twenties, soon after she began to write professionally, she further complicated her problem by vowing that she would write "like a man of the world of intellect and action" and not "like a woman, of love and hope and disappointment"; she would keep "behind the curtain" all that she knew about "human nature" (Works 3: 303). She understood that a price would have to be paid for this subterfuge. "One should be either private or public. I love best to be a woman; but womanhood is at present too straitly bound to give me scope. At hours, I live truly as a woman; at others, I should stifle; as, on the other hand, I should palsy, when I would play the artist." (Emerson, Channing, and Clarke 1: 297).

She labored under the constant strain of doubleness; like all romantics, she complained often that she could not find a home on earth. The effort to protect her inner self produced in others serious misunderstandings; to mask the vulnerabilities of her private self, she forged a public persona and public voice. Her severest critics, like Nathaniel Hawthorne, who called her "a humbug," thought she was insincere (Hawthorne 156). Even her admirers found that her writing, for all its erudition, variety, and power, was often forced and unnatural. Yet everyone marvelled at her extraordinary power of speech. Elizabeth Barrett Browning went so far as to say that all of her writings were inferior to her conversation (Browning 3: 309). Even Henry

Thoreau, whom his friend Emerson described as one who "will never like anything," conceded that she wrote her best when her writing read like "talking with pen in hand," (Emerson Letters 3: 183) and Emerson wondered why she bothered to write at all when she "spoke so well" (Manuscripts 17: 15). These faint praises from canonical figures of her time have until recently discouraged a considered evaluation of her thought and writing. She was vivacious, moody, and outspoken; she approached people with a frank intimacy and directness that was unusual in a woman of old New England stock. This led Bronson Alcott and Emerson to say that one would have thought that she had been born and bred in some foreign country with a southern climate and an unselfconscious and sensuous response to living, instead of austere, a village of 5,000 in 1810, her natal year.

But Fuller claimed nothing exotic in her background. In an autobiographical fragment she described her father as a "character, in its social aspect, of quite the common sort. A good son and brother, a kind neighbor, an active man of business . . . but one of a class, which surrounding conditions have made the majority among us." Her mother, Margarett Crane Fuller was, in her daughter's problematic reconstruction of her childhood, the revered, gentle mother of the "True Woman" era. She was "angelic" and "a creature not to be shaped into a merely useful instrument, but bound by one law with the blue sky, the dew, and the frolic birds" (Emerson, Channing, and Clarke 1: 12).

The only unusual feature of her upbringing, Margaret wrote, was the strenuous program of intellectual forcing that her father imposed on her from the age of three. In her adult years she vacillated as to whether the regime had been to her advantage, but she held Timothy Fuller, and not her mother, Margarett Crane Fuller, responsible for her inability to accept passively the conventional role of the unmarried elder sister in a New England family in the years before the Civil War.

Timothy Fuller, Jr. was a hard-working and ambitious lawyer and politician who served in the Massachusetts legislature and as representative in Washington for four terms (1817-25). He upheld austere standards of conduct and inflexible political principles in a style not unlike that of his father who had also been known for his uncompromising and somewhat eccentric rectitude. Early in 1776, the elder Timothy Fuller, a country parson, was dismissed from his parish for preaching against the revolutionary fervor; some nine years later, when his townsmen sent him to the Massachusetts convention convened to ratify the new federal constitution, he voted against ratification because the proposal recognized slavery.

At Harvard, Timothy Fuller, Jr., of the Class of 1801, became an enthusiastic Jeffersonian. He assumed that the future of the new country would follow the Jefferson model; despite his modest beginnings, his obvious virtues and intelligence would win him a favored place in the natural aristocracy that would make up the new elite. When he began his career, the Jefferson party in Massachusetts was just beginning to gain power. He rose with the tide. When he married at the age of thirty-one, he was a member of the state Senate and had a substantial law business.

But his forward-looking politics did not in any way mollify his role as an authoritarian father. Even his loyal wife was forced to admit that he brooked no disobedience. With the intention of giving Margaret, his first child, the benefit of the education that had won him distinction at college—he graduated second in his class and always insisted he would have been first if he had not participated in a student riot—he began early to inculcate the Roman virtues and the mental discipline of a classical education.

When Margaret was three, he began teaching her to read; and arithmetic was introduced a year later. By six, after a year of studying grammar, she began Latin. Soon she was expected to complete a daily Latin assignment and be ready to render the passage in perfectly phrased English at an evening session. Kept to a rigorous daily schedule of household tasks and studies, she was allowed little personal freedom. Her friendships, mostly with the daughters of relatives and family friends were as carefully regulated as her studies. Acts of rebellion set in at an early age; christened Sarah Margaret, she insisted on being called Margaret, her mother's name and one she thought closer to her self-image. Although the Fuller family was large and gregarious, Margaret, as an adult, constructed her early years along a romantic model—she pictured herself, rightly or wrongly, as an emotionally deprived and lonely child. Her strongest early memory was of the death of an infant sister, two years younger, who, if she had lived, would have provided the constant youthful companionship that Margaret thought her childhood so lacked. Her nearest sibling was her brother, Eugene, born when she was five. Thereafter, at two-year intervals, there were six more Fuller children; only one of them was a girl, Ellen, who was ten years Margaret's junior.

Ellen was named after a well-bred English woman, Ellen Kilshaw, who visited Cambridge for a few months when Margaret was seven. She befriended the Fuller family, made a special pet of Margaret, and kept up a correspondence with the Fullers for several years. When at thirty Margaret looked back on her childhood, she emphasized the impact that this seemingly refined English woman had on her youthful fantasies; she credited Kilshaw with sparking in her the fascination with Europe and the yearning to visit the Old World that later on became an obsession.

In Margaret's mind, Europe, unlike wild, untamed America, was the cradle of culture and a continent of cultivated landscapes that stimulated the imagination. To evoke her own fantasies, she made a refuge from family pressure in her mother's garden, a carefully tended, fenced-in half-acre beside the Fuller family house that stood in an undeveloped section of Cambridge overlooking a marshland. The latent power of gardens and flowers surfaces frequently in her writings. Gardens and flowers were firmly associated with her mother who was an avid gardener; for Margaret her mother's garden seemed an Eden where she could return to her earliest years when, except for the months that her infant sister lived, she was the only child, enjoying the undivided attention of her mother and of her father who showered her with his eagerness to teach her all he knew.

Margarett Crane Fuller, the daughter of a gunsmith, had taught in a country school for a few months before she married, but she made no pretense to learning. In the early years of her marriage, at her husband's behest, she was ambitious to continue her education; she made reading lists and worked at penmanship and arithmetic, but she was often ill during her pregnancies and soon found that child-rearing took up all of her time. Her family shrouded her in the anonymity required of a respectable woman in the nineteenth century; biographies usually portray her as a mere cypher in her elder daughter's life, but her many affectionate letters to her husband during the first years he was in Congress record her resourceful and sensible responses to daily demands as she raised a large young family through the New England winters while he served his country in Washington, D.C. Although she occasionally indulged in simpering airs and coaxings for bonnets and crinolines, her spontaneous accounts of the Fuller homelife, including sensitive comments on Margaret's development, reveal a hardworking, pious and liberal-minded woman, proud of her husband's distinction, ambitious for her family, and willing to make the necessary sacrifices. "[Y]ou are ambitious, & alas! so am I," she wrote him in an exchange of letters regretting their long absences from each other, "so we must take the consequences" (Manuscripts 6: 117).

When Timothy Fuller began to spend his winters in Washington, Margaret was seven; it was assumed that she would take on some of the responsibilities of an elder sister in a rapidly expanding family. This was the first generation of Fullers or Cranes who lived the middle-class model of family life with a house in town, the father working in an urban office, the mother in charge of the home and children, and most of the necessities of life purchased instead of provided by home industry. In Timothy Fuller's absence, his brothers held the family pursestrings, which provided one source of family tension. Another irritation was the frequent presence of various of Timothy's five sisters, at least two of whom were as officious and opinionated as their brothers. A hot-house atmosphere resulted in which Margaret was under constant critical surveillance.

When Margaret started her formal education at the age of ten, she had already begun the study of Greek. At the one-room Port School (Cambridgeport Grammar School) where she shared the classroom with ten-year-old Oliver Wendell Holmes and five-year-old Richard Dana, Jr., both of whom later became literary celebrities, she intimidated the other pupils with her sophisticated language and self-conscious mannerisms. Two years later she transferred to Boston's most outstanding school for young women, Mr. Park's School (the Boston Lyceum for Young Ladies); there she had a year and a half of solid training in modern languages, history, geography and some science. The school had been founded by a group of Brahmin Yankee fathers expressly for their daughters. In such a preserve of privilege, the social distinctions were too strong to disregard Margaret's country manners. She acquired good work habits, but was received coolly by most of her schoolmates.

At Miss Prescott's School in Groton where her father next sent her to learn proper deportment, she was surprised to find herself far happier. After a year there she returned home at the age of fifteen with a small collection of life-long friends, a firm attachment to the headmistress, Susan Prescott, and the material for a short story (probably autobiographical) which she wrote sixteen years later and incorporated into her book *Summer on the Lakes* (1843).

The story of "Mariana" recounts the spiritual crisis of a creative, strong-willed and moody young woman—notably of Creole parentage—whose unconventional behavior makes her an outcast at a restrictive country boarding school. Her revengeful attempts to gain power over her schoolmates through lies and behind-the-scenes maneuverings provoke a dramatic confrontation that results in the young woman's breakdown. Nursing her guilt until she grows feverish from a "terrible nervous affection," Mariana resists help until the understanding attentions of the school headmistress affect a cure: the penitent has learned the consequences of nonconformance to the cost of her developing artistic spirit (*Summer*, 90). No longer the angel of destruction, the chastened Mariana returns home and marries for love but unwisely; most of her husband's charms lie in her imagination. In the privacy of her home life, her passionate, powerful spirit revives and seeks response, but her husband and friends again find her too overpowering. Unable to find an outlet for her questing spirit, she succumbs to "the mind's disease" and dies (*Summer*, 98-9).

Although the themes of the Mariana fable—resentment and loneliness, guilt, and mental disorder resulting from the struggle of a passionate nature with society's norms—surface frequently in Fuller's adult attempts to reconstruct her childhood, these concerns did not seem to plague her unduly when she returned to Cambridge in 1825 and took up her life as the elder daughter of a prominent citizen. Even though source material for this period is sparse, it would seem that for the next few years, she was fired with optimistic enthusiasm about her future. She wrote Susan Prescott in Groton that she was "determined on distinction" and had settled on a daily schedule of study, exercise and social life designed to continue her optimum development (*Letters* 1: 152). When she was to attend a reception with her father in honor of the Marquis de Lafayette, who was making a tour of the United States on the fiftieth anniversary of the American Revolution, she entered wholeheartedly into the spirit of patriotic gratitude that surrounded the event and wrote the sixty-eight year-old general a letter of appreciation for his sacrifices on behalf of liberty.

His example had instilled in her "a noble ambition" and the hope that someday if "it is possible to a female, to whom the avenues of glory are seldom accessible," she would be able to meet him on more equal ground (*Letters* 1: 150).

In 1825 her father retired from Congress and returned to Massachusetts politics where he became Speaker of the House. He bought one of the finest homes in the area, the Dana Mansion. There the Fullers entertained President John Quincy Adams and Margaret gathered around her a lively group of young friends, many of whom were Harvard students. During the first few years in the Dana Mansion, Margaret was more contented than earlier; her father believed that he was now enjoying the fruits of his labors and the family reflected his complacency. Yet he had miscalculated the rapidity of change in the early republic. No sooner had he come home to rest on his laurels than the realignment of interests and ideas that resulted in the election of Jackson to the presidency in 1828 wrought similar changes in Massachusetts politics. He was left stranded between the new major parties, unable to call himself either a Whig or a Democrat. As his political power diminished, so did his legal business. His bitterness and the resulting decision to retire to the country, pulled the rug out from under the expectations that had been so carefully nurtured in Margaret from early childhood.

Beginning in the fall of 1829, Margaret suffered several major disappointments. In November, her infant brother, Edward Breck, with whose care she had been charged, died in her arms, leaving her devastated with grief and a sense of failure. At the same time, she realized that George Davis, a distant cousin in the Harvard class of 1829, who was her favorite figure in her social group, had begun to avoid her without explanation. His defection intensified in Margaret an already deep-seated sense of abandonment rooted in her early childhood; it resurfaced in her later life as a feeling of betrayal whenever she felt herself the object of neglect.

She took refuge in the companionship of one of Davis's close friends, James Freeman Clarke. Together they dedicated themselves to learning German. When Margaret fell warily in love with him, he adroitly resisted romance; they managed to preserve the friendship. Margaret continued to nurture intense relationships with women; at least two of these—with Anna Barker and Caroline Sturgis—included erotic episodes. By her late teens she accepted as a mark of her nature that in any relationship she would be the more intensely involved.

At this time, Eliza Rotch Farrar, an author of advice books and children's stories, as well as the wife of a Harvard professor of mathematics and astronomy, was impressed with Margaret. To Margaret's great advantage she took Margaret under her wing and helped her social adjustment.

By the time an embittered Timothy Fuller moved the family to the country town of Groton in the spring of 1833, Margaret had decided that she would have to make her future independently of her family. But, cast as the family governess until the younger children were educated, she saw no way out of her dilemma. During her free time she read widely, discovering a special affinity with Goethe whose writings responded to her emotional needs. As Margaret's sense of exile increased, she considered going to the west and teaching in a school. An opportunity to explore the possibilities in Cincinnati was offered, but she declined, feeling that her mother was too dependent on her. Her response was enthusiastic to an invitation to contribute to a new journal, *The Western Messenger*, to be published by several of her former Harvard friends who were now Unitarian ministers in various frontier towns.

Her father now kept her on a very short leash. When the Farrars invited her on a vacation trip to Trenton Falls, she had to promise to increase her family workload in order to extract from him the trip's expenses. When she returned, she fell seriously ill, possibly from typhoid fever. Her father, who had hardly ever praised her—he "abstained from praise as hurtful to his children"—at her bedside told her, "You have defects of course, as all mortals have, but I do not know that you have a single fault" (Manuscripts 3: 379). The wave of gratitude that overcame her at this moment hints at an important source of the romantic sense of loneliness and abandonment that she both nurtured and bewailed for most of her life.

Within a week of Margaret's recovery her father was dead of cholera; he left no will; his financial affairs were in a tangle, and his domineering brother Abraham was his executor. Timothy Fuller's death coincided with an invitation to Margaret from the Farrars to accompany them on a Grand Tour of Europe. They would be joined by Samuel Gray Ward, a young man with artistic tastes whom Margaret greatly favored, as well as the famous British feminist and social commentator, Harriet Martineau, who was returning after a year's tour of America. Martineau was impressed with Margaret and was urging her to write the first American biography of Goethe. Forced by financial considerations to forego the trip, Fuller was certain that she had been deprived of her last best chance to widen her experience, broaden her education, and make the contacts that would launch her into a more satisfying life.

Neither of the two older Fuller sons, now in their twenties, was in a position to assume family responsibilities, so Margaret took over more than her share. Since money was always short and every possible chance in life was to be provided to the younger children, Margaret's life was tailored to the fulfillment of this goal. Though bouts of bad health—frequent headaches and back trouble—plagued her for the rest of her life, she dedicated herself to hard work. With the recommendation of Ralph Waldo Emerson, who was impressed with her erudition and personality, she took up teaching as a career, but in no ordinary sense. Bronson Alcott hired her as his assistant in the Temple School in Boston, where his unorthodox philosophy of education and methods of teaching young children were becoming the center of controversy. Working with Alcott, Fuller was introduced to an extreme example of that combination of religious and philosophical questioning, social criticism, and attitudes of mind that became known as Transcendentalism. Distrustful of Alcott's methods and many of his ideas, but admiring his right-minded aims and his single-minded dedication, she persisted through the winter of 1837, making enough of a reputation as a teacher to be offered a post at a far higher salary at the Greene Street School in Providence, Rhode Island, where she taught from June 1847 through December 1838.

Recognized as a stimulating if sometimes intimidating teacher, and welcomed enthusiastically by the self-appointed "literati" of Providence, Fuller fell into a demanding schedule that inhibited progress with both her Goethe biography and a translation of *Eckermann's Conversations with Goethe* which she, on Emerson's recommendation, had promised to a publisher. Teaching courses in moral philosophy, literature, history, and languages to young women from middle-class families, she was shocked at their ignorance and poor training. In a paper presented to the Coliseum Club, a local literary group, she articulated for the first time her concern over the sorry condition of women in modern society. ". . . I might easily be tempted to write a volume on this subject . . .," she noted prophetically. It was the first indication in her writing of her emerging feminism (Hoffman 50).

During her year and a half in Providence, Fuller kept up her ties with her friends at home. For all her proclamations of self-reliance, she was inordinately dependent on her friendships. Her relationships to the people with whom she had the strongest bonds—both in the real world and in the ideal world of her inner life—made up such a large part of her identity and self-acceptance that any rebuff from one of them undermined her. During her vacations from teaching in Providence she cemented her friendship with Ralph Waldo Emerson; he invited her to join in meetings of the informal conversation group that came to be known as the "Transcendental Club." She chose him for her spiritual guide, and flattered him by calling him "Sanctissime" (Letters 1: 160). When the Fuller family was selling the Groton Farm, he tried to find them a suitable home in Concord. (They moved to Jamaica Plain on the outskirts of Boston instead.) Each of the Transcendentalists was drawn to the movement by different interests and concerns. Unitarian ministers made up the majority of the early members of the so-called Transcendental Club. German scholarship was challenging the divine origins of Christianity; the Transcendentalists questioned their church's stance on such thorny problems as the historicity of the miracles and on more general issues of how to make the church more responsive to the rapid changes going on in society. Most of them had a sense that a new era was approaching in which humanity would be challenged to realize its potential.

Frederick Henry Hedge, a Unitarian minister who had been educated in Germany, first suggested the idea of regular meetings—Hedge's Club was, indeed, the Transcendental Club's first name. He had read widely in German philosophy, and was a recognized interpreter of Kant, whose idealism, somewhat roughly understood, was central to the underpinnings of the theological and philosophical side of the transcendental movement. Emerson's *Nature* (1836) was one of the first books to announce "The Newness" to the public. Through his lectures and his essays Emerson became the movement's recognized leader in the public mind. Margaret's restless temperament had a natural affinity with the rebellious tone of the book, the fluidity of its ideas, its call for self-reliance, and the claim that an intuitional relation with the natural world can effect an identity with the Divine.

Emerson's doctrine of human perfectibility gave focus to Fuller's uncertainties and supported the program of religious self-culture that already animated her life. She had been brought up as a Unitarian when William Ellery Channing was the dominant voice in the liberal church. From early childhood she had been instructed in Channing's affirmation that Christianity had "but one purpose, the perfection of human nature, the elevation of men into nobler beings" (quoted. in Wolf 27). Indeed, her father's frequent injunctions relied on perfection as the goal of life. The European Romantics who particularly appealed to Fuller—Wordsworth, Shelley, Byron, Schiller, Novalis, and Boehme—reinforced the idea of dedicating herself to the "continual spiritual growth" of her soul (Robinson 84). But it was Goethe who inspired her to adopt the doctrine of self-culture conscientiously as her own. His ideal emphasized the importance of experiencing everything that life offered in order to reach human maturity; he stressed that to experience life in all its intensity one should live consciously and temper one's passions with reason so as to reach that harmony between thought and feeling which marks the complete human being. Goethe accepted that certain mystical forces were at work in the world—one's personal Daimon at the mercy of chance was one of his ideas that influenced Fuller—yet his aim was not unity with a mystical divine force, which figured in Fuller's credo; he aspired to a state of being in which one had learned how to overcome oneself. In the introduction to her translation of *Eckermann's Conversations with Goethe*, published in 1839, Fuller expressed her admiration for Goethe's profound understanding of human nature.

She was influenced by several versions of the self-culture ideal but all saw the process as continual and highly personal, as indeed it was to Fuller. Her later difficulties with Emerson may have been due in part to the nuances in their understanding of the process by which the divine core of identity in an individual was led—or called—out of itself to unite with the Divine will. Emerson's approach, expressed in his famous "transparent eyeball" metaphor, emphasized the position of the solitary thinker, "without intervention or mediation" single-mindedly awaiting the moment of confrontation with the Divine principle (Wolf 36).

Fuller described her first mystical experience in two different recollections. In the first account, emotion engendered by distress over failed personal relations triggered the experience, and she used sensual language to denote the supreme instant of insight. Twenty-one, and suffering from "deceived friendship, domestic discontent, and bootless love (Letters 1: 347)", she had been so distraught in church that she ran outside and kept running through the fields until the sun came out. At that moment, she felt herself "taken up into God"; she saw "there was no self; that selfishness was all folly, and the result of circumstance," and that if she could "live in the idea of the ALL," she would no longer suffer (Emerson, Channing, and Clarke 1: 139-42). In the second version Fuller presents the episode more in terms of a mystical experience's possible practical application. She claimed that the experience left her with a special "talismanic" power of influencing others. At the moment in which she "touched the secret of the universe," it was revealed to her that her miseries she thought resulted from fractured friendships were illusory—those friends were not meant to serve her future spiritual growth. Her insight revealed that the pains that accompanied active human involvement were essential to her growth (*Letters* 1:347); she proceeded in the assurance that her particular path to enlightenment would be well-worn with human interaction.

She relished belonging to the Transcendental circle, as well as being welcomed into a smaller group that was forming around Emerson in Concord at the time she returned from Providence. She introduced two highly-valued friends to the inner circle, Samuel Gray Ward, now a young banker with literary interests, and Anna Barker, a beautiful cousin of Eliza Rotch Farrar,—Fuller had erotic fantasies about both of them at times—and enjoyed a happy season of intellectual and social life in the midst of an entourage of her own creation. That idyll ended when Barker and Ward were married in the fall of 1840.

By then Margaret was involved in two enterprises that were lasting contributions to the Transcendental movement. From the fall of 1839 until the spring of 1842, she was the editor of the movement's journal, *The Dial,* and for five winter seasons, beginning in November 1839 until the spring of 1844, she led the Conversations, an innovative series of weekly classes initiated to encourage educated women to discuss aesthetic, philosophical, and moral subjects in a social setting. In both capacities she served transcendentalism as a versatile and powerful publicist. By the time Fuller stepped into these two roles, the cause was understood to be nothing less than to change the nation's soul. Margaret described her fellow Transcendentalists as "a small minority" who had become "aware that political freedom does not necessarily produce liberality of mind, nor freedom in church institutions—vital religion; and, seeing that these changes cannot be wrought from without inwards, they are trying to quicken the soul, that they may work from within outwards" (*Letters* 2: 108). The purpose was to change people, to encourage individuals to reexamine their values and purposes, to activate the moral life so that Americans would need, desire, and thus effect the changes in public life that would lead to a society sympathetic to a rich development of human potential.

When the need for a journal was recognized, but none of the male candidates—Emerson, Theodore Parker, and George Ripley— was prepared to undertake the task of editor, Fuller agreed to take the job. It is unlikely that there would have been a *Dial* without her. With the small field of possible contributors widely scattered, she had considerable difficulty, in attracting quality material, but she persisted and managed to put out eight issues before retiring exhausted and unpaid, eager for a change of pace but worried that Emerson, who took her place, would use the periodical to represent his own taste rather than follow her policy of letting "all kinds of people have freedom to say their say, for better, for worse" (*Letters* 3: 58).

Although the effort had been discouraging—the *Dial* never had more than five hundred subscribers and was in debt from the beginning—it gave a voice to Transcendental philosophy; the literary press in New England and New York City had to take notice, sometimes only to ridicule, but more often with increasing respect.

In her work as a tough-minded editor who often quarreled with Emerson over editorial decisions, Fuller laid the foundation for her own future career as a journalist and a literary critic. Beginning with her forceful "Essay on Critics," in the first issue, she demonstrated originality and command of a wide field of subject matter. Her essay on Goethe was admired until late in the century. In a number of experimental essays in the form of mystical contemplations, "The Magnolia of Lake Pontchartrain", "Klopstock and Meta," "Leila" and "Yuca Filamentosa," she gave expression to her personal search for a universal concept of womanhood that would include power, intelligence, and energy, qualities she felt in herself but which in the culture of the "True Woman" that dominated antebellum society were considered masculine. Her most famous *Dial* essay, "The Great Lawsuit: Man *versus* Men; Woman *versus* Women," was later revised and expanded to become her most famous work. Its value to the transcendental cause was to apply the doctrine in Emerson's *Nature* to the lives of American women in an effort to change their thinking and their lives.

Fuller pursued this aim on a practical level in her Conversations, a novel idea in woman's education that tapped the latent hunger of educated women for mental exercise at a time when society offered them only too few such opportunities. Using a format Alcott had developed, Fuller offered a forum in which women were encouraged to think systematically, express themselves precisely, and to choose "what pursuits are best suited to us in our time and state of society, and how we may make the best use of our means of building up the life of thought upon the life of action." Over a five-year period as many as two hundred women took advantage of her classes. Whether they discussed Greek mythology, poesy, the fine arts, women, or health, Fuller—interpreter and mediator—tried to provoke them into thinking, "What were we born to do? How shall we do it?" (Letters 2: 87). Fuller saw the series as an educational venture, but part of its success was due to the opportunity it offered for female bonding. It created a setting for exploring and interpreting women's interests, thought processes, attitudes and language; the one meeting that included male participants was deemed a failure (Ellison 239-256). This comradeship of the Conversations filled a personal need for Fuller at times when she needed reassurance. During the 1840-41 sessions she was experiencing a religious crisis that seems to have arisen when the group intimacy she had been enjoying with Anna Barker, Samuel Gray Ward, and Emerson was broken. That autumn the marriage of Barker and Ward followed abruptly an upsetting period of unresolved tension between Emerson and Fuller. For several months she withdrew into self-absorption and religious study, emerging with the assertion that she was conquering her overweening drive to "claim", as she put it, the souls of people for whom she had an attraction (*Letters* 2:160). And it did seem that thereafter she gradually became better at repressing social disappointments and redirecting her energies.

The responses and discontents of women to the changing conditions of American life was one of the themes she wove through her first original book, *Summer on the Lakes* (1844). Based on a trip she took to the west in the summer of 1843, it is a travel book with an original format. It contained a series of vignettes describing her observations of the western settlers, the disjointed quality of their lives, the shocking condition of the Indians, the plundering of the land, as well as some extraneous pieces. One of these, an explication of *The Seeress of Prevorst*, a book she had been reading at the time, reveals her continual interest in unusual psychic phenomena. In a dialogue between voices called 'Good Sense,' 'Old Church,' 'Self-Poise' (Emerson), and 'Free Hope' (Fuller), she clarifies her distance from Emerson. She was no longer in thrall to his influence. Thereafter, the relationship settled into one of mutual friendship with Emerson perhaps more needful, as their paths separated, of her stimulating company than she was of his (Urbanski, *Ambivalence*).

The originality of *Summer on the Lakes* drew the attention of Horace Greeley, the editor of the Whig newspaper, the *New-York Daily Tribune*. In the autumn of 1844 Fuller accepted his offer to join the *Tribune* staff as literary editor. Greeley also encouraged her to expand her *Dial* essay, "The Great Lawsuit." The publication of her controversial *Woman in the Nineteenth Century* in early 1845 established her as a literary presence in New York. The book's publication in England at the end of the year brought her to the notice of British writers and reformers. Even so, the work's importance as a synthesis of American social idealism, as a feminist statement introducing an original theory of feminine psychology and morality, and as a primary transcendentalist document was largely ignored for over a hundred years (Fuller's *Woman*).

A romantic dalliance with James Nathan, a German immigrant with literary ambitions, filled Fuller's personal life for several months after her arrival in New York. Although this episode is usually considered an aberration in Fuller's commitment to self-reliant feminism, her letters to Nathan (most of his to her are missing) indicate that she approached the experience—somewhat naively and foolishly—as an experiment in the Goethean "union of souls" model, seen in *Woman in the Nineteenth Century* as the basis for the highest relationship between the sexes.

From December 1844 until July 1846, Fuller wrote a newspaper column—usually bi-weekly and front-paged—on social, cultural and literary subjects. Often conflated into a general essay, the treatment was sometimes chatty and sometimes analytical. In her 1845 New Year's column, she created the role of national critic. Using rousing millennial language suggestive of evangelism, she measured the political and cultural scene against her standard of potential perfection. Her sense of national destiny was securely tied to democratic ideals. In *Woman in the Nineteenth Century*, she had written "[T]his country is as surely destined to elucidate a great moral law, as Europe was to promote the mental culture of Man" (15). Using the comparative method, she presented examples of literature from England, Germany, France, Italy and Spain, and measured American efforts against them. In 1846 a selection of her critical work was published in book form as *Papers on Literature and Art.* Her concluding article, a survey of the work of prominent American writers, won her a number of admirers such as Walt Whitman, as well as several influential enemies,—Edgar Allan Poe, James Russell Lowell, and Henry Wadsworth Longfellow among them—because of its sharp judgements and notable omissions.

She occasionally translated articles from the New York foreign language press. "Social Movements in Europe," taken from the *Deutsche Schnellpost*, introduces Socialism as "the great idea of the age;" the article's references to Karl Marx's *Holy Family* and its summary of Frederick Engel's *On the Situation of the Laboring Class of England* were among the earliest discussions of their theories in America (5 Aug. 1845, 1). Later, in a commentary on the newspaper of the German Social Reform Association in New York, Fuller announced that although she professed "to belong to the 'extreme left' of the army of progress", she recommended moderation in these European reform measures (17 Jan. 1846, 1). She adopted enthusiastically the genteel, progressive causes that Horace Greeley advocated in his Whig newspaper—abolitionism, opposition to the Mexican War, anti-slavery, anti-nativism, anti-capital punishment—and campaigned for interests of her own—programs to rehabilitate prostitutes, reforms in the treatment of prisoners and the mentally ill, and enforceable authors' contracts.

She occasionally put in a good word for Fourierism, the French socialist phalanx plan that Greeley supported. But there is no evidence that she had retreated substantially from the scepticism salting her idealism that she had expressed at the time George Ripley was recruiting for his Transcendentalist Utopian experiment, Brook Farm early in 1840. "Utopia it is impossible to build up," she wrote at the time:

> At least, my hopes for our race on this one planet are more limited than those of most of my friends. I accept the limitations of human nature, and believe a wise acknowledgment of them one of the best conditions of progress. Yet every noble scheme, every poetic mani- festation, prophesies to man his eventual destiny" (*Letters* 2: 109).

Through Greeley, the Unitarian minister William Henry Channing, who edited a series of short-lived Socialist publications, and Anne Lynch, a writer friend, Fuller met a prosperous young Quaker couple, Rebecca Buffum Spring and her husband, Marcus. They were anti-slavery activists and, along with Greeley, financial backers of Brook Farm and the North American Phalanx in Red Bank, New Jersey. Rebecca's family had a two-generation connec- tion with British social reformers. In 1846 she and her husband invited Fuller to accompany them to Europe. By offering to pay Fuller as a foreign correspondent, Greeley encouraged the plan. Aided by additional loans from family and friends, Fuller finally realized her long-cherished dream of visiting Europe; she departed for Liverpool at the end of July 1846.

Before leaving, Fuller wrote a farewell letter to the *Tribune's* readers announcing that her purpose in Europe was to cull ideas that would be useful if transplanted to the New World. Visiting Liverpool and Manchester soon after arrival, Fuller was introduced early to the urban squalor of Britain's industrial center. The Springs, whose philan- thropic concerns were based on Quaker and Unitarian social values, had contacts with many reform leaders. Moving through the Lake District, after an awkward reunion with Harriet Martineau and a satisfactory meeting with the elderly Wordsworth, Fuller and her party continued on to Scotland. There they conferred with philanthropic, business and church leaders and Fuller received the news that James Nathan, whom she had hoped to meet in Europe, was engaged.

She seemed to bear this disappointment stoically; a few days later she found herself further tested when, in the course of a late afternoon climb with Marcus Spring, she lost the way on Ben Lomond and had to spend the night alone, wet and cold. But, typical for Fuller, once she resigned herself to the "stern, stark reality" of her situation, she was responsive to "Ossianic visions" and the "sublime" aesthetic and sensuous pleasures of being centered in the natural world (*Sad Days* 75-77).

She recovered from her adventure in time to react with shock to the shiftless, forsaken poor on the streets of Glasgow. By the time she arrived in London she clearly saw that social conditions were serious enough to politicize poets and authors. Her reputation as an American author having preceded her, she was entertained in London by several writers active in reform movements, William Johnson Fox, Hugh Doherty, Garth Wilkinson, Thomas Cooper, William Thom, and Mary and William Howitt, editors of *The People's Journal*, as well as two women authors she had long admired, Joanna Baillie and Mary Berry.

None of these drew her interest as much as Thomas Carlyle whose early books and translations of German works had fired social rebellion among many of her friends in the late 1820s. Carlyle had already heard about Fuller's work on the *Dial* and about her forceful opinions from Emerson and Henry James, Sr. (The elder Henry James was responsible for launching the anecdote about Carlyle and Fuller in which James reported that Fuller had announced that she accepted the universe, and Carlyle replied, "Egad she'd better" (Ehrlich 473-475; Wm. James 41).

Carlyle's middle-aged cynicism disappointed Fuller. She attached herself instead to Jane Carlyle's friend and confidant, the exiled Italian revolutionary, Giuseppe Mazzini; he was living in London awaiting the propitious moment to return to his country. Before departing England for France, Fuller lectured at Mazzini's school for Italian immigrants, and agreed to be his emissary while in Italy. (A plan to help smuggle him onto the Continent fell through at the last moment.) For the next three years Fuller's sympathy with Mazzini's ambitions to establish an Italian republic focused her attention on the political unrest in Europe.

Fuller's stay in France coincided with the hard winter of 1846-47 when the failures of Louis Philippe's government were dramatically apparent. Along with a busy tourist program of museums, theatre, opera, the Chamber of Deputies, lectures at the Collège de France, and even a royal ball at the Tuileries, she accompanied the Springs on visits to several institutions for the disadvantaged whose programs Fuller recommended for use in America. At Mazzini's suggestion she was able to have her essay "American Literature" translated and published in the February 1847 issue of *La Revue indépendente*, a democratic republican journal in Paris. Her associations there led to meetings with Félicité-Robert Lamennais, the revered republican priest, and the poet Béranger whose witty verses satirized the monarchy of Louis Philippe. None of the French celebrities Fuller heard or met in Paris—Guizot, Berryer, Arago—measured up to these two republicans whom she hailed as the "true kings" of France (*Sad Days*, 111).

Before Fuller arrived in Europe she had thought that improvement in the social conditions there would follow in the wake of the collapse of monarchy and the establishment of democratic institutions. This assumption conformed to her belief that humanity was proceeding in steady steps toward a common Edenic goal. In France, where most of the leading republicans (including George Sand whom Fuller visited twice) took for granted that the establishment of a republican government would require radical social reorganization, Fuller began to view the socialist movement as part of the inevitable forward march of mankind. Recognizing that associative measures could have important practical applications in alleviating suffering as that march proceeded, Fuller now recommended Fourierism, despite its neglect of the individual soul, as an example of the kind of preventive measure that might assuage future social unrest in America.

The figure she met in France whose character and program were fully in tune with this heroic forward march was Adam Mickiewicz, the Polish national poet who was living in exile in Paris, while organizing an army of Polish exiles prepared to fight under a banner proclaiming universal human rights for all, including women, in any battle for national sovereignty. When Mickiewicz responded to Fuller's request for spiritual guidance, she formed a bond with him that was as important in influencing her personal life for the next three years as her connection with Mazzini was in giving direction to her public concerns.

Fuller's arrival in Italy was at a dramatic moment. In early April 1847, a rousing spirit of hope and renewal (the Risorgimento) was spreading through the populace; in Rome the new pope, Pius IX, Pope Nono, born of the people himself, had begun to signal by a series of decrees that the Vatican was ready to take some beginning steps toward a more representative government of the Papal States. Joining in the general euphoria, and eager to identify with the Italian spirit for which she had long believed she had an affinity, Fuller at first sublimated her role as critical observer, hailed the Pope and his program, and prophesized a new era for Italy and Europe.

During Easter week 1847 the ceremonies of the Church had an especially strong hold on her imagination. After hearing the Miserere in the Sistine Chapel on Holy Thursday, Fuller became separated from the Springs; a handsome young Italian offered to help her find her friends. He was the Marchese Giovanni Angelo Ossoli, the youngest son of a noble family of very small fortune. Out of this encounter a private romance developed quietly over the next two months even as Fuller aggressively pursued an intimacy with the young American student-artist, Thomas Hicks, whose early response of panic, she soon subdued. She and Hicks became devoted friends.

Though Fuller remained a loyal supporter of Mazzini, whose aim was a unified, secular, and republican Italy, she now made the friendship of the Marchesa Costanza Arconati Visconti, a prominent moderate who believed that Italy could only be united under a constitutional monarchy or a council of princes that provided some, as yet undecided, role for the Catholic Church. Though the differences in the two women's political views widened, during Fuller's European years their relationship continued to deepen.

The Springs' travel plans required Fuller to leave Rome after a two-month stay; she left with her mind set on finding a way to return. While the party was stopping in Florence, the news that freed her to do so arrived; her Uncle Abraham had died in Cambridge, leaving her a small inheritance.

She continued with the Springs through northern Italy—to Milan, where she met the Italian novelist Manzoni and conferred with Italian revolutionary activists, Anselmo Guerrieri Gonzaga and Pietro Maestri. In Bologna she hailed the city's honored Renaissance women, Properzia Di Rossi, Elizabeth Sirani and Lavinia Fontana, as well as Matilda Tambroni, professor of Greek. At Venice, instead of continuing on through Austria to Goethe's Germany, she separated from the Springs and returned to Rome where she settled into an apartment on the Corso.

She and Ossoli were now lovers. Without mentioning this connection, her letters home glowed with personal happiness and enthusiasm for the Italian cause. She wrote one friend that she expected to remain in Europe two years more. In November 1847

Ossoli, whose two older brothers were in the Papal service in positions that had become Ossoli family sinecures, risked disinheritance and family censure when he joined Rome's new Civic Guard. Clerical authorities had only recently conceded to the people of Rome the right to form this citizen army; its smart uniform and kepi cap denoted liberal democratic leanings. Earlier, Fuller had written Adam Mickiewicz about Ossoli; his replies admonished her for prudery and sensual restraint. "You have pleaded the liberty of woman in a masculine and frank style. Live and act, as you write," he wrote. "Emerson says rightly: *give all for love*, but this *love* must not be that of the shepherds of Florian nor that of schoolboys and German ladies. The relationships which suit you are those which develop and free your spirit, responding to the legitimate needs of your organism and leaving you free at all times"(Wellicz 105-6).

She quietly made a life for herself in Rome, continuing her friendship with Thomas Hicks and with other members of the American artist colony. In an effort to defend Mazzini against mounting criticism in the British press, she sent an article to *The People and Howitt's Journal* in London. She included a rousing sonnet "To a Daughter of Italy," celebrating the role of women in Italian legend and history and appealing to them to join the national movement for Italian unity (4 (Oct. 1847): 327).

Her dispatches to the *Tribune* now took on the crisp urgency of a compelling narrative. Italy's heroic struggle, she preached to her American readers, represented a spirit now sadly lacking at home—a fervent and heroic commitment to the advancement of humanity expressing itself in the hunger for democratic forms of government. Part of her New Year 1848 dispatch reads like a jeremiad with its indictment of Americans for betraying the values of the War of Independence. She scored her country's "boundless lust of gain," its toleration of "this horrible cancer of Slavery," and the Mexican War. As an antidote "against the evils that have grown out of the commercial system of the old world," she prophesied "that voluntary association for improvement of these particulars will be the grand means for my nation to grow and give a nobler harmony to the coming age" (*Sad Days* 165).

With the fall of Louis Philippe in France (February 1848), she quoted the spirited language of Alphonse de Lamartine, the French deputy who believed that a revolution of the working class was inevitable. Exhorting the people of America to understand "the real meaning of the words FRATERNITY, EQUALITY," she called on them to "learn to reverence, learn to guard the true aristocracy of a nation, the only really noble—the LABORING CLASSES" (*Sad Days* 211).

Her stance softened by May when she wrote to a friend at home that she had become an "Associationist"; that "the next form society will take . . . will be voluntary association in small communities" (*Letters* 5:71). Though Fuller was clearly sophisticated about class and understood that the numerous European socialist plans and theories had developed in response to a flawed commercial and social system, there is no solid evidence that her concept of socialism included a theory of radical economic and social transformation for Europe, let alone for America. She continued to use phrases such as "the march of Reform," that suggest that she never relinquished the basic tenets of her romantic and transcendental belief in a millennial historical purpose driven by moral law. In her role as interpreter and prophet, she sought to convey to her readers that social unrest as well as fervent nationalism underlay the turbulent upheavals of 1848 Europe; in the future march of history measures to satisfy both human desires would be required.

By January 1848 Fuller knew she was pregnant. Perhaps the socialism she advocated included the Fourierist view of the marriage bond; in all events whether there was a Fuller-Ossoli marriage ceremony, either legal or symbolic, remains unresolved. She struggled through the winter worrying about money, gathering material for a book on the Italian revolution, and observing carefully the events surrounding Piedmont's declaration of war against the Austrian occupiers, including the arrival of Mazzini and Mickiewicz in Milan. In the spring, she travelled to several towns in the Roman Campagna, where she may have married Ossoli. In June, anxious and fearful of dying alone—Ossoli's duties permitted only infrequent visits—she retreated to Aquila in the Appenines intending to have her child there, but later moved to Rieti, nearer to Rome, where a son Angelo (Angelino or Nino) was born in early September 1848.

She rejoiced in the child but the need to be at the center of events so as to continue with her *Tribune* column forced her to leave him with a wetnurse and return to Rome where she lived apart from Ossoli. She went to great pains to keep their liaison secret because, as she explained later, his brothers would have disinherited him if they knew he was connected with a Protestant foreigner who supported Mazzini.

The political situation in Rome was moving rapidly toward a show-down. In April the hope that Pope Nono would be a champion of change was dispelled when he backed away from confrontation with Austria. In November, after one of his counselors, Count Rossi, was assassinated, he escaped to his fortress in Gaeta and thus opened the way for the republicans to call for democratic elections for a constituent assembly and to establish the Roman Republic of 1849.

Now observing these events as a partisan, identifying with the people, and calling Rome her home, Fuller had uneasy forebodings; early and rightly, she prophesized that the French would eventually lend decisive military aid to restore the Pope's power.

Before that crisis occurred, she welcomed Mazzini as one of the Triumvirs of the new Roman government and observed the beginnings of an orderly transition to democratic government. But by the end of April her fears were realized. The city was under siege from the French and she was cast in a new role. The Princess Belgioioso, a liberal republican activist whom Fuller had known for over a year, appointed her Director of the Fate Bene Fratelli Hospital on the Tiber Island. Throughout the months of May and June, until the Roman Republic capitulated, she cared for the wounded while worrying constantly about Ossoli who was defending the city.

Having served as a captain in the National Guard of the Republic, Ossoli was now persona non grata in the Vatican States. Fuller, too, a foreigner who had helped the republicans, was required to leave Rome. She turned to Lewis Cass, Jr., the American chargé d'affaires of the Vatican States, who had become a solid friend. He provided her with transportation to Rieti; there she found Angelino ill and badly undernourished. While nursing him and recovering from shock and depression herself, she and Ossoli decided that they would move to Florence and live there together openly as a family.

Fuller had written only one person about Angelino, her friend Caroline Sturgis; and Sturgis had been sworn to secrecy. Fuller found it painful to break her long silence over this important matter, especially to her mother who may have suspected something of the sort. Even so Fuller's letters are unforthcoming about an actual marriage ceremony. Her reticence led to conjectures among her friends at home (as well as future scholars) about "a Fourierist or Socialist marriage"(Bremer 1:170). Margaret Crane Fuller received the news warmly, as did Margaret's Italian friend, Costanza Arconati, but others, even those who remained loyal, worried that Fuller had created enough doubts to injure her reputation.

The couple's immediate problem in Florence was the Tuscan police who threatened to deport Ossoli if he could not present a recent passport or papers proving Roman citizenship. He wrote a friend in Rome, Gaeto Suarra, begging him to get from the Roman police a proper "Pontifical passport" to be made out in the name of "Gio

Angelo Marchese Ossoli with wife and family." He added that there was no point in applying to officials in his home parish because they could only provide a passport for him alone. "I never informed them that I had married an American woman outside of Rome" (Manuscripts 11: 37). This passage suggests the possibility that they were married in a ceremony that would not have been recognized by the Catholic Church. When Suarra did not succeed with the Roman police, Fuller engaged the help of Lewis Cass, Jr. (who clearly believed the couple were married) and the American sculptor, Thomas Crawford; they managed to arrange for residence papers.

The family, hard-up for money, settled into a frugal life enlivened by a small circle of rewarding friends, including Elizabeth Barrett and Robert Browning. Fuller (or the Marchesa Ossoli, as she called herself now) continued to work on her history of the Italian revolution. She had written Thomas Carlyle asking for help in finding a publisher; he had replied that he would do his best to find one if she could provide him with a finished manuscript (Manuscripts 11: 132). Fuller's conviction that she could make a better bargain with a publisher in the United States if she could negotiate a contract in person influenced her decision to return home in the coming summer (1850).

In her penultimate *Tribune* columns Fuller wrote that before she came to Europe, she had believed that "what is called Socialism" would be the eventual consequence of the "tendencies and wants" of the time, but she now thought that "these vast changes in modes of government, education and daily life" would come about much more quickly (*Sad Days* 320). In a letter to Rachel and Marcus Spring, notifying them that she was coming home, she wrote that she had become "an enthusiastic Socialist" (*Letters* 5: 295). But she remarked in her journal just before the siege of Rome, "I take an interest in some plans, *our* socialism, for instance, for it has become mine too, but the interest is as shallow as the plans. They are needed, they are even good, but man will still blunder and weep, as he has done for so many thousand years" (quoted in Fellman, 80).

Unable to afford the cost of a Cunard steamship from Le Havre, the Ossoli family booked passage on the *Elizabeth*, an American cargo bark that sailed from Livorno in the middle of May. The voyage was beleaguered from the start. After a week at sea, the captain fell ill with smallpox and died just as they reached Gibralter. After a quarantine period, the ship continued with its inexperienced master serving as captain. Two days later Angelino developed smallpox symptoms. The ship made little headway for over a month for lack of wind while his parents nursed him constantly and pulled him through.

After the first week in July, the winds changed. On the evening of July 18, the ship's master announced that they would enter New York harbor the next morning. He had seriously miscalculated his position. That would not have been fatal had there not been a hurricane proceeding up the east coast. It hit the New York City area in the early morning. The *Elizabeth* went aground on the rocks off what is now Point O' Woods, Long Island. Land was in sight and many on board, including most of the crew, managed to reach shore safely by riding on spars.

During lulls in the storm, Fuller, who could not bear to be separated from either Angelino or Ossoli, delayed action in hope of rescue. Efforts to launch a lifeboat failed. At noon the tide turned and the ship broke up. A mate jumped into the sea with Angelino in his arms; the bodies of both were found later on the shore.

At Emerson's request, Henry Thoreau went to Long Island the next day to search for information about Fuller. Neither her body nor that of Ossoli was ever found. Nor did the manuscript of her book on the Italian revolution turn up; her papers that survived the wreck barely covered a table top.

In her last *Tribune* column, Fuller forsook her polemical position. In a powerful hosanna reminiscent of Schiller's "Hymn to Joy" and the millenial language at the end of *Woman in the Nineteenth Century*, she transmuted her suffering and anguish, her anger and disappointment, into a triumphant announcement—"the Newness," the awakening of a mass consciousness of human potentiality that she and her fellow Transcendentalists had prophesized and promoted fifteen years earlier had now arrived in both America and Europe:

> The New Era is no longer an embryo; it is born; it begins to walk— this very year sees its first giant steps, and can no longer mistake its features. . . .
>
> Joy to those born in this day: In America is open to them the easy chance of a noble, peaceful growth, in Europe of a combat grand in its motives, and in its extent beyond what the world ever before so much as dreamed. Joy to them; and joy to those their heralds, who, if their path was desert, their work unfinished, . . . yet holy-hearted in unasking love, great and entire in their devotion, fall or fade, happy in the thought that there come after them greater than themselves, who may at last string the harp of the world to full concord, in glory to God in the highest, for peace and love from man to man is become the bond of life (*Sad Days* 321-323).

Works Cited

Bremer, Fredrika. *The Homes of the New World: Impressions of America*. Vol. 1. New York: Harper & Brothers, 1853.

Browning, Elizabeth Barrett. *The Letters of Elizabeth Barrett Browning*. Eds. Meredith B. Raymond & Mary Rose Sullivan. Vol. 3. Waco: Tex., Armstrong Browning Library of Baylor University, 1983.

Clarke, James Freeman. *The Letters of James Freeman Clarke to Margaret Fuller*. Ed. John Wesley Thomas. Hamburg: Cram, de Guyter, 1957.

Eliot, George. "Margaret Fuller and Mary Wollstonecraft." Essays of George Eliot. Ed. Thomas Phinney. New York: Columbia UP, 1963.

Ellison, Julie. *Delicate Subjects: Romanticism, Gender, and the Ethics of Understanding*. Ithaca: Cornell UP, 1990. 239¬256.

Emerson, Ralph Waldo. *The Journal and Miscellaneous Notebooks of Ralph Waldo Emerson*. Ed. William H. Gilman et al. Vol. 11. Cambridge, Ma.: Harvard UP, 1960-.

—. *The Letters of Ralph Waldo Emerson*. Ed. vols. 1-6, Ralph L. Rusk. Vol. 3. New York: Columbia UP, 1939. Vols. 7-8, ed. Eleanor M. Tilton, 8 vols. to date.

Emerson, R.W., Channing, W.H., and Clarke, James Freeman. *Memoirs of Margaret Fuller Ossoli*. Vol. 1. Boston: Phillips, Sampson, 1852.

Fellman, Michael. *The Unbounded Frame: Freedom and Community in Nineteenth Century American Utopianism*. Westport: Greenwood Press, 1973.

Fuller Manuscripts and Works. Houghton Library. Harvard University.

Margaret Fuller Papers. Massachusetts Historical Society.

Fuller, Margaret. "Daughter of Italy." *People's and Howitt's Journal*. 4 (1847): 528.

—. *The Letters of Margaret Fuller*. Ed. Richard N. Hudspeth. 5 Vols. to date. Ithaca: Cornell UP, 1983-.

—. *Summer on the Lakes in 1843*. (1844) Nieukoop: B. De Graaf, 1972.

—. *"These Sad But Glorious Days"*: Dispatches From Europe, 1846-1850. Eds. Larry J. Reynolds and Susan Belasco Smith. New Haven: Yale UP, 1991.

—. "The Social Movement in Europe." *New-York Daily Tribune*. 5 Aug. 1845: 1.

—. "Der Volks-Tribun: Organ der Deutschen Sozial Reform-Association in New York." *New-York Daily Tribune*. 17 Jan. 1846: 1.

—. *Woman in the Nineteenth Century*. New York: Greeley and McElrath, 1845.

Hawthorne, Nathaniel. *The French and Italian Notebooks*. The Centenary Edition of the Works of Nathaniel Hawthorne. Vol. 14. Ed. Thomas Woodson. Columbus: Ohio State UP, 1980.

Hoffman, Tess. "Miss Fuller among the Literary Lions: Two Essays Read at "The Coliseum'in 1838." *Studies in the American Renaissance* (1988). Ed. Joel Myerson. Charlottsville: Virginia UP, 1988. 37-53.

James, Henry. *William Wetmore Story and His Friends.* Boston: Houghton, Mifflin, 1903.

James, William. *Varieties of Religious Experience: A Study in Human Nature.* New York: Longmans, Green & Co., 1903.

Robinson, David. "Margaret Fuller and the Transcendental Ethos." *Publications of the Modern Language Association of America.* 97 (1982). 83-98.

Urbanski, Marie Olesen. "The Ambivalence of Ralph Waldo Emerson Towards Margaret Fuller." *Thoreau Journal Quarterly.* 10:3 (July 1978): 26-36.

—. "Margaret Fuller's Woman in the Nineteenth Century: The Feminist Manifesto." *Nineteenth-Century Woman Writers of the English-Speaking World.* Ed. Rhoda B. Nathan. Contributions in Women's Studies, 69. New York: Greenwood Press, 1986. 201¬207

Wellicz, Leopold. "The Friendship of Margaret Fuller D'Ossoli and Adam Mickiewicz." *Bulletin of the Polish Institute of Arts* and Sciences in America. 4 (1945-1946). 83-122.

Wolf, Bryan Jay. Romantic Re-vision: *Culture and Consciousness in Nineteenth Century American Painting and Literature.* Chicago: Chicago University Press, 1982

Renate Delphendahl

How I Met Margaret Fuller

M Y FIRST ACQUAINTANCE with Margaret Fuller dates back to January 1984 when my friend and colleague Marie Urbanski presented me with a copy of her book *Margaret Fuller's Woman in the Nineteenth Century*, introducing me to Fuller's intellectual accomplishments. A lecture, given by Joseph Jay Deiss at the University of Maine, highlighted other aspects of Fuller's multi-faceted personality and I subsequently read his book *The Roman Years of Margaret Fuller*. Thus, my acquaintance with Fuller was still confined to reading about her in secondary sources. Sigrid Bauschinger's book, *Die Posaune der Reform*, especially sparked my desire to read some of Fuller's own work. I was most impressed by Fuller's knowledge of the German language, her interpretations of German literature, and her translation skills. I have great respect for the task a translator faces, based on my experience as a student when I served as an interpreter at a Lutheran World Conference. My experience as an interpreter allows me to fully appreciate Fuller's accomplishments as a translator, especially her resourcefulness and daring.

My interest in Fuller's writing was heightened when I realized that she was one of the first Goethe scholars in the United States. Through her clear-sighted criticism and sensitive interpretations of Goethe's works—both from a philosophical and artistic point of view—she greatly increased the awareness of Goethe among her compatriots. As early as 1833/34, Fuller translated Goethe's *Torquato Tasso*, which, however, was only published posthumously. She identified herself with German thought by referring to herself as *Germanico*, and it is not surprising that her first book publications were translations from German. In 1839, she published Eckermann's *Conversations with Goethe*, which served as a basis for John Oxenford's translation, published in London in 1850, and which is considered to this day the standard English-language version. In 1842, Fuller published an excerpt from Bettina von Arnim's epistolary novel *Die Günderode*, entitled "Bettine Brentano and her friend Günderode," in the *Dial*, and an expanded version in book form under the title *Günderode*.

Fuller's linguistic skills and her wide knowledge of German literature, at a time when the study of the German language and literature was still in its infancy in the United State, placed her at the cutting edge of the study of a new language, and made her a disseminator of new cultural information. As an interpreter/translator Fuller was creative, mediating between two different cultures and reconciling them through her translations.

When the American Association of Teachers of German chose as its topic "German Literature in American and European Contexts" for its international meeting in Baden-Baden, Germany in July 1992, I presented a paper on Margaret Fuller, commenting on her work as an interpreter and translator of German literature. The paper sparked lively discussion and convinced me that Fuller scholarship is of interest to German scholars and no longer confined to American scholars.

Renate Delphendahl

Margaret Fuller: Interpreter and Translator of German Literature

ARGARET FULLER used her language skills to create a revisionary model of reading, first, for herself by reading and interpreting German authors, and secondly, by translating. Early on, translation became the cornerstone for her intellectual development in a patriarchial society. When she was a child, her father required her to translate Latin poetry and prose into her native tongue; and when she was a young adult, prominent men in the Transcendentalist movement, such as, James Freeman Clarke, Frederic Henry Hedge, William Ellery Channing, and Ralph Waldo Emerson encouraged her to publish a series of translations from German. While Fuller's engagement with translation is associated with powerful male figures, she used her language skills and translation to gain her intellectual independence. It should be remembered that German is a language she taught herself; it was not the language of her father or a tutor but a language she acquired of her own choosing. Besides German, she also learned Italian by herself "unassisted except as to pronunciation" (*Memoirs* 1: 241). Indeed, Fuller's intellectual make-up is grounded in a linguistic versatility and competence unusual for any time. Her language skills enabled her to search for a concept of universal womanhood that included power, intelligence, energy, and a voice.

It is well known that Fuller used her voice effectively. In her "Conversation Classes" for intellectual women in Cambridge, she was a gifted leader of conversations. Fuller possessed intelligence and energy, which she displayed in her studies, her teaching, her Conversation classes, her letters, her interactions with her friends, her essays in the *Dial*, and in her creative writing. In her description of her youth, she says *"very early I knew that the only object in life was to grow"* (*Memoirs* 1: 133). Growth meant self-development and intellectual discipline, which Fuller regards as synonomous with self-culture. Fuller admired Goethe as the great apostle of individual self-culture, a concept that included self-trust, self-reliance and also superb balance of character. Yet, long before she became familiar with his writing, she gives evidence that she possessed self-culture as a fifteen year old girl. In a letter to her teacher, Susan Prescott, written on July 11, 1825, Fuller gives an account of how she spent a typical day: it begins by getting up before five o'clock in the morning and is filled with practicing on the piano, reading French, Greek, and Italian authors, and also attending Mr. Perkins's school. The afternoons are filled with more studying and recitations until eleven o'clock when she retires to write in her journal and to do exercises on what she has learned during the day (*Letters* 1: 151). Concerning her aims and ambitions, she writes in that same letter:

> I feel the power of industry growing every day, and, besides the all-powerful motive of ambition . . . I have learned to believe that nothing, no! not perfection, is unattainable. I am determined on distinction, which formerly I thought to win at an easy rate; but now I see that long years of labor must be given to secure even the *succes de societe*, — which, however, shall never content me. . . . my powers of intellect, though sufficient, I suppose, are not well disciplined. Yet all such hindrances may be overcome by an ardent spirit. If I fail, my consolation shall be found in active employment. (*Letters* 1: 151-152)

With her notion of "active employment" Fuller indicates that she wants to take control of her life. By Fuller's own account, she values ambition, discipline, and intellect. In the 1820s, these were characteristics associated with male privilege. It is not surprising that Clarke attributed to Fuller "a masculine mind; that is, its action was determined by ideas rather than by sentiments" (*Memoirs* 1: 95). In the framework of the twentieth century, a "masculine mind" can be equated with a feminist mind that focuses on ideas that involve change within a given system. Fuller wanted to change her own literary outlook and expand her cultural horizon by studying the German language and the literary works of the German poets; she was especially interested in reading and interpreting the works of Goethe.

Fuller commenced her study of German in 1832, which, incidentally, is also the year of Goethe's death. Clarke reports that within the brief period of three months, Fuller was reading the masterpieces of German literature "with ease" (*Memoirs* 1: 114). Within the span of one year, she had read

> Goethe's *Faust, Tasso, Iphigenia, Hermann and Dorothea, Elective Affinities,* and *Memoirs*; Tieck's *William Lovel, Prince Zerbino,* and other works; Körner, Novalis, and something of Richter; all of Schiller's principal dramas, and his lyric poetry. (*Memoirs* 1: 114)

This amount of reading in German literature which Fuller accomplished in a year is extraordinary and one can only marvel at the scope of the material covered. In addition to reading the selections cited above, Fuller also read in due time the dramas of Lessing, the works of La Motte Fouqué, Klopstock, Schlegel, Schelling, and Herder; the poetry of Heine and Uhland; and the philosophic works of Kant, Fichte, and Hegel. While the literary and poetic works inspired her with fresh thought, the philosophical works apparently were of little influence in her own writing. In 1833, Fuller wrote in her diary, "I have now a pursuit of immediate importance: to the German language and literature I will give my undivided attention. I have made rapid progress for one quite unassisted" (Higginson 41). Although Fuller was "self-taught" (*Memoirs* 1: 241) and did not attend a university, she was fortunate to live near Harvard College, where she came in contact with distinguished men interested in German literature. Foremost among her friends who encouraged her study of German were James Freeman Clarke and Frederic Henry Hedge. Hedge had studied in Germany and had the reputation of being "a fountain of knowledge in the way of German" (Higginson 44). While both shared Fuller's enthusiasm for German literature and supported her in her studies, Hedge also assisted her with the pronunciation of the German language. Moreover, in regular meetings with Dr. William Ellery Channing, Fuller translated the works of Herder and the German theologian de Wette. Her interest in translation simultaneously engaged her in issues of interpretation, conversation, and pedagogy.

Shortly after she began her studies of German, Fuller demonstrated her comprehensive command of the language by successfully teaching it in private lessons in 1834, at Bronson Alcott's school in Boston in 1836, and at the Greene Street School in Providence, Rhode Island, in 1837. She reports that her pupils at the end of three months "could read twenty pages of German at a lesson, and very well" (*Memoirs* 1: 174). With more advanced pupils, she read in 24 weeks Schiller's

Don Carlos, the long poems *Der Künstler* and *Das Lied von der Glocke;* Goethe's *Hermann und Dorothea, Götz von Berlichingen, Iphigenie, Clavigo,* and in three weeks the first part of *Faust;* Lessing's *Nathan der Weise, Minna von Barnhelm* and *Emilia Galotti;* parts of Tieck's *Phantasus,* and nearly the whole first volume of Jean Paul's *Titan* (*Memoirs* 1: 174). This extensive list demonstrates Fuller's preference for German at a time when the teaching of German literature was only in its formative stages in the United States.[1] Furthermore, the literary works she selected have remained to this day universal favorites and serve as a testimony to Fuller's critical discernment. In spite of the adverse criticism of Goethe prevalent in the 1830s, Fuller chose to include in her instruction more of Goethe's works than of any other writer. Emerson observed that Fuller knew German literature "more cordially than any other person" (*Memoirs* 1: 204-205). In 1836 Fuller wrote that she wished to interpret German authors because "this kind of culture would be precisely the counterpoise required by the utilitarian tendencies of our day and place" (*Memoirs* 1: 168). Fuller welcomed the new European influences and was primarily interested in interpreting German literature as distinct from theology and philosophy, which already had made an impact on Unitarian Boston. In 1846 she proudly noted that she had done "a good deal to extend the influence of the great minds of Germany" among her compatriots (*Memoirs* 1: 168; and also *Art, Literature, and the Drama* 7).

Fuller's work as a teacher, translator, and interpreter of German literature placed her at the cutting edge of the study of a new language in the United States. O. W. Long points out that instruction of German at Harvard began only in 1825 when "New England was still stumbling over the correct pronunciation of Goethe's name" (173). Victor Lange reports that between 1816 and 1830, approximately sixteen Americans visited Goethe in Weimar. Among these was Joseph Cogswell, a scientist at Harvard, who was a frequent and welcomed guest at Goethe's house and was responsible for Goethe's donation of a selection of his works to Harvard in 1819 (Lange 66). It was not until 1874 that a Goethe Club was organized in New York City, which played an important role in the cultural life of this country in the latter part of the nineteenth century (Long 173).

The history of the reception of Goethe in the early part of the nineteenth century is characterized by extreme reactions. The annals of criticism present a record in which Goethe is either proclaimed with enthusiasm or criticized by thinkers, who were offended by Goethe's sensuality. The lack of appreciation of Goethe's work was largely due to strong religious views. Goethe's view on God and nature, or what he called *das Sittlich-Sinnliche*, which recognized the sensuous side in the development of character, had been neglected by orthodox traditional churches, which, in turn influenced the Unitarians and Transcendentalists, who therefore condemned Goethe as a pagan, and his work as immoral. However, Goethe's genius and poetic mastery were praised in the British Isles—notably by Thomas Carlyle, whose essays and translations were held in high regard by New Englanders. Long observes: "With the influence of Carlyle's essays, and the work of Longfellow and others, especially the *Dial* coterie, Goethe became . . . the central figure in the introduction and progress of German letters" (173).

Fuller was the first editor of the *Dial*, a magazine of literature, philosophy, and religion, published from 1840 to 1844. It was intended as a "Journal in a new spirit," and its contributors were united in "a common love of truth" (*Dial* 1: 1-2). Fuller was chosen as editor because of her literary interest, tact, and ability to avoid theological disputes in which other Transcendentalists frequently became involved. It is interesting to note that she identified herself closely with German thought when she told her friends, "I fear I am merely 'Germanico' and not 'transcendental'" (Higginson 141; compare also her letter to Frederic H. Hedge of March 6,1835 in *Letters* 1: 226). Her editorship provided her with an opportunity to serve as a disseminator of German literature. She was assured of an educated readership that was open-minded and eager to learn about the cultural currents of foreign countries. The January 1841 issue of the *Dial* contains her essay "Menzel's View of Goethe" in which she denounces Wolfgang Menzel by stating "Menzel's view of Goethe is that of a Philistine" (*Dial* 1: 340). Menzel was a well respected scholar: his *History of German Literature* had been translated by Professor Cornelius Felton of Harvard College and appeared in George Ripley's *Specimen of Foreign Standard Literature.* Despite Menzel's sterling reputation, Fuller did not hesitate to challenge his judgment. She wrote:

> [Menzel] is a man of talent, but talent cannot comprehend genius. He judges of Goethe as a Philistine, inasmuch as he does not enter into Canaan, and read the prophet by the light of his own law, but looks at him from without, and tries him by a rule beneath which he never lived. (*Dial* 1: 340)

Fuller holds that Goethe "obliges us to live and grow," and paraphrases Bettina Brentano, a fascinating author, closely associated with the German romantic school, who says that Goethe's works "lead us on and on (*fort und fort*) till we live in them" (*Dial* 1: 341). Demonstrating her independent judgment, Fuller says "historically considered, Goethe needs no apology . . . Man should be true, wise, beautiful, pure, and aspiring. This man was true and wise" (*Dial* 1: 341). Fuller admonishes the reader, "if you want a moral enthusiast, is there not Schiller? If piety, or pure mystic sweetness, who but Novalis?" (*Dial* 1: 341-342). She concludes that Goethe was "neither epicurean nor sensualist, if we consider his life as a whole" (*Dial* 1: 346), and praises his serenity, self-trust, and perseverance.

In the July 1841 issue of the *Dial*, Fuller wrote a long essay on Goethe, noteworthy for its excellent analysis of the poet's major works. She touches upon the important ideas in *Werther, Tasso, Faust,*

Wilhelm Meister, Iphigenie, and *Die Wahlverwandschaften* with the assured knowledge of the central import of each, and explains their profound meaning for the life of their author and his age. She absolved *Meister* and *Die Wahlverwandschaften* of the charges of immorality and coldness by emphatically stating that they are "works of art" (*Dial* 2: 34). She concedes that "if [Goethe's] genius lost sight of the highest aims . . . ceasing to be a prophet poet, he was still a poetic artist" (*Dial* 2: 21). Yet, Fuller was also attuned to the moral judgment of her society when she said concerning the *Wahlverwandschaften* that "any discussion of the validity of the marriage vow [makes] society tremble to its foundation" (*Dial* 2: 31).

More importantly, Fuller commended Goethe for his treatment of fictional women characters, noting that "Goethe always represents the highest principle in the feminine form" (*Dial* 2: 26). In *Faust,* Fuller singles out Margarete (Gretchen) as the representative of the redeeming power, and in *Die Wahlverwandschaften* she comments on Ottilie's saintliness "that seems to point heavenward" (*Dial* 2: 32). *Wilhelm Meister*—the work so little appreciated in New England at that time—fascinated Fuller, who considered it "the continuation of Faust in the practical sense of the education of man" (*Life Without and Life Within* 38). Fuller regarded the representation of Goethe's women characters as symbolical of the stages of development through which each individual must pass. Fuller also praised *Iphigenie* at some length as Goethe's representation of the feminine principle because Iphigenia is self-reliant, "obeys her own heart . . . and purifies all around her" (*Dial* 2: 41). By appealing to the king's humanity, Iphigenia is able to transform the barbarous custom of human sacrifice to one of forgiveness and reconciliation. Fuller perceived Goethe's women characters as archetypal figures, possessing intelligence and wisdom, or what she termed "the Minerva side of the feminine nature" (*Woman* 115). What fascinated Fuller most among the ideas expressed in Goethe's works was the concept of *das ewig Weibliche* and the redemption of man by woman.

Goethe's influence on Fuller is apparent in her essays in the *Dial*. In "The Great Lawsuit," published in the *Dial* in 1844 (4: 1-47), Fuller discusses substantially the same material she had utilized in her earlier essay on Goethe. In *Woman in the Nineteenth Century* (1845), she added her thoughts on Swedenborg and Fourier, as prophets of the coming age. In contrast to her earlier essays, Fuller no longer apologizes for Goethe's life-style. Applying his ideas to her focus on women, she writes:

> He aims at pure self-subsistence, and free development of any powers with which [women] may be gifted by nature as much for them as for men. . . . Accordingly the meeting between man and woman, as represented by him, is equal and noble. (*Woman* 115)

The idea of "self-subsistence, and free development" and especially equality between men and women is analogous to the concept of each individual's uniqueness. Fuller shared with Emerson and others in the Transcendentalist movement the emphasis on individualism and self-trust. Her egalitarian attitude motivated her to champion Goethe's works before they were widely accepted in the United States; it made her bold enough to translate some of them.

In 1910, Frederick Augustus Braun praised Fuller as a sensitive interpreter and translator of Goethe's works in his book *Margaret Fuller and Goethe*. However, other scholars in the early part of the twentieth century acknowledge Fuller's contributions only marginally. Among these are Harry Slochower[2] and O. W. Long, both writing in 1932. Long claims that "Longfellow . . . became the first important interpreter in this country of [Goethe's] genius and fame" (145). It should be noted that Longfellow's *Poets and Poetry of Europe* was not published until 1845, whereas Fuller had written her interpretations and translations between 1834 and 1842. Clearly then, she deserves the distinction as the first literary interpreter of Goethe in America. Arthur B. Schultz does acknowledge Fuller's contribution when he states: "with the exception of Carlyle, there was no one who before 1845 had revealed to the English-speaking readers in such an authoritative, stimulating, and informative manner the nature of German literary achievements of the recent past" (204). Fuller's achievements as an interpreter of Goethe's works have been evaluated more favorably by critics in the second half of the twentieth century. Among those who deserve mention are Margaret Vanderhaar Allen[3], Russel E. Durning[4], Henry A. Pochmann[5], and Sigrid Bauschinger. In *Die Posaune der Reform*, Bauschinger states that reading German authors had a decisive influence on Emerson and Fuller and credits Fuller more than any other as the disseminator of German literature in America (15). Hertha Marquardt commemorates Fuller's attempt to write a Goethe biography with an article entitled, "Die erste Goethe-Biographin in Amerika, Margaret Fuller's geplantes *Life of Goethe*."[6] Fuller is beginning to be recognized for her pioneering spirit in bringing Goethe's works into the American orbit.

Fuller's role as interpreter and translator is nowhere more clearly delineated than in her essay "Goethe" (*Dial* 2: 1-41), which Emerson considered "her best paper" (*Memoirs* 1: 243-244). Clarke echoes Emerson's sentiment by stating, "her strength was in characterization and in criticism. Her *critique* on Goethe, in the second volume of the *Dial* is, in my estimation, one of the best things she has written. And as far as it goes, it is one of the best criticisms extant of Goethe" (*Memoirs* 1: 96). Excerpts from Fuller's essay are reprinted here because the material is often inaccessible to today's reader and because this particular essay best shows her dual role as interpreter and translator. Alternating between a critical analysis of several of Goethe's works, she also presents a translation of Goethe's *Der Neue Paris* ("The New Paris") and passages from *Iphigenia*, both of which have been largely overlooked by critics, who comment mostly on her book-length translations of Goethe's *Torquato Tasso*, Johann Peter

Eckermann's *Conversations with Goethe*, and Bettina von Arnim's epistolary novel *Die Günderode*.

Before discussing Fuller's work as a translator, I want to point out some slight orthographic mistakes which Fuller made in her German quotation which she prefixed as a motto to her essay on "Goethe" (*Dial* 2: 1-41) and which have been reprinted in anthologies without correction. My illustration also serves as an example for Fuller's eclectic method of work, which is symptomatic of all her translations. Her tendency to select what appears to be best is evident throughout her contributions in the *Dial*. There are spelling mistakes in the German text, which of course might be attributed to typographical errors, and also an occasional omission of sources; on the positive side Fuller demonstrates her ability as a translator. The typographical errors in the German motto are as follows:

> Wer Grosses will muss sich zusammen raffen [sic]
> In der Beschrankung [sic] zeigt sich erst der Meister,
> Und der [sic] Gesetz nur kann uns Freiheit geben. (*Dial* 2: 1)

Goethe's verse reads:

> Wer Großes will, muß sich zusammenraffen;
> In der Beschränkung zeigt sich erst der Meister,
> Und das Gesetz nur kann uns Freiheit geben. (*Goethe Werke* 1: 153)

To clarify, the German verb *zusammenraffen* is one word; *Beschränkung* has an umlaut (a diacritical mark) placed over the *a*, and the article before *Gesetz* must be *das*. Reprinting Fuller's essay in *Writings of Margaret Fuller*, Mason Wade writes *Beschränkung* correctly but leaves the other orthographic mistakes (242). Similarly, Perry Miller's reprint of that same essay in *Margaret Fuller: American Romantic* retains the orthographic mistakes from Fuller's quotation and makes an additional mistake by capitalizing the modal auxiliary *kann* (79).

Moreover, neither Wade nor Miller copy Fuller's Latin quotation faithfully but capitalize the Latin words *Deum* and *Deus*, presumably in accordance with the custom of Christians to use capital letters for the word *God*. Goethe's Latin motto "Nemo contra deum nisi deus ipse" is written in lower case letters in accordance with Latin orthography and Fuller copied it correctly.

Concerning the obscuring of sources, Fuller simply states: "The first of these mottos is that prefixed by Goethe to the last books of "Dichtung und Wahrheit" (*Dial* 2: 1). Goethe's *Dichtung und Wahrheit* comprises more than 700 pages and it is difficult to locate the motto in his work. Goethe prefixed the Latin motto to Part IV, Book 16 (603), and then, within his text, explicates what the concept of the demonic denotes in Book 20 (698-700). Fuller draws from various sources, selecting what appears to be best. In her discussion of the demonic, she presents what Goethe expressed in *Dichtung und Wahrheit* and also in *Conversation with Eckermann*. In her essay, she retains the German word "Dämonische" (*Dial* 2: 18-19) and provides an excellent exegesis of what that concept denotes. Not content to provide her interpretation of Goethe's thoughts on the demonic, she somewhat abruptly states: "But hear Goethe himself" (*Dial* 2: 18). Because Fuller succeeds very well in paraphrasing Goethe's ideas on the subject, her abridged translation is reprinted here:

> The boy believed in nature, in the animate and inanimate, the intelligent and unconscious to discover somewhat which manifested itself only through contradiction, and therefore could not be comprehended by any conception, much less defined by a word. It was not divine, for it seemed without reason, not human, because without understanding, not devilish, because it worked to good, not angelic, because it often betrayed a petulant love of mischief. It was like chance, in that it proved no sequence; it suggested the thought of Providence, because it indicated connexion. To this all our limitations seem penetrable; it seemed to play at will with all the elements

of our being; it compressed time and dilated space. Only in the impossible did it seem to delight, and to cast the possible aside with disdain. This existence which seemed to mingle with others, sometimes to separate, somtimes to unite, I called the Dämonische, after the example of the ancients, and others who have observed somewhat similar. —*Dichtung und Wahrheit.* . . . The Dämonische is that which cannot be explained by reason or understanding; it lies not in my nature, but I am subject to it. Napoleon was a being of this class, and in so high a degree, that scarce any one is to be compared with him. Also our late Grand Duke was such a nature, full of unlimited power of action and unrest, so that his own dominion was too little for him, and the greatest would have been too little. Demoniac beings of this sort the Greeks reckoned among their demi-gods.—*Conversations with Eckermann.* (*Dial* 2: 18-19)

While Fuller condensed Goethe's thoughts on the subject of the demonic, she captures well his essential ideas. For Goethe, the demonic had a universal character and is an entity which puts human beings at risk; it can equally elevate or destroy individuals, and can be equated with inner conflict or with the concept of dualism that sustains both good and evil. It constitutes the enigma of life, which the artist and the creative person or the genius experiences more intensely than the ordinary person. Goethe portrayed masterfully the enigmatic character of demonic forces in human nature in such figures as Egmont, who succumbed; Tasso, who could not resolve his inner conflict; and Iphigenia, who was able to overcome the demonic curse of barbaric human sacrifice through her humanity. It is important to understand that the demonic is not associated with evil as Fuller points out elsewhere. Rather, it is "an instinctive force, which at once, without calculation or foresight, chooses the right means to an end" (*Dial* 2: 18). Goethe used the word *daemon* in reference to its Greek origin which implies nothing evil. Fuller understood the secret forces of the demonic and even identified them within herself when she says, "with me, for weeks and months, the daemon works his will. . . . As to the Daemoniacal, I know not that I can say to you anything more precise than you find from Goethe. There are no precise terms for such thoughts. The word *instinctive* indicates their existence" (*Memoirs* 1: 225). Fuller derived her conception of the demonic from Goethe; her reference to the *instinctive* could equally refer to the concept of the uncanny that cannot be analyzed by the rational mind. In the twentieth century, the concept of the instinctive could be linked to Freud's conception of the *id*.

Fuller provides no source reference for the second motto she prefixed to her "Goethe" essay and the reader presumes that this motto is also taken from *Dichtung und Wahrheit*. However, it is taken from Goethe's poem *Natur und Kunst* (*Goethe Werke* 1: 152-153) and consists of four verses in the original. Fuller selected only the last stanza of the poem and provides a translation of it in her discussion of Goethe's "expansive genius," stating that the "secret may be found in the second motto of this slight essay." She translates the poem as follows:

> He who would do great things must quickly draw together his forces.
> The master can only show himself such through limitation, and the
> law alone can give us freedom. (*Dial* 2: 29)

Fuller's translation of this verse is excellent. Even though she does not retain the metrical line of Goethe's poem, she conveys the thought very well. What appealed to Fuller is the idea that temporal laws can be superseded by a higher spiritual law if human beings transcend their limitations and achieve mastery. Elsewhere in her writing she prefers to use the German word *Beschränkung* in place of the word "limitation" (*Dial* 2: 41).

Her "Goethe" essay serves as an excellent example of Fuller's eclecticism. She alternates between her analysis of Goethe's works, denunciations and also praise by critics. To show how Goethe was praised, Fuller includes extracts from remarks made by celebrated persons, such as Rahel von Emse "whose discernment as to his work was highly prized by Goethe" (*Dial* 2: 28). Fuller provides the extract in English without giving an indication if the extract were translated by herself or if Rahel von Emse wrote in English. Similarly, Fuller includes an "extract from a letter of Beethoven to Bettina Brentano, Töplitz, 1812" (*Dial* 2: 30) without indicating if she herself translated the letter or where it can be found. Fuller interprets both extracts in praise of Goethe and as a sign that "Goethe has a natural taste for the trappings of rank and wealth, from which the musician was quite free" (*Dial* 2: 31). While Fuller's eclectic method of providing information and drawing on various sources may be disconcerting to the scholar of the twentieth century, her sketches show her as a widely-read person, knowledgeable in German letters.

Fuller's tendency to intersperse her critical comments with translations can be found in her insertion of a translation of Goethe's fairy tale entitled "The New Paris" (*Dial* 2: 8-17). Fuller introduces this fairy tale rather abruptly with the following words: "Exceedingly characteristic of his genius is a little tale, which he records as having frequently been told by him to his companions when only eight or nine years of age. I think it is worth insertion here" (*Dial* 2: 8). As source reference, Fuller gives Goethe's *Dichtung und Wahrheit* (*Dial* 2: 17). Originally, "Der neue Paris" was published in Book II (*Goethe-Werke* 5: 43-75). Goethe remiscences about his childhood at age seven and tells the story of how he as a young boy told his playmates a fairy tale that excited his and their imagination. However, the fairy tale does not originate in Goethe's youthful writing but is the product of his mature years. He wrote it in 1811 when he was sixty-two years old (*Goethe Werke* 5: 718). "The New Paris" alludes to the Trojan prince Paris, chosen by Eris, the Greek goddess of discord, to give the golden apple to the fairest of the three goddesses: Aphrodite, Athena, or Hera. While Goethe alludes to the Greek prince Paris as the darling of the gods, his New Paris is led by Mercury to enter the magical garden of poetry, when he crosses the golden bridge into fantasy land and encounters hostile as well as benign forces. The fairy tale stands as a paradigm of Goethe's belief in the active imagination of the poet, who has to reconcile the power of the imagination with the reality of life. The allusions to Greek mythology and the subject of reconciliation between poetry and life provided the impetus for Fuller to translate this fairy tale. The emphasis on the creative process signifies Goethe's genius when she declares that this tale marks "well the man that was to be" (*Dial* 2: 17). Fuller's translation is not abridged; it is her best literal translation, which captures the playful spirit of the original accurately. Only in one instance does Fuller avoid a literal rendering of Goethe's text by deleting the words "ganz nackt schritt ich . . ." (*Goethe Werke* 5: 58), which translate into "entirely naked I walked . . .," a phrase that may have offended her Victorian readers. While Fuller briefly comments on the artistic merits of the tale, she does not integrate an analysis of it in her commentary, which may be the reason why Wade and also Miller chose to omit the "New Paris" in their respective reprints of Fuller's "Goethe" essay. Because Fuller scholarship has hardly taken notice of this particular translation, it is reprinted in the appendix to this volume.

In her discussion of Goethe's *Faust*, Fuller introduces one German passage from that work, followed by her translation:

> Kannst du mich schmeichelnd je belügen
> Dass ich mir selbst gefallen mag,
> Kannst du mich mit Genüs [sic] betrügen:
> Das sey für mich der letzte Tag.
> Werd ich zum Augenblicke sagen:
> Verweile doch! du bist so schön!
> Dann magst du mich in Fesseln schlagen,
> Dann will ich gern zu Grunde gehen.

Canst thou by falsehood or by flattery
Make me one moment with myself at peace,
Cheat me into tranquility? Come then
And welcome, life's last day.
Make me but to the moment say,
Oh fly not yet, thou art so fair,
Then let me perish, &c. (*Dial* 2: 22)

While Fuller condenses the eight lines of the original into seven, her translation accurately reflects the thought content of the model. The omission of line seven "Dann magst du mich in Fesseln schlagen," which Wayne translates as "Then bind me with your fatal chain" (87), and Arndt as "Then forge the shackles to my feet" (41), can be dispensed with because Goethe's focus is on the wager for Faust's soul. Thus, Fuller's condensation is not detrimental to an understanding of the pact between Faust and Mephistopheles. In her essay, Fuller states that the passage refers to "the compact, whose condition cheats the fiend at last" (*Dial* 2: 22). She does not specifically indicate that her quotation alludes to the wager between Faust and Mephistopheles, presuming that her readers are intelligent and would be able to place the quotation in its proper context.

For the sake of comparison, I would like to cite one translation of these lines by Philip Wayne, made in 1949, published in the Penguin Classics, and widely adopted at American universities in the 1950s; and another one by Walter Arndt, made in 1976, and published in the Norton Critical Edition. The excerpt from the translation by Philip Wayne is:

If ever flattering lies of yours can please
And soothe my soul to self-sufficing,
And make me one of pleasure's devotees,
Then take my soul, for I desire to die.

If to the fleeting hours I say
'Remain, so fair thou art, remain!'
Then bind me with your fatal chain,
For I will perish in that day. (*Faust*, trans. Philip Wayne 87)

The excerpt from the translation by Walter Arndt is:

When first by flattery you lull me
Into a smug complacency,
When with indulgence you can gull me,
Let that day be the last for me!
If the swift moment I entreat:
Tarry a while! You are so fair!
Then forge the shackles to my feet.
Then I will gladly perish there! (*Faust*, trans. Walter Arndt 40-41)

Arndt's translation in particular shows strict adherence to the form of the original in metric and rhymic patterns, maintaining a line-by-line correspondence. However, a comparison of all three translations demonstrates that each translator uses slightly different words, yet each conveys the essential meaning of Goethe's lines.

Fuller concludes her "Goethe" essay by inserting an extract of her translation of Goethe's *Iphigenie auf Tauris*, providing at the same time her assessment of Iphigenia and a synopsis of the plot, so that her readers could become familiar with the content. Because it illustrates well Fuller's scheme of combining commentary, analysis, and translation into a coherent whole, this part of the essay, reprinted from the *Dial* 2: 34-41,[7] may be found in the appendix.

Fuller was aware of the pitfalls of translation when she indicated that the heroic dignity expressed in the cadence of the original by the words

Zwischen uns
sey Wahrheit!
Ich bin Orest!

can only be approximated in English, pointing out that the two syllables in the name "Orest" are more forcible for the pause than the three syllables in "Orestes," and therefore, she pauses after the word "truth" in her translation:

> between us
> Be truth! —-
> I am Orestes!   (*Dial* 2: 39)

It should be pointed out that Goethe's play is entitled *Iphigenie auf Tauris*. Fuller shortened the title to *Iphigenia*, omitting the reference to the Greek locality. One can speculate that Fuller rightly considered this dramatic poem to be universal; by omitting a reference to a nation and an era, she underscored its universality and its validity in any time and in any place. Fuller's literary analysis indicates that she is a discerning critic of Goethe's work. When she wrote her essay in 1841, she had been studying the works of Goethe for almost a decade and could affirm his concern with the universal. She perceived the individuality of the character of Iphigenia and the universality of thought expressed in this play. Elsewhere, writing as a critic, Fuller states that Iphigenia is "a work beyond the possibility of negation; a work where a religious meaning not only pierces but enfolds the whole; a work as admirable in art, still higher in significance, more single in expression" (*Life Without and Life Within* 51). In her preface to *Conversations with Goethe*, she says, "Iphigenia, by her steadfast truth, hallows all about her, and disarms the powers of hell" (xiv). Fuller's translation is remarkably successful in respect to the quality of composition. She followed closely the original and succeeded in the exact transmission of thought. Her translation does justice to the structure and tone of Goethe's verses.

Fuller's eclecticism is also evident in her review of R. H. Wilde's book *Conjectures and Researches concerning the Love, Madness, and Imprisonment of Torquato Tasso* (*Dial* 2: 399-401) when she inserted an abridgement from her translation of Goethe's *Torquato Tasso* (*Dial* 2: 401- 407). It demonstrates that for Fuller, reviewing, interpretation, and translation were valid variables. At the end of her review, without any proper introduction, she interpolates: "Let me add as the best criticism . . . one of those matchless scenes in which Goethe represents the sudden blazes of eloquence, the fitful shadings of mood, and the exquisite sensitiveness to all influences, that made the weakness and power of Tasso" (*Dial* 2: 401). Fuller then presents her own translation of the first two scenes of the second Act without indicating that she is the translator. Her failure to identify herself may be one of the reasons why critics have largely overlooked the fragment of *Tasso* as it appeared in the January issue of the *Dial* in 1842.

In her article, "Feminism in Translation: Margaret Fuller's *Tasso*," written in 1990, Christina Zwarg expresses her intention of writing an essay that examines how Fuller "used her review of a book about the historical figure Tasso to publish a section from her translation of Goethe's dramatic reading of the same, . . . [intending to scrutinize] the complex theory of reading that [Fuller] develops during her book review career" (474). Moreover, in her discussion of Fuller's translation of *Tasso*, Zwarg cites from Fuller's fragment in the *Dial*, claiming that Fuller's brother "made some revisions in Fuller's manuscript when he published *Tasso*" (474). As an example, Zwarg cites the following words which Tasso says to the Princess:

> For as I gazed, *my* world sank in the distance
> Behind steep rocks,— on which I seemed to fade—
> To Echo—to poor shadow of a sound,—
> Bodiless,— powerless. (*Dial* 2: 402)

The translation, which Arthur Fuller published, reads as follows:

> For as I gazed, *my* world sank in the distance
> Behind steep rocks, on which I seemed to fade

To echo—to poor shadow of a sound—
Bodiless—powerless. (*Art, Literature, and the Drama* 380)

In these lines, Arthur Fuller spelled "echo" with lower case letters. Zwarg holds that the German substantive "Echo" refers to the mythical figure of Echo and when he spelled echo in lower case letters, he did "considerable damage to this pivotal moment in the text; closing down the classical reference closes down the infinite complications of gender imposed upon the moment by the classical text of Echo" (478-479). As far as I can ascertain, the spelling of "Echo" is the only substantive change Arthur Fuller made. Spelling "echo" in lower case letters can also be interpreted as an example of verbal logic supplanting the fidelity of the original text because nouns are not capitalized in the English language; it may also signify a diminution of the character's narcissistic obsessions. A line for line comparison between Fuller's translation as published by her in the *Dial* and the translation published posthumously by Arthur Fuller reveals that he made some slight changes in punctuation; where Margaret Fuller's translation had commas and dashes, he chose either one or the other. I noticed only slight deviations in two lines when Tasso says to the Princess: "When most I sigh to approach" (*Dial* 2: 403), which Arthur Fuller changed to read: "When I most sigh to approach thee" (*Art, Literature, and the Drama* 382). Another example is from Tasso's soliloquy in which he says: "Let the born blind think what they will of colors" (*Dial* 2: 407), which Arthur Fuller rendered as "Let those born blind think what they will of colors" (*Art, Literature, and the Drama* 387). These changes are not substantial but merely stylistic and actually improve Fuller's original translation.

Fuller never considered herself a translator *per se* but rather as a mediator who conveyed to her compatriots the thoughts expressed in the German literature of the nineteenth century. These ideas enriched her own thinking and she was convinced that they would enrich the minds of her American readers. J. Wesley Thomas writes that Fuller, "like Carlyle . . . resolved to aid in the dissemination of the German masterpieces among her monolingual compatriots" (89). Fuller translated in order to expand her own cultural horizon and that of the New World. In her review of *Faust*, she writes: "We cannot but wonder that anyone who aims at all at literary culture can remain ignorant of German . . . the acquisition of which . . . would give . . . access to such wide domains of thought and knowledge" (*Dial* 2: 134). Since Fuller considered her translations as instruments of thought and knowledge, her method of translation closely resembles the attitude of the German romantics who equated *übersetzen* (to translate) with *verdeutschen* (to germanize). Their translations were informed by a strategy of linguistic incorporation much in the same manner as the Roman Empire incorporated Greek culture into its own. For the Romans, translation was a form of conquest that enriched their civilization. Fuller was familiar with the writings of the German romantics, who not only were writers and poets, but also gifted translators.[8]

By analogy, Fuller produced "Americanized" translations of German literature that represent a strategy of linguistic incorporation in regard to word choice, phrasing, and syntax. She shortened the long German sentences, adhering to the rules of syntax of the English language. She made use of American idioms favored in mid-nineteenth century New England, selecting expressions which allude to dominant values in the target language in order to enhance her readers' understanding of the translated work. She often condensed statements by focusing on their important aspects and by omitting the non-essential parts. She also shortened the titles of works such as Goethe's *Iphigenie auf Tauris* into *Iphigenia*, and *Torquato Tasso* to *Tasso*. Fuller's decision to delete "Torquato" from Goethe's title may be nothing more than to create a distance between herself and the historical man. Zwarg suggests that when Fuller's friends, "having read her translation, spoke of "Tasso," they were no longer speaking of . . . the poet of literary history, nor of Goethe's construction of the man . . . they were . . . referring to Fuller's criticial redaction of all three" (473). Yet, Fuller's synoptical style still conveyed a general view of the whole. She interspersed her translations with interpretations, commentaries, and compelling reasons why the study of German literature would widen the intellectual horizon of her American readers. Thus, Fuller's translations served a multiple purpose: to convey the new ideas inherent in the foreign text, to persuade her readers of the merit of the piece, and also to express these ideas in idiomatic language familiar to her readers. To illustrate my point, I would like to cite a short passage from Fuller's translation of *Tasso*, where the Princess Leonora and the poet Tasso debate the respective merits of liberty and law. Fuller renders the conversation between the Princess and Tasso as follows:

PRINCESS: Change in thy maxim but one single word,
All is explained. All which is *meet* is lawful.

TASSO: Might then a synod of the wise and good
  Decide on what is meet; for now each one
Says that is meet which to himself is pleasing,
And to the crafty and the powerful
  All is permitted, whether just or not.

(*Art, Literature, and the Drama* 384)

Fuller retained the word "meet" as it was used in the Book of Common Prayer in her time; it is a term her American contemporaries understood. By comparison, a present-day translator might replace the phrase "all which is *meet* is lawful," with "what is proper or befitting is allowed" when translating the original *erlaubt ist, was sich ziemt* (*Goethe Werke* 2: 339; translation mine). Also, in Fuller's translation the word "synod" alludes to an ecclesiastical realm with which her American readers could identify and which was a timely expression in mid-nineteenth century America. Goethe used the words *ein allgemein Gericht* (*Goethe Werke* 2: 339), which I would translate as "a general court." Fuller's rendition of Goethe's lines reflects the circumstances and times of the translator in word choice, phrasing, grammar, and syntax. It can be argued that her use of the word *synod* reflects the ideologies of the intended readers. Having recourse to familiar concepts about a culture makes the text more meaningful because the readers can relate to them better and their understanding is enhanced. Fuller's utilization of American idioms may well be the result of her early training under her father's influence, who demanded that her translation should "give the thoughts in as few well-arranged words as possible, and without breaks or histations, . . . [making the] meaning perfectly intelligible to the person addressed" (*Memoirs* 1: 17). Elsewhere, Fuller notes "in what I did and said I learned to have reference to other minds" (*Memoirs* 1: 18). Her father's early disciplined tutoring influenced her to study Roman history and literature so that she was sensitive to other cultures. Indeed, Fuller's translation is not only characterized by references to her reader's mind but also by common sense.

This discipline in common sense, Fuller learned from the "great Romans, whose thoughts and lives were [her] daily food during those plastic years [of her childhood] as Jeffrey Steele points out in *The Essential Margaret Fuller* (28). Earlier, I considered Fuller's decision to call herself *Germanico* as a reference that she identified herself with German thought. However, given her classical education and her admiration of the "genius of Rome" (Steele 28), her designation of *Germanico* can also be read as an allusion to Germanicus Caesar (15 BC–AD 19), a successful and popular general, who led his Roman army to the Teutoburg forest in the north of Germany, where he defeated Armenius at "Idistaviso on the Weser" in AD 16 and was subsequently given command of the Eastern territories (*The Oxford Companion to German Literature*, "Armenius" 36, "Germanicus" 287).

Fuller's pioneering spirit can also be linked to her desire to conquer new territory in the intellectual sphere of nineteenth century America by incorporating German thought in her writing. In military terminology, Fuller is both, a conquerer and a defender. In her discussion of the Roman virtues and the greatness of Caesar, she alludes to her own tendency "to conquer obstacles" (Steele 31). Many critics have commented on her spirited defense of Goethe's liberal ideas. Miller states that in her preface to *Eckermann's Conversations with Goethe*, Fuller "defended Goethe even more *militantly*" than in her famous *Dial* essay of January 1841 (79; italics mine). Zwarg maintains that Fuller's "translating from German becomes a way to revise the terms of both Germanic and American cultures" (470).

As early as 1833/34, after having studied German for less than two years, Fuller translated Goethe's *Torquato Tasso*. It was her first literary endeavor, yet, as Thomas points out, it "was the last of her writings to be printed" (92). Mason Wade specifies that Fuller's translation of *Torquato Tasso* first appeared in the Crosby/Nichols edition in 1856 (595). The basis for my evaluation is Fuller's translation as it appeared in *Art, Literature, and the Drama*, edited by her brother, Arthur B. Fuller, published in 1859.

Goethe published his *Torquato Tasso* in 1790. His source was a biography of the poet Tasso by Giovanni Batista Manso, entitled *Vita di Torquato Tasso* (1621). Goethe himself considered his work as a meditation on the art of poetry more concerned with poetic structure than with its dramatic effect. Thematically and structurally, it is one of the most complex plays Goethe has written; it anticipates in several respects the artistic production of his middle and late period. The emphasis lies on the written and not the spoken word. The diction is elevated and decorous and is at times allusive and stiff. The characters often speak obliquely through generalizations or *sententiae*, never quite engaged in animated dialogue. The speeches tend to be long; there are many monologues and the discourse rarely involves more than two speakers. In its form, *Torquato Tasso* resembles a drama in the French neo-classical style consisting of five acts in verse, representing the events of a single day and confined to one locale, Belriguardo, the summer residence of the dukes of Ferrara. There are only five characters: Duke Alfonso II of Ferrara; Princess Leonora d'Este, sister of the duke; her friend the Countess Leonora Sanvitale; Antonio Montecatino, minister to the Duke; and the poet Tasso. *Torquato Tasso* represents an account of the intricate relationship among the poet Tasso, his patron, the Duke, the two Leonoras, and the statesman Antonio, whose steadfastness and adherence to moral law stands in sharp contrast to Tasso's emotional, imaginative, and poetical mind. Tasso suffers a sense of inadequacy in comparison to the competent Duke, who views the poet and his poetry for political purposes, which enhance the power structure of his court. The poet has just completed his great epic poem *Jerusalem Delivered* for which he is praised by the Duke and the two ladies. Tasso is in love with the Princess, but in order to avoid impropriety, he addresses her primarily through poems written for "Leonora." The Princess and the Countess share the same first name, Leonora, which introduces an element of ambiguity, which at the same time fuses the two female characters into a composite whole and also confuses the reader in terms of Tasso's emotional involvement with the two Leonoras. The subject of *Tasso* is the intense suffering of an artist, his unrequitted love for the Princess Leonora, a woman of high-ranking nobility, his self-absorption in poetry and his impending mental disintegration.

Zwarg advances an interesting theory of why *Torquato Tasso* appealed to Fuller, pointing out that the "gathering of identities into lethal oppositions and the circling of desire and pain that it produces—Tasso and siren, poet and philosopher, master and slave—enable Fuller to use translation as a demonstration of its radical imperative" (472). She furthermore holds that the "drama touches upon so many relevant themes discussed among members of the

Concord circle that 'Tasso,' the name, became for Fuller and her friends, particularly Emerson, the signal of their own complicated interaction" (473). Fuller herself provides a more modest reason of why this play appealed to her, stating: "In Tasso Goethe has described the position of the poetical mind in its prose relations with equal depth and fulness" (*Dial* 2: 6). While the subject of poetic creativity attracted Fuller to this work, I might add that the theme of suffering and anguish, which the creative person experiences, and in which poetry has its origin, inspired Goethe to write his drama, and motivated Fuller to translate it. In *Goethe: The Poet and the Age*, Nicholas Boyle quotes Goethe as saying, the "anguished yearning of a passionate soul, irrestistably drawn into an irrevocable exile, runs through the whole drama" (530). In his introductory remarks to a more recent translation of *Torquato Tasso*, published in 1966, Charles E. Passage considers the merits of the play as they appeal to "twentieth century minds . . . in terms of the theme of 'non-communication'" (xii), claiming that the five characters, who speak at length with one another, "understand nothing of what is said" (xiii). The verbal communications are bound to lead to misunderstandings, especially between the statesman Antonio, who feels contempt for the emotionality of Tasso and does not acknowledge the unique vocation of the poet, and Tasso, who cannot comprehend the world of reality and statesmanship. Also, Tasso's compassionate feelings for the Princess make him verbalize his inner turmoil in words the Princess considers inappropriate. Mistakenly, he feels encouraged in his love because the Princess seeks out his company and because his poetry gives great consolation to her spiritual nature. While the verbalization of each character's thoughts results in misunderstanding, the symbolic gestures of friendship and solidarity, based on common objectives and interests, often coincide.

In her preface to the translation, Fuller apologizes for the shortcomings of her work, stating that she made a "somewhat paraphrastical translation" and that she "deemed the rendering of the spirit, on the whole, more desirable than that of the letter," comparing her method of translation to Coleridge's translation of *Wallenstein* (*Art, Literature, and the Drama* 355). While Fuller remained true to the general thought of the original, her accent on the "rendering of the spirit" shifts the emphasis away from a translation to the translator's interpretation of the work, which makes it—at times—prone to misinterpretation. One such example is found in the following lines: Goethe's Tasso says:

> Nur eines bleibt:
> Die Träne hat uns die Natur verliehen,
> Den Schrei des Schmerzens, wenn der Mann zuletzt
> Es nicht mehr trägt—Und mir noch über alles—
> Sie ließ im Schmerz mir Melodie und Rede,
> Die tiefste Fülle meiner Not zu klagen: (*Goethe Werke* 2: 402)

Fuller translates these lines as follows:

> No: 'tis vain.
> There's a last refuge, nature's providence
> Supplies to miserable men like me—
> Tears, sobs of pain, when the overladen heart
> Can bear no more. I have, besides, the gift
> To make my sighs and groans melodious
> To express my anguish in the deepest, saddest,
> Most piercing notes. (*Art, Literature, and the Drama* 448-449)

Here, Fuller's translation does not reflect accurately Goethe's language in its simple dignity. Fuller's words seem ornate, marked by elaborate rhetoric, accentuating the emotional turmoil Tasso feels. By using superlatives alluding to music only and not to speech, she overlooks the important function of speech which Goethe attributed to the poet Tasso. On this occassion, a more literal translation of these lines, keeping Goethe's stress on the role of nature and on the poet's ability to express his anguish through speech/poetry, would read as follows:

> Only one thing remains:
> Nature gave us the gift of tears
> The cry of anguish, when at last a man
> Can no longer bear the pain—to me above all else—
> She (nature) gave the ability to express my anguish in melody and speech.
>
> *(translation mine)*

There is one other example of what might be called a misinterpretation of Goethe's intended meaning. Goethe's Tasso, addressing Antonio, says:

> Zerbrochen ist das Steuer, und es kracht
> Das Schiff an allen Seiten. Berstend reißt
> Der Boden unter meinen Füßen auf!
> Ich fasse dich mit beiden Armen an!
> So klammert sich der Schiffer endlich noch
> Am Felsen fest, an dem er scheitern sollte. (*Goethe Werke* 2: 403)

Fuller's translation reads:

> The rudder breaks; the trembling skiff gives way,
> And rocks beneath my feet. With both my arms
> I clasp thee. Stir not. Here is all my hope.
> The mariner thus clings to that rude rock
> Which wrecked his friends, his fortune and his home.
>
> (*Art, Literature, and the Drama* 449)

The sentiment expressed here by Tasso informs the reader that the poet is no longer ashamed to admit his weakness by considering himself a broken man. The image of shipwreck, i.e., the broken rudder and the trembling skiff, serves as a metaphor for Tasso's recognition of his mental disintegration, which Fuller's translation conveys adequately. However, the last line and a half of her translation misses the fundamental thought of Goethe's poem, when she says, ". . . that rude rock/ which wrecked his friends, his fortune and his home." In Goethe's text, there is no reference to friends, fortune, or home. By comparison, Passage's translation renders the last lines more accurately:

> I now throw both my arms around you. Thus
> The helmsman at the very last clings to
> The rock on which he was about to founder. (104)

The image of the "helmsman" depicts metaphorically the poet Tasso, and the image of the "rock" refers to Antonio, who earlier in the play had been Tasso's antagonist. But now, at the conclusion of the play, the image of Tasso clasping Antonio as the man who saves him from the brink of madness symbolizes a gesture of friendship. The opposing extremes of inadequacy and competency are reconciled. Tasso's final moment of recognition draws attention to the role of art which transfigures the suffering of the artist, who had been at risk and almost foundered, had it not been for the solidarity shown by Antonio in the end.

Fuller's translation of poetry does not follow the metrical pattern exactly; there are many broken or lengthened lines and—at times—her translation lacks the subtlety of the original, as demonstrated by the following lines. Goethe's Tasso says,

> Und wenn der Mensch in seiner Qual verstummt,
> Gab mir ein Gott, zu sagen, wie ich leide. (*Goethe Werke* 2: 402)

Fuller's rendition of these lines does not reflect the eloquence of the original:

How many grieve in silence!
The gods have gifted me to tell my sufferings.

(*Art, Literature, and the Drama* 449)

A more literal translation would be: "And if men in their torment must fall silent/ A god gave me the strength to tell my suffering" (translation mine). However, seven years later, in her "Goethe" essay of July 1841, Fuller translated the last line more accurately, stating "To me gave a God to tell what I suffer" (*Dial* 2: 6). Here, she captures Goethe's dignified and artistic sentiment.

Fuller is keenly aware of the difficulties encountered when translating, because the German language has "a condensed power of expression" (*Art, Literature, and the Drama* 355), which English has lost. She points out that "a great variety of compound words enable the German writer to give a degree of precision and delicacy of shading to his expressions nearly impractical with the terse, the dignified, but by no means flexible English idiom" (*Art, Literature, and the Drama* 355). A comparison between her translation and the original reveals that Fuller avoids a word for word translation and succeeds well in making use of idiomatic English, which enhances her translation. On the whole, her translation conveys the tone of the original, as evidenced by the following lines:

Ein edler Mensch zieht edle Menschen an
Und weiß sie festzuhalten, wie ihr tut. (*Goethe Werke* 2: 314)

Only the noble can attract the noble
And hold them firmly bound as you have done.

(*Art, Literature, and the Drama* 361)

This translation is superb and transmits the delicate sensibility inherent in the original. Fuller's wording approaches the quality of a *sententia* or an aphorism, which must have appealed to New Englanders, well trained in classical languages. By comparison, Charles E. Passage's translation, made in 1966, does not capture the refined tone of Fuller's translation. Passage translates:

> A noble person will attract the noble
> And can retain them firmly, as you do. (4–5)

Comparing a few passages, line for line, indicates that Fuller had a clear perception and a "feel" for Goethe's play. Her translation is faithful to the original except for the few passages cited above. Whereas the original text enjoys autonomy and is hardly criticized, the translator puts herself at risk of being criticized. The translator does not enjoy the autonomy of an author but operates at his peril. Fuller's resourcefulness preserves the enigmatic quality of the original and the coherence and profundity of Goethe's thoughts.

When translating poetry, it is extremely difficult to find idioms in the target language that correspond exactly to those of the original. Braun asserts that Fuller's "translation is expressed in good idiomatic English and has all the qualities of an *original composition*" (218; italics mine). Braun also indicates his intention of writing "a criticism of Margaret Fuller's translation of Goethe's *Tasso*, analyzing and comparing it carefully with the original" (220), an undertaking which apparently has not come to fruition. One is tempted to speculate that the complexity inherent in a translation of such magnitude is one of the reasons for scarce secondary sources on the subject of Fuller's translation of *Tasso*. Because Fuller's translation of *Torquato Tasso* captures well the thought content of the original, and because the topics touched upon in *Tasso*, i.e. failed communications, complicated interactions, and the suffering and anguish of the poetical mind are still relevant today, Fuller's *Tasso* is reprinted in an appendix to this volume. Making Fuller's translation available may spark new interest in Goethe/Fuller scholarship, especially as it pertains to Fuller's role as a translator.

In "A Hithero Unpublished Textual Criticism by James Freeman Clarke of Margaret Fuller's Translation of 'Tasso'," Thomas cites a letter of June 1833 in which Clarke discussed Fuller's translation, offering "detailed criticism of the versification of the first act" (89). Clarke writes:

> I am delighted with Tasso. I agree with you that the style has not the precision of Goethe, but it has a beautiful life of its own. It is a new birth of Goethe's ideas, & bears not the least trace of a translation. As to the versification you take freedoms which may be allowable, but which I do not remember to have met with before in English blank verse. (89)

Clarke then proceeded to make specific suggestions of how some lines should be changed. Clarke had occupied himself with translations from the German and Fuller could trust his good judgment. While he made some suggestions for improvement, his assessment of her translation is positive and congruent with Braun's evaluation of Fuller's translation. Thomas cites another letter by Clarke, dated June 21, 1833, which contains textual criticism of Fuller's translation of *Tasso*:

> The more I read your Tasso the more I am charmed with it. I think that its defect is an occasional obscurity arising from the connexion not being clearly determined. I find this also in your notes, & think it arises from the quickness with which your mind apprehends relations which are not so clear to others, & thereby they are left in doubt between two meanings. . . . I have marked some of these. . . . It appears also that the syntax of your sentences is somewhat free. (92)

Again, Clarke offers specific textual changes especially in regard to syntax. Furthermore, Thomas points out that Fuller's manuscript was "criticized—first by Frederick Henry Hedge in 1834, and also possibly by Emerson" (92). Since Thomas does not elaborate on Hedge's or Emerson's criticism, it is left to future Fuller scholars to investigate how Fuller's contemporaries evaluated her translation.

A discussion of Fuller's work as a translator would not be complete without mentioning her translation of Johann Peter Eckermann's *Gespräche mit Goethe in den letzten Jahren seines Lebens.* Fuller's translation, entitled *Conversations with Goethe from the German of Eckermann,* was published by George Ripley in *Specimens of Foreign Standard Literature* in 1839 and constitutes Fuller's first book publication. Eckermann (1792-1854) was Goethe's companion and secretary from 1823-1832. In 1836, Eckermann published the first two volumes of *Gespräche mit Goethe,* which are a valuable source for Goethe's life and opinions in his last years. Goethe was born in 1749 and died in 1832; thus, he was seventy-four years old when the *Conversations* began and eighty-two when they terminated.

Fuller's early rigorous language training worked to her advantage in this prose translation, which shows her superb command of the English language. Bauschinger observes that Eckermann's introductory remarks about his own background sound in Fuller's translation just a bit more sophisticated than in the original (95). Fuller compressed the original, excluding Eckermann's "meagre record of his visit to Italy" as she points out in her introductory remarks (xxv). She omitted all passages that deal with Goethe's *Farbenlehre,* because the theory of colors was "scarcely known" in the United States and also because she herself had "no clear understanding of the subject" (xxiv-xxv). Thus, Fuller used prudent judgment in deleting the information pertaining to Goethe's scientific experiments. Fuller offers a practical reason for her condensed translation, stating, "—it being found that the two German volumes would not, by any means, make two, yet were too much for one of the present series,—it seemed necessary, in some way, to compress or curtail the book" (xxiv). Fuller's translation of *Conversations with Goethe* comprises 414 pages; Eckermann's *Gespräche mit Goethe,* Part I covers 218 pages and Part II, 222 pages, bringing the total to 440 pages. Without examining the respective texts more closely, one can conclude that Fuller's condensations were minor ones. Another plausible reason for shortening the original text can be attributed to the nature of the book. Fuller writes, "for a book of table-talk, so much greater liberty would be allowed . . . than for a classical work" (xxiii). She asserts that nothing has been "omitted which would cast either light or shade on [Goethe's] character, [stating], I am sure that nothing has been softened or accentuated, and believe that Goethe's manners, temper, and opinions, wear here the same aspect that they do in the original" (xxvi). Early on, Fuller had wanted to write a biography of Goethe, but she was unable to do so because she was not able to obtain the necessary research material. Her translation of the *Conversations* became a substitution for her intended biography.

A perusal of Fuller's text discloses that she made a faithful translation and presents a portrayal of Goethe in his interaction with Eckermann and representative men of letters and the sciences, which affords an extraordinarily full picture of Goethe's old age and his era. Eckermann also had noted in his preface that the *Conversations* complete the portrait of Goethe and his era (6). To the end of his life, Goethe maintained an unceasing interest in all that happened in the world of literature, the arts and the sciences. Goethe paid attention to many leading foreign writers, among whom were Byron, Carlyle, Beranger, and Manzoni, whose works undoubtedly appealed to the rebellious side of Fuller's nature. To offer a glimpse of Fuller's excellent translation, I will quote her last passage from *Conversations with Goethe*, which concludes her translation as well as Eckermann's volume, published in 1836.

> The morning after Goethe's death, a deep longing seized me to look yet once again upon his earthly garment. His faithful servant, Frederic, opened for me the chamber in which he was laid out. Stretched upon his back, he reposed as if in sleep; profound peace and

security reigned in the features of his noble, dignified countenance. The mighty brow seemed yet the dwelling-place of thought. I wished for a lock of his hair; but reverence prevented me from cutting it off. The body lay naked, only wrapped in a white sheet; large pieces of ice had been placed around to keep it fresh as long as possible. Frederic drew aside the sheet, and I was astonished at the divine magnificence of the form. The breast was so powerful, broad, and arched; the limbs full, and softly muscular; the feet elegant, and of the most perfect shape; nowhere, on the whole body, a trace either of fat or of leanness and decay. A perfect man lay in great beauty before me; and the rapture which the sight caused, made me forget, for a moment, that the immortal spirit had left such an abode. I laid my hand on his heart—there was a deep silence—and I turned away to give free vent to my tears. (413-414)

This excerpt demonstrates that Fuller captured the sentiment of Eckermann's emotions very well. There is great fidelity to the original in its simplicity of wording and style. Fuller's prose translation stands out for its faithful adherence to the original as well as for its strong stylistic appeal. She succeeded in transmitting the substance and the essential features of Eckermann's *Conversations*. Emerson reports that Fuller's translation "makes the basis of the translation of Eckermann since published in London by Mr. Oxenford" (*Memoirs* 1: 243). Emerson refers to John Oxenford's edition, published in 1850. In the "Translator's Preface," Oxenford acknowledges Fuller's translation with the following words: "I feel bound to state that, while translating the First Book, I have had before me the translation by Mrs. Fuller, published in America. The great merit of this version I willingly acknowledge, though the frequent omissions render it almost an abridgement" (vi).[9] The term "abridgement" seems an exaggeration since Fuller's translation consisted of 414 pages in comparison to Eckermann's 440 pages. By Fuller's own admission, she purposely omitted Eckermann's record of his visit to Italy, and all the passages that deal with Goethe's theory of colors.

Moreover, a word for word comparison between Fuller's translation and that of Oxenford of the passage cited above reveals that Oxenford uses the identical language which Fuller had used in her translation, with a few minor exceptions: where Fuller says "a deep longing seized me" (413), Oxenford says, "a deep desire seized me" (572). Fuller's translation is more accurate because the German word "Sehnsucht," used by Eckermann, is best translated by "longing" and not by "desire." Some other minor deviations between the two translations are put in italics for easier recognition of Fuller's and Oxenford's respective word choices. Fuller's translation reads: "profound peace and security reigned in the features of his *noble, dignified* countenance," where Oxenford's translation reads "*sublimely* noble countenance." Fuller's wording, "large pieces of ice had been placed *around*," is replaced by the words "*near it.*" Where Fuller states, "I was astonished at the divine magnificence of the *form*," Oxenford substitutes the word *limbs*. Fuller's sentence, "the breast was so powerful, broad, and arched; the *limbs* full, and softly muscular," reads in Oxenford's translation, "the *arms and thighs were full*." Fuller's last sentence reads, "I turned away to give free vent to my tears," to which Oxenford adds the word *suppressed* tears, which corresponds to a literal translation of the original, *verhaltenen Tränen* (477). For a word-for-word comparison between the two translations and the original, see Eckermann 477, Fuller 413-414, and Oxenford 572.[10] In essence, Oxenford used Fuller's translation. When he made changes, they were often less precise, as demonstrated in the passage cited above. One of the chief merits of Oxenford's translation lies in his inclusion of the third volume of *Conversations with Goethe*, which Eckermann published in 1848. Eckermann compiled these additional Conversations from his own notes and those of another friend of Goethe's, M. Soret, covering the years from 1822 to 1832.

Fuller's last translation from the German was an excerpt from Bettina von Arnim's epistolary novel *Die Günderode*. Fuller published her essay, entitled "Bettine Brentano and her friend Günderode," in the January 1842 issue of the *Dial* (*Dial* 2: 313-357); an abridgement—consisting of eight pages—can be found in Steele's book. Subsequently, Fuller expanded her translation and published it in book form under the title *Günderode* in 1842. In a letter to Elizabeth Palmer Peabody on December 26, 1844, Fuller writes, "should I ever get a name, probably I may be able to finish the translation on good terms, but shall, at present, do nothing about it" (*Letters* 3: 254). Minna Wesselhoeft revised Fuller's translation, added her own translation, and published the expanded version as *Correspondence of Fräulein Günderode and Bettina von Arnim* in 1861 (Wade 595).

Bettina von Arnim (1785-1859) published *Die Günderode* in 1840 in two volumes. Her book constitutes a fictionalized account of her correspondence with the young Canoness Karoline von Günderode (1780-1806) in the years between 1804 and 1806. Bettina was orphaned at age fifteen and lived with relatives in Frankfurt between 1800 and 1808. Her friendship with the five years older Karoline, who was also a poet—writing under the pseudonym Tian—highlights the emotional bond between two trusted friends and also their intellectual aspirations. Both women were highly educated and sophisticated in their tastes for art, music, and philosophy. Bettina and Karoline developed their own philosophy, which they called *Schwebereligion* (Bronfen 10 and 17), roughly translated as "hovering religion." The credo of their religion emphasized emancipation from the limitations of conventional morality and rebellion against the restrictions of society. Bettina's and Karoline's utopian vision focused on women's development of their inner nature and an evolution of the self that does not define itself in relation to a man.

On a historical note, Bettina Brentano had been closely associated with the *Frühromantiker*, the so-called Heidelberg School of romantics. She was the granddaughter of the writer Sophie von Laroch, the sister of the poet Clemens Brentano, and married to the poet Achim von

Arnim. As the wife of von Arnim, she presided over a literary salon in Berlin. Among her friends were many writers of the romantic period, and the composers Liszt, Brahms, and Beethoven. As a young girl, Bettina corresponded with Goethe's mother and during frequent visits with her, she heard first-hand accounts of the poet's life and work, which culminated in her book *Goethe's Briefwechsel mit einem Kinde*, published in 1835. This book represents the fictionalized account of an admiring young girl who imagines herself in the company of the great poet. The English edition appeared in 1838 under the title *Goethe's Correspondence with a Child* (Bronfen 38). The book was widely circulated and read by the Transcendentalists. Pochmann reports that "Emerson was fond of Bettina's 'pure and poetic' nature, 'her wit, humor, will, and pure aspirations,' . . . but *Margaret was the first to notice Bettina*, for she owned, or at last was reading, the book in May 1838" (241; italics mine).

In her introduction to "Bettine Brentano and her Friend Günderode," Fuller criticizes Bettina's book *Goethe's Correspondence with a Child* as "youthful idolatry" (*Dial* 2: 313), stating, "we must feel that the relation in which [Bettina] stands to Goethe is not a beautiful one" (*Dial* 2: 314) . . . "it is too unequal . . . [and] compels us to demand some conscious dignity of her as a woman" (*Dial* 2: 316). In a letter to William H. Channing on 19 February 1841, Fuller writes "I meant to have translated for you the best passages of 'Die Günderode' (which I prefer to the correspondence with Goethe. The two girls are equal natures, and *both* in earnest)" (*Letters* 2: 202).

Fuller's introductory remarks criticizing Bettina's first book stand in sharp contrast to her positive assessment of Bettina's second book. Fuller was delighted with the account of the friendship between two sophisticated young women as recorded in *Die Günderode*. The vivacious Bettina and the more delicate and at times melancholy Karoline were equal in age, intellectual training, and aspirations. Both women wanted to develop a voice to express their own thoughts regarding friendhsip, nature, poetry, philosophy, and a woman's place in society. Female friendship founded upon equality appealed to Fuller as well as the idea of women writing poetry and engaging in philosophical discourse. Fuller held that the friendship between the two young women was "essentially poetic" (*Dial* 2: 319), and saw them both having been influenced by the philosophy of Fichte and Schelling (*Dial* 2: 320). The importance of Fuller's Brentano/ Günderode essay in relation to *Woman in the Nineteenth Century* lies in its exploration of a close friendship between two women, their cultured tastes and high aspirations. For Fuller, these letters not only present a "view of the interior of German life, and of an ideal relation realized, but the high state of culture in Germany which presented to the thoughts of those women themes of poesy and philosophy as readily, as to . . . the American girl come[s] the choice of a dress" (*Dial* 2: 320). Here, Fuller expresses disappointment with the mundane interests of American girls, and admires the poetic aspirations of the two German girls, who symbolize to her "Nature and Ideal" (*Dial* 2: 318-319).

Steele holds that Fuller's *Günderode* essay "introduces several of her most important feminist arguments" (xx), stating, "no longer portrayed as the victim of men who 'cast' her out, . . . [Günderode] possesses the intellectual capacity to 'interpret' Bettine, the natural woman of beauty. The conjunction of Bettine and Günderode sets up the central dynamic of Fuller's feminist model of interpretation" (xxi). Steele is oblivious of the irony of Günderode's real life situation and makes no mention of her suicide over the rejection by her lover, Professor Friedrich Creuzer. Günderode was despondent when her lover informed her that he would break off their relationship and that he would not divorce his wife. Günderode committed suicide in 1806 by stabbing herself with a dagger; she had prepared a towel filled with stones, which she put around her neck wishing to drown in the Rhine river. Because she fell backwards, she landed on the bank of the river, where she was found by a local farmer (Bronfen 385-386). Fuller was aware of Günderode's "voluntary death," as she stated in her concluding remarks of her essay: "On this subject I have said nothing; it involves too much for the space to let me venture" (*Dail* 2: 353).

In her translation, Fuller successfully reproduces the vivacity and youthful spirit of Bettina's letters as well as the more tempered and solemn responses of Günderode's. Fuller translates their fluent conversational style into equally flowing American idiom, retaining the tone of the original in its vitality. Fuller imitates Bettina's exuberant style as far as possible, including her childish punctuation that consisted of many dashes, question marks, and exclamation marks, as the following sentence demonstrates. In Fuller's translation, Bettina writes: "In the summer-house where we last saw one another for the first time,—yes, a whole year have we been good friends to one another???!!!!!" (*Dial* 2: 325). This sentence mirrors Bettina's joyful exuberance in feelings of friendship; Fuller's translation also simulates Bettina's German sentence structure that results in an awkward English sentence. Another example of Fuller's Germanized English is the following: "I would wish for thee Bettine (to speak between ourselves, for this may no man hear)" (*Dial* 2: 355). In her last translation from German, Fuller no longer condenses the long German sentences but reproduces the German sentence structure in her English translation. While Fuller captured the exuberant tone of the originals, the *Letters* sound sentimental to today's readers.

In general, the eloquence of an original work cannot be duplicated in any translation. The original has enduring qualities; it is a monument to human genius that transcends the linguistic and cultural changes of time and space. In *Rethinking Translation*, the noted translator Lawrence Venuti writes, "the original is a form of self-expression appropriate to the author, a copy true to his personality or intention, an image endowed with resemblance" (3). By comparison, a translation is only a replica, derivative by its nature, which by neccessity conveys an image of approximation. Since translations reflect the circumstances and times of the translator in word choice, phrasing, grammar, and syntax, they are dated in contrast to the original work which is timeless. Venuti sees the translator as "a paradoxical hybrid, at once dilettante and artisan" (1). This image of the dilettante/artisan also applies to Fuller. In its positive sense, *dilettante* denotes an admirer of the arts and Fuller certainly admired Goethe and German literature. Her language skills made her an artisan, striving for self-expression. Fuller's self-expression was guarded and her translations were not so much a literal expression of the translator's self, but a mediation between two languages. At the level of language, she could be creative and her translations signify a passage from one culture to another. In her article, "Translation as (Sub)version," Suzanne Jill Levine, a scholar and a translator, supports my contention, stating: "translation—an activity caught between the scholarly and the creative, between the rational and intuitive—is a route, a voyage if you like, through which a writer/translator may seek to reconcile fragments: fragments of a text, of language, of oneself. More than a moment of interpretation, translation is a (w)rite of passage" (85).

As to the question of the merits of a translation, and whether or not one can profitably gain from translations, Fuller voices her opinion positively. Discussing her readings from Greek masterpieces in translation she states:

> And so with these translations from the Greek. I can divine the original through this veil, as I can see the movements of a spirited horse by those of his coarse grasscloth muffler. Beside, every translator . . . feels his subject inspired, and the divine Aura informs even his stammering lips. (*Woman* 194)

This graphic image of the "spirited horse" in comparison with a "coarse grasscloth muffler" indicates that a translation, in Fuller's assessment, hides much of the beauty of the original. Yet, while a translation offers a clouded vision that shrouds the original, and may be an imperfect transcript, it, nevertheless, is of value. In *Life Without and Life Within*, Fuller writes "no great Poet can be well translated. . . . Translations come to us as a message to the lover from the lady of his love through the lips of a confidante or menial—we are obliged to imagine what was most vital in the utterance" (102). Thus, Fuller views translations as a substitution for authenticity. The translator mediates between the author's work and the reader's acquisition of it; while the translator conveys the message, the reader still has to read it perceptively for the implied meaning.

Notes

1. For a concise account of the early reputation of the German writers in America, see S. H. Goodnight's *German Literature in American Magazines Prior to 1848*. Bulletin of the University of Wisconsin, Philology and Literature Series, vol. 4, no. 1 (Madison: University of Wisconsin, 1907) 40-55 and 61-104.

2. Concerning Fuller's appreciation of Goethe, Slochower concludes his essay by stating, "it was her tragedy that she was able to appreciate this man without being able to follow him" (144). "Margaret Fuller and Goethe," *The Germanic Review*, vol. VII (April 1932): 130-144.

3. *The Achievements of Margaret Fuller* (University Park and London: The Pennsylvania State University Press, 1979). See especially the chapter "Goethe and Humanism," 45-65.

4. *Margaret Fuller, Citizen of the World*. (Heidelberg: Winter, 1969).

5. *German Culture in America*. (Madison: University of Wisconsin Press, 1957) Rpt. in *Critical Eassays on Margaret Fuller*. Ed. Joel Myerson (Boston: G. K. Hall & Co., 1980) See chapter "Margaret Fuller and Germany," 228-246.

6. In: *Festschrift zum 75. Geburtstag von Theodor Spira*. Eds. H. Viebrock and W. Erzgräber (Heidelberg: Winter, 1961) 309-317.

7. Another reason for inclusion here is the fact that this part of Fuller's essay was excluded from Miller's reprinting of the "Goethe" essay in his anthology of 1963 and the reprint thereof in 1969.

8. Foremost among these were Ludwig Tieck (1773-1853), a prominent and versatile representative of early German romanticism, who produced several translations of Shakespeare's works and also August Schlegel (1767-1845), who is considered one of the most gifted translators, whose verse renderings of Shakespeare's plays—seventeen plays between 1797-1810—made many Germans believe that Shakespeare's works were part of the German literary canon.

9. In his introduction to the 1930 edition of Oxenford's translation, Havelock Ellis echoes Oxenford's earlier remark, stating: "Sarah Margaret Fuller's translation appeared in 1839. Her version, however, was very incomplete" (xv n. 2). Compare also Margaret V. Allen, who states that Oxenford's translation became the standard English-language version and was based on "Fuller's translation which appeared in 1839" (185 n. 5).

10. Compare also R. O. Moon's translation, published in 1950 of the passage cited, which shows a greater resemblance to Fuller's translation than to Oxenford's (Moon 403-404). Moon's translation comprises 404 pages for Part I and II in comparison to Fuller's 414 pages. Yet, I have not seen a reference that Moon's translation is abridged.

Works Cited

Allen, Margaret Vanderhaar. *The Achievement of Margaret Fuller.* University Park: Pennsylvania State UP, 1979.

Arndt, Walter. Trans. *Faust, Part I and II.* Ed. Cyrus Hamlin. New York: W. W. Norton, 1976.

Bauschinger, Sigrid. *Die Posaune der Reform: deutsche Literatur im Neuengland des 19. Jahrhunderts.* Bern and Stuttgart: Francke, 1989.

Braun, Frederick Augustus. *Margaret Fuller and Goethe.* New York: Henry Holt and Company, 1910.

Boyle Nicholas. *Goethe: The Poet and the Age.* Oxford: Clarendon Press, 1991.

Bronfen, Elisabeth. Ed. *Bettina von Arnim: Die Günderode*. München: Mathes & Seitz, 1982.

The Dial: A Magazine for Literature, Philosophy, and Religion. 4 vols. 1840-1844. Rpt. New York: Russel & Russel, Inc., 1961. Cited as *Dial*.

Durning, Russel E. *Margaret Fuller: Citizen of the World*. Heidelberg: Winter, 1969.

Eckermann, Johann Peter. *Gespräche mit Goethe in den letzten Jahren seines Lebens*. 2 vols. Ed. Fritz Bergemann. Baden- Baden: Insel, 1981.

Emerson, Ralph Waldo, William Henry Channing, and James Freeman Clarke. *Memoirs of Margaret Fuller Ossoli*. 2 vols. Boston: Phillips, Sampson and Company, 1852.

Fuller, Margaret [Margaret Fuller Ossoli]. *Art, Literature, and the Drama*. Ed. Arthur B. Fuller. Boston: Roberts Brothers, 1859.

—. *Conversations with Goethe from the German of Eckermann*. (Translation) Vol. 4 of *Specimens of Foreign Standard Literature*. Ed. George Ripley. Boston: Hilliard, Gray and Company, 1839.

—. *The Letters of Margaret Fuller*. 5 vols. to date. Ed. Robert N. Hudspeth. Ithaca: Cornell UP, 1983- . Cited as *Letters*.

—. [Margaret Fuller Ossoli]. *Life Without and Life Within*. Ed. Arthur B. Fuller. Boston: Roberts Brothers, 1859.

—. *Woman in the Nineteenth Century*. New York: Greely & McElrath, 1845. Cited as *Woman*.

Goethe, Johann Wolfgang von. *Goethe Werke*. 6 vols. Frankfurt am Main: Insel, 1979.

Goodnight, S. H. *German Literature in American Magazines Prior to 1848*. Madison: University of Wisconsin, 1907.

Higginson, Thomas Wentworth. *Margaret Fuller Ossoli*. 5th ed. Boston: Houghton Mifflin and Company, 1886.

Lange, Victor. "Goethe's Amerikabild. Wirklichkeit und Vision." *Amerika in der deutschen Literatur*. Eds. Sigrid Bauschinger, Horst Denkler, and Wilfried Malsch. Stuttgart: Reclam, 1975.

Levine, Suzanne Jill. "Translation as (Sub)version: On Translating *Infante's Inferno*." *Rethinking Translation*. Ed. Lawrence Venuti. London and New York: Routledge, 1992. 75- 85.

Long, O. W. "Goethe and Longfellow." *The Germanic Review*. 7. 2 (April 1932): 145-175.

Marquardt, Hertha. "Die erste Goethe-Biographin in Amerika. Margaret Fuller's geplantes *Life of Goethe*." *Festschrift zum 75. Geburtstag von Theodor Spira*. Eds. H. Viebrock and W. Erzgräber. Heidelberg: Carl Winter, 1961. 309-317.

Miller, Perry. *Margaret Fuller: American Romantic*. Ithaca: Cornell UP, 1963. Rpt. Gloucester, Mass.: Peter Smith, 1969.

Oxenford, John. Trans. *Conversations of Goethe with Eckermann and Soret*. London: George Bell & Sons, 1850. Rpt. 1874.

—. Trans. *Conversations of Goethe with Eckermann*. Introduction by Havelock Ellis. New York: E. P. Dutton & Co., 1930.

The Oxford Companion to German Literature. 2nd ed. Ed. Mary Garland. Oxford: Oxford UP, 1986.

Moon, R. O. Trans. *Eckermann's Conversations with Goethe*. London: Morgan, Laird & Co., LTD., 1950.

Passage, Charles E. Trans. *Torquato Tasso*. New York: Ungar, 1966.

Pochmann, Henry A. "Margaret Fuller and Germany." *German Culture in America*. Madison: University of Wisconsin Press, 1957. Rpt. in *Critical Essays on Margaret Fuller*. Ed. Joel Myerson. Boston: G. K. Hall & Co., 1980. 228-246.

Schultz, Arthur R. "Margaret Fuller—Transcendentalist Interpreter of German Literature." *Monatshefte für Deutschen Unterricht*. 32 (April 1942): 169-182. Rpt. in *Critical Essays on Margaret Fuller*. Ed. Joel Myerson. Boston: G. K. Hall & Co., 1980. 195-208.

Slochower, Harry. "Margaret Fuller and Goethe." *The Germanic Review* 7 (April 1932): 130-144.

Steele, Jeffrey. Ed. *The Essential Margaret Fuller*. New Brunswick, New Jersey: Rutgers UP, 1992.

Thomas, J. Wesley. "A Hithero Unpublished Textual Criticism by James Freeman Clarke of Margaret Fuller's Translation of 'Tasso'." *Monatshefte für Deutschen Unterricht*. 41 (February 1949): 89-92.

Venuti, Lawrence. Ed. *Rethinking Translation: Discourse, Subjectivity, Ideology*. London and New York: Routledge, 1992.

Wade, Mason. *The Writings of Margaret Fuller*. New York: Viking, 1941.

Wayne, Philip. Trans. *Faust, Part I*. Baltimore: Penguin, 1949.

Zwarg, Christina. "Feminism in Translation: Margaret Fuller's *Tasso*." *Studies in Romanticism*. 29. 3 (Fall 1990): 463-490.

Marie Mitchell Olesen Urbanski

My Struggle for Margaret Fuller

O N MAY 31, 1971, my brother-in-law called me in Lexington, Kentucky to tell me my Mother had died. I finished typing my dissertation prospectus on Margaret Fuller's *Woman in the Nineteenth Century* and left it in the mail box of my dissertation director. My friend, Colleen Herrmann (Demaris) made plane reservations for my two daughters and me for Macon, Georgia to attend the funeral of Esther Mitchell Olesen.

I had been struggling with my Ph.D. director to accept Margaret Fuller as a writer worthy of a dissertation for a year, and at last he had acquiesced. When I first broached this subject, he replied: "I don't like Margaret Fuller and I don't know anything about her." I did not dare to question his logic but his words haunted me. In those days students were deferential to professors. Each month I would appear at his office with a new topic about Fuller. I began with her literary criticism and avoided her feminist writing, since he made no effort to conceal his antipathy to the women's movement. Month after month, I suggested various aspects of Fuller's literary output and was turned down. Meanwhile, my colleagues were making progress on safe and acceptable dissertations about Herman Melville and William Faulkner, but the more I read Fuller, the more enmeshed I became. Despite my poverty with two children to support on a graduate teaching assistant's stipend, and a shrinking job market, I refused to compromise my dissertation choice. As I did more research, I realized that of all of Fuller's writing, her *Woman in the Nineteenth Century* had the least study. Then my struggle with this dissertation director was to convince him to accept a feminist masterpiece as my thesis topic. Finally, on March 9, 1971, he wrote to me a letter of capitulation if I would meet certain research criteria. He was disturbed by my "emotionalism" that would work against "scholarly objectivity," as well as my choice of a figure that had been so "thoroughly worked over as Margaret Fuller with nine biographies and six dissertations." He found it "absurd" to bring so much knowledge to a "simple, little book." I was overjoyed.

Fortunately for me from then onward, our contacts were by mail from Orono, Maine, where I had obtained a teaching position. Looking back at his frustration and my frustration after twenty-two years, I can understand his reluctance to validate Margaret Fuller. She was not a member of the literary canon and had, in fact, been denigrated by the literary establishment ruled over by Perry Miller, who, to quote Madeleine Stern, "not only belittled but patronized" her. Had my director been enthusiastic, I might not have worked so hard. His negativity was a favor as it forced me to read everything written about Fuller; and his bias against her foreshadowed problems I would encounter in the future.

Certain patterns emerged in the parroting of generations of critics of the same repetitive denigration. Clearly Fuller posed a great threat to patriarchal power. The counter-offensive was to ridicule her rather than to deal with her ideas. (However, there was an exception at the University of Kentucky; Guy Davenport, a member of my committee, was a poet who understood Fuller's importance and supported my work.)

My next struggle was to publish. I soon learned that unlike my dissertation director, younger scholars were well aware that Fuller's work offered a fertile field for research opportunities. Nevertheless, traditionalist attitudes still controlled access to grant money as well as to journal and book publication. In 1980 Greenwood Press published my book, *Margaret Fuller's Woman in the Nineteenth Century.*

Perhaps because they were not dependent as a profession on the academic establishment, scholars outside of the "Ivory Tower" were often more courageous and more willing to challenge received opinion than professors. Fuller's biographer, Madeleine Stern, a rare book dealer and writer, and Howard Meyer, a lawyer and writer, were making new interpretations of Fuller and were sources of encouragement. Other writers, Joseph Jay Deiss from Wellfleet, and Dale Spender from Australia, also challenged previously held assumptions about Fuller.

Meanwhile, the feminist movement was beginning to transform the universities as it did society at large. No longer so deferential, students pressured faculty to reevaluate the canon, to validate women writers, to study the history of women's oppression. Assumptions about gender were being questions. I began to put my struggle to acknowledge Fuller and my sense of isolation in perspective. Women were talking to each other as they had once talked in Fuller's consciousness raising sessions in the 1840s. After twenty years, as Fuller's writing became more accessible, newer scholars were responding to the influences of the feminist movement and were forced to reevaluate Fuller.

But it was R. Buckminster Fuller, Margaret's grandnephew, whose genius as a thinker and architect has been acknowledged, who in the name of the Fuller family thanked me for my work in behalf of

Margaret. As a child and as a student attending Harvard, Buckminster Fuller had heard and accepted the same negative comments about his great aunt. It was during his spiritual crisis in his thirties that he discovered her on his own. From that time on, he identified with Margaret in much of his thinking. He, too, believed in the power of intuition and clairvoyance. In his book, *Ideas and Integrities*, he quoted from her in a chapter called, "Margaret Fuller's Prophecy." In Sunset, Maine, he asked me to sit in Margaret Fuller's chair. Not long before his death, he was attempting to have my essay, "The Ambivalence of Ralph Waldo Emerson towards Margaret Fuller" republished in a major journal and to collaborate with me in a second edition of my book. One of his letters to me is included in this volume. He understands that he might not be physically present for the second edition he hoped to see, so he gives suggestions for areas future scholars need to investigate. Bucky Fuller understood that in order to educate people about his great aunt Margaret, that a film needed to be made about her life. This effort continues today.

R. Buckminster Fuller is linked to his great aunt and the others who have worked for a just society. It was part of the Grand Design of the Universe that my Mother (who was a suffragette at Woman's College in Greensboro, North Carolina) should have died on the day of a significant stage in my struggle to validate Margaret Fuller's genius. I hope that the next link, the generation which my daughters, Jane Urbanski Robbins and Wanda Urbanska, represent, will be able to live in a world that respects women and acknowledges their genius.

Marie Mitchell Olesen Urbanski

The Ambivalance of Ralph Waldo Emerson Towards Margaret Fuller

See you not that I cannot spare you? that you cannot be spared? that a vast & beautiful Power to whose counsels our will was never party, has thrown us into strict neighborhood for best & happiest ends?—A letter from Ralph Waldo Emerson to Margaret Fuller, October 24, 1840

I N ANY STUDY of Margaret Fuller's life and work, the role of Ralph Waldo Emerson has always elicited considerable comment. Some scholars tend to interpret her relationship with Emerson as one of mutuality, whereas others see the emotional involvement as one-sided. Supporting the latter view, Carl F. Strauch's analysis has been accepted as valid by a large part of the scholarly community. It is Strauch's conjecture that Fuller declared a love from which Emerson recoiled, but that she served as a major catalyst in his poetic output. To be sure, Strauch's evaluation of Fuller's importance as an inspiration to Emerson at the time of his high poetic creativity is significant, but his dismissal of their letters after December, 1844 as inconsequential invalidates his argument. This period in which they no longer saw each other is an important factor in an analysis of their relationship because it reveals Emerson's continued preoccupation with Fuller. Revelation of Fuller's involvement with a young man influenced Emerson's feelings about her. Her memory so disturbed him after her death that his evaluation of her writing was clouded and his criticism of her work lacked the requisite objectivity for a canonical judgment. Dorothy Berkson has published a more current analysis of their relationship in which she argues it was an intellectual friendship, but she does not adequately explain Emerson's change of attitude about Fuller's writing after her death.

An examination of their journals, essays, poetry, the *Dial*, the *Memoirs*, and especially their correspondence over a period of fourteen years reveals that the nature of their intimacy changed from an intellectually centered one to one which suggested greater passion. In a remarkable exchange of letters that lasted from 1836 to 1850, Waldo and Margaret penned words to each other which at times reached high poetry. Emerson wrote to her in the nature metaphors of transcendentalism: "We once have risen to yonder bank of rich flowers and have reflected a heaven of stars." At other times, he hints at desperate longing: "Wonderful sleepless working loving child, with such aspiration! and with all this doubt and self reproach! Whether to admire or chide or sooth you? I can no less than do all at once, if there existed any word of such a wondrous mixture of meaning . . . Yet that is a compliment too costly to be paid." And Fuller's letters express the frustration of Heloise writing to Abelard: "All this music is played upon me almost too fully: I have scarcely force to bear it." Although Emerson called her the "new Corinne,"

Margaret was no Corinne. Unlike the heroine of Madame de Stael's novel, Fuller refused to waste away and die of a broken heart, to worship indefinitely at the Emersonian shrine. Instead, after telling Emerson he was "intellect," but she was "life," she moved to New York and discovered James Nathan, and then to Italy where she found a lover in a handsome nobleman. With the sting of Fuller's marriage to the Marchese Giovanni Angelo Ossoli fresh on his mind, Emerson established a critical canon, in the *Memoirs of Margaret Fuller Ossoli*, not the least damaging of his assertions being "her pen was a non-conductor." Emerson lacked the detachment to be a proper critic of her writing and her character due to his reaction to her life style in Europe and his long time emotional involvement with her.

At age thirteen, she wrote her father twice, expressing her wish to attend Mr. Emerson's school for girls in which both William and Ralph Waldo taught (1:130, 135). For years she continued to seek Ralph Waldo Emerson's acquaintance. In the small milieu of New England's intelligentsia, Fuller had heard of Emerson well before she met him. No doubt, her friends dropped discreet hints about Emerson, the eligible widower, who had recently returned from an extended sojourn in Europe. In an 1834 letter, she wrote: "He spoke with due admiration of the Rev. W. Emerson, that only clergyman of all possible clergymen who eludes my acquaintance. *Mais n'importe!* I keep his image bright in my mind (1:210). Then she asked the Rev. F.H. Hedge, to give her translation of *Tasso* to Emerson for corrections. "It gratified me that a mind which had affected mine so powerfully should be dwelling on something of mine. . ." (1:213). Fuller's selection of Emerson as the recipient of her translation is significant. Princess Leonara in *Tasso* asks:

> And in the fair companionship of Muses
> May not a lady hope to meet some poet
> Who rapturously may recognize in her
> The treasure he was seeking far and wide?

Certainly she could not have been oblivious of the parallel between herself and the princess. Nevertheless Emerson soon married Lidian, after a pallid courtship that suggests a *marriage de convenance*.

When Fuller learned of Emerson's marriage to Lidian Jackson, she made unflattering comments about her in a letter to Frederic Hedge written March 6, 1835. Nevertheless, it was Lidian who extended to Margaret the invitation she had wanted for so long. Since Emerson was no longer an eligible widower, Fuller sought him as a mentor. At twenty-six, she arrived as a guest in the Concord household, which was depressed over the recent death of Emerson's brother, Charles. In addition, Lidian was well over six months into her first pregnancy. But, as Emerson later admitted in the *Memoirs*, Fuller charmed this serious thirty-three-year-old scholar by making him laugh more than he liked, and by studying his tastes. During the three-week visit, Emerson recorded the impact Fuller made upon him in a letter (August 8, 1836) to his brother, William. "She is quite an extraordinary person for her apprehensiveness, her acquisitions and her powers of conversation." During the visit, Fuller had already begun discussion on a personal level. In his journal (August 6, 1836), Emerson records: "'I know not what you think of me,' said my friend. 'Are you sure? You know all I think of you by those things I say to you.'" (5:187).

Once their acquaintance was established, Emerson was equally aggressive in maintaining it. Almost immediately after she left, Emerson began making plans to see her again. A preacher at Groton had written to Emerson on March 23, 1835, asking him to give a sermon there. Emerson acceded to this request made over a year previously, soon after he met Fuller who was living in Groton at the time. Then he learned she would not be there for the Sunday committed. She wrote from Boston on September 21, 1836 and implored him to postpone his engagement: "Do not go, dear Sir, I intreat you . . . I think you will do it for my sake, for I would do twenty times as much for yours." While Emerson was unable to change the date, he suggested that she visit him in Concord instead.

Details of another early visit Fuller made to the Emerson home are described in Emerson's journal. Just prior to her visit, he was ruminating the disillusion of marriage:

> In life all finding is not that thing we sought, but something else. The lover on being accepted, misses the wildest charm of the maid he dared not hope to call his own. The husband loses the wife in the cares of the household. Later, he cannot rejoice with her in the babe for by becoming a mother, she ceases yet more to be a wife.

On April 16, 1837, he again returned to the subject, this time in relation to courtship: the "youth and maiden who are glancing at each other across a mixed company with eyes so full of mutual intelligence" immediately after marriage begin "to discover incongruities, defects. Thence comes surprise, regret, strife." Into a marriage gone stale in which the husband felt neglected by a wife absorbed with a baby, household chores, and the feeding of houseguests, came the admiring, young Margaret Fuller. Emerson found that she cheered him up, and carried with her an aura of excitement he found in no other persons. In a letter to a friend, Fuller ecstatically describes her drive with "the author of *Nature.*" She cites the singing birds, and the pine-trees sighing "with their soul-like sounds," in a day that was beauteous, while "care and routine fled away." She was happy there, but she was anxious, too: "The excitement of conversation prevents my sleeping" (1:212). After their foray to Watertown, Emerson noted in his journal that she read *Vivian Gray* to him "and made me very merry," and that she insisted on giving him lessons in his German pronunciation "against my will" (5:319).

The period of the electric, idealized relationship of Emerson with Fuller roughly coincided with Lidian's childbearing years—from October 30, 1836 when Waldo was born, to July 10, 1844, Edward's birth. Lidian was not a woman who took pregnancy lightly, as described in a letter Emerson wrote to his brother, June 17, 1844:

> Lidian's hour draws near, and between this and the 4 July, she promises me a babe; a work which dear nature in civilized countries seems to take sadly to heart, and one way or another to make us pay high prices for, - tears, groans, indispositions, wondrous discomforts and spleens, and very shattered constitutions.

There was little feeling of closeness between them. Emerson generally announced the birth of a baby with "I have a son," or "a daughter was born to me," instead of using "we" or "us." He lacked sympathy for his wife's chronic ill health, and once referred to her as a "miserable Dyspeptic."

Comparison of his letters to Fuller with those he wrote to his wife reveals that the former are exalted, whereas the latter are matter-of-fact. He asks his wife about his children and mother; he frequently discusses people he has met, money, discomfort of the journey, the size of his audience, but his expressions of affection are perfunctory.

That his letters to Fuller were *composed* suggests the importance he attached to them. They abound with literary allusions and references to nature. Their letters contain the ambiguities peculiar to courtship. For example, Emerson writes on March 3, 1840: "For you, as I remember, are one who can never comprehend how any affairs or knots of affairs should operate a moments diversion from the allegiance due to a lady so sovereign . . . How many things are worth our doing if only life were longer or more elastic." Towards the end of the month, he writes again: "I fancy I can divine reasons why so wise a woman and my good friend lets me read no syllable from her pen whilst I remain in this town, and I will use philosophy for that and many things." Nevertheless, both writers were careful to express their love either for, or from, Lidian and mother.

The tone of his letters gradually became more personal. On May 30, 1837 he was writing to her: "Seeing the stage stop this afternoon I gladly left my corn, threw down my Admiral Vernon's hoe and hastened to receive you — and was much dissatisfied to find it was only some books." He began trying to persuade Fuller to move to Concord. "Will you commission me to find you a boudoir?" (October 12, 1838). For several months, he continued to write about houses in Concord, but to his regret, she moved to Jamaica Plains. "But truly I am sorry that you have sat down in a place so inaccessible to me." (June 7, 1839).

As the correspondence accelerated, he made other tantalizingly ambiguous remarks that could be interpreted romantically by a reader eager to do so. Fuller reciprocated, hinting at her own feelings. She wrote September 19, 1840, after describing Lidian as "saintly," she herself was indeed "no saint," but a "great soul born to know all, before it can return to the creative fount."

During this highly creative time of their lives, it is clear that Fuller was the major inspiration for Emerson's ideas and his writing. *La Vita Nuova*, which she challenged Emerson to translate, became their guidebook. Together they pored over the conversations which Walter Savage Landor reconstructed from historical documents. Emerson especially liked Landor's *Pericles and Aspasia*, in which the love story of the great Athenian orator with the famous courtesan was reconstructed. He even read the novels of the notorious George Sand which Fuller recommended. When he asked her to return letters or copy sentences he had written to her to use in his essay on "Friendship," he was acknowledging her inspiration. Other ideas first used in the correspondence later surfaced in their poetry. On December 23, 1839, he wrote her referring to a forthcoming lecture, "I wish you were here to find me my subject for next week."

By this time, as many biographers have noted, their emotions were becoming explosive, and reached a climax in the fall of 1840. Because Fuller had become the first editor of the *Dial*, they needed to write to each other frequently about the journal. By February 2, 1840, Emerson regrets her "hurrying away . . . as this fragment of a visit seems only argument for a long conversation," and continues suggestively, "These are the days of passion when the air is full of cupids and devils." In the summer, their confrontation began. Emerson noted on August 16, 1840 in his journal that as he rode with Margaret to the Plains, "She taxed me, as often before, so now more explicitly, with inhospitality of Soul." Emerson's letters are available during the crisis in their relationship, but Fuller's written October 22, 1840 has disappeared. Conjecture must be made from Emerson's letters and journal as to the content of her letter. On September 25, 1840, he acknowledges to Fuller some misunderstanding and mentions at the beginning of his letter that perhaps they should part. Then in a kind of rhapsody he changes his mind:

> You, O divine mermaid or fisher of men, to whom all gods have given the witch hazel-wand, or caduceus, or spirit-discerner which detects an Immortal under every disguise in every lurking place . . . do say, . . . that I am yours and yours shall be, let me dally how long soever in this or that other temporary relation. I on the contrary do constantly aver that you and I are not inhabitants of one thought of the Divine Mind, but of two thoughts, that we meet and treat like foreign states, one maritime, one inland, whose trade and laws are essentially unlike.

Next he mentions his recent speculation about "The Protean energy by which the brute horns of Io become the crescent moon of Isis." In view of the nature of his predicament—a married man in an untenable position—it is notable that he chooses the image of Io, one of those loved by Zeus, who driven by gadflies, was forced to wander. His journal entry of the next day provides further explanation of their dilemma:

> You would have me love you. What shall I love? Your body? The
> supposition disgusts you. What you have thought and said? Well,
> whilst you were thinking and saying them, but not now. I see no
> possibility of loving anything but what now is, and is becoming; your
> courage, your enterprise, your budding affection, your opening
> thought, your prayer, I can love,—but what else?

That Emerson writes that Fuller was disgusted by the supposition of
"body" loving means this subject was raised. This passage suggests
that some kind of sexual confrontation had taken place.

A few days later (October 7, 1840), Emerson continued his debate
with Fuller in his journal: "Settle with yourself your accusations of
me." After a meeting with Bronson Alcott and the Ripleys to discuss
Brook Farm, Emerson and Fuller were still at an impasse. Emerson
wrote to her October 20, 1840: "I should gladly have talked with
you another day that we might have brought things to speech somewhat more reverently than in a cold room at abrupt and stolen
moments. Yet what would another day have done to reconcile our
wide sights?" He is not able to let their relationships simmer down,
however; two days later he writes to her to make "amends" to one
"whom he loves in his flinty way." On October 24, he writes again
in response to a Fuller letter (which was either lost or destroyed),
which he calls "frank and noble," but wishes could be unwritten. As
Strauch and others have pointed out, he asks that she not expect him
to write on the topic of their relationship "for a very long time."
Simultaneously in the same letter, it is also important to note that
Emerson pens the words used as the epigraph for this paper, which in
the romantic tradition implies that their involvement is fated, to
which their will was "never party," and tells her he cannot spare her.
Two days later in his journal Emerson wrote: "Our little romances,
into which we fling ourselves with so much eagerness, end suddenly,
and we are almost sad to find how easily we can brook the loss"
(7:526). The tone of their correspondence cooled, but their letters

and meetings continued. Although Fuller's letter to Emerson is missing, one she wrote to Caroline Sturgis the same day is available. She said her letter to Waldo gave her "pain," and yet, "his call bids me return" (2:167).

Emerson's emotions became more ambivalent, as indicated by his journal entry of October 12, 1841:

> I wish that I could, I know afar off that I cannot give the lights and shades, the hopes and outlooks that come to me in these strange, cold-warm, attractive-repelling conversations with Margaret, whom I always admire, most revere when I nearest see, and sometimes love, yet whom I freeze, and who freezes me to silence, when we seem to promise to come nearest.

Fuller's journal, written the next summer during a long visit to the Emerson household, reveals her expectations have moderated, and gives a picture of the Emerson's unhappy marriage and of Lidian's jealousy. After Margaret's arrival, Lidian confined herself in her chamber for two days with a "slow fever." As F.B. Sanborn was later to observe, Fuller showed "a rather marked disregard of Mrs. Emerson's position as hostess" (251). When after two days, Margaret finally appeared at her hostess's room, Lidian burst into tears. She cried again at the dinner table, when at first Margaret declined her invitation to a walk because she planned to walk with Waldo. During this scene, Emerson's response was to stare at the floor, with "his sweetness of look." In general, Margaret did not sympathize with Lidian's complaints and concluded Lidian made her feel "anti-Christian, and anti-Marriage." Later, on one of their frequent evening walks during which they talked as they "always" did "on Man and Woman, and Marriage," Waldo delineated the phenomenal nature of love, "a contrivance of nature," and reiterated his belief in the love of one soul for another. Although a married woman says her aim is to further the genius of her husband, Emerson added with "a satirical side glance" at her, in reality her conduct is to claim daily devotion which is injurious to him. Later writing in her journal, Margaret imagined that if she were married to Waldo, she would "acquiesce" in his relations, and that "nothing could be nobler, nor more consoling than to be his wife."

By April 1844, both of them wrote for the last issue of the *Dial* an ambivalent work each would recognize was intended for the other. "The Visit" begins with the question:

> Askest, 'How long thou shalt stay?
> Devastator of the day!

Emerson's poem concludes with the couplet:

> If Love his moment overstay,
> Hatred's swift repulsions play.

Fuller reciprocated with a Landor-style conversation concerning the death of love. Aglauron (Emerson) in an ostensible discussion about Ophelia and Hamlet says:

> But lovely as she was, and loved by him, this love could have been only the ornament, not, in any wise, the food of his life. The moment he is left alone, his thoughts revert to universal topics; it was the constitution of his mind, no personal relation could have availed it, except in the way of suggestion.

Thus Fuller gives her view of Emerson's aloofness. In the following exchange by means of her dialogue, she refers directly to their discussions of friendship and his coldness:

> *Laurie.* (Fuller) No, I do not understand being both friendly and cold.
> *Aglauron.* Thou wilt, when thou shalt have lent as well as borrowed.

Fuller concludes her ironic dialogue by suggesting that Emerson's ideas are static:

Aglauron. Good night, and farewell.
Laurie. You look as if it were for some time.
Aglauron. That rests with you. You will generally find me here,
and always I think like-minded, if not of the same mind.

In April when that issue of the *Dial* came out, Emerson looked for her in Boston, only to find she had gone to New York for a visit. He acknowledged in his letter April 11, 1844 to her they both suffered: "But Fourier and Miller and Dr. Buchanan will not heal us of our deep wound."

In July of 1844 Lidian gave birth to their last child, and Fuller visited Concord but did not stay with the Emersons. As a farewell to Waldo, Margaret wrote a poem, alluding to "The Visit."

> In that temple so divine
> She sought at once the inmost shrine
>   And saw this thought there graven,
>   'Earth and fire, hell and heaven,
> Hate and love, black and white,
> Life and death, dark and bright,
>   All are one
>   One alone: (Stern 218)

A verse near the end of the poem admonishes: "Don't lure me here again with your sweet smile." This poem was the epitaph of her love for Emerson.

Having overcome the lure of Emerson's "sweet smile," Fuller moved to New York in December to work for the *Tribune.*[1] When Emerson saw her there in August of 1845, she was in love with James Nathan, so their contacts and letters were scant. Fuller, thereafter, expended little more emotional energy on Emerson. He, however, tried to revive their "romance" in Europe.

Fuller's trip to Europe opened new doors for her as she became absorbed in her life abroad. Emerson, however, wrote February 28, 1847 that he had been invited to lecture in England but would only accept the invitation if terms were satisfactory. "So perhaps I shall wait for you at home." As in previous days, he began his letter affectionately: "That you are very generous and noble, that your great love makes your memory tenacious of all it ever held." He was enthusiastic (April 30, 1847) about her description of George Sand, and glad Margaret was "out of the coop of our bigoted societies." As previously he writes in an ambiguous style, ostensibly in connection with a proposed magazine: "I suppose, you are not one of those sleepers who dream the same dream over many times. — It seems I am." From Manchester, England, he writes on December 5, 1847 that he is glad she is happy in Italy but that she must not stay long alone. Then in an attempt to revive Fuller's interest, Emerson suggests he is again ready to be her victim:

> Shall we not yet — you, you, also —as we used to talk, build up a
> reasonable society in that naked unatmospheric land, and effectually
> serve one another? In some sense I certainly do not grow old, —
> perhaps 'tis the worse for me — but, I believe, all the persons who
> have been important to my — imagination — shall I say? personal
> imagination (is there no such thing in just psychology?) retain all their
> importance for me. I am their victim, and ready to be their victim, to
> the same extent as heretofore. When we die, my dear friend, will
> they not make us up better, with some more proportion between our
> tendencies and our skills; that life shall not be such a sweet fever, but
> a sweet health, sweet and beneficient, and solid as Andes?

On March 2, 1848 he is writing her that he would be very glad to see her in Paris. And he reverts to his earlier idea that she should move to Concord: "How much your letter made me wish to say, come live with *me* (italics mine) at Concord!" The long-suffering Lidian objected to Emerson's proposal. In a letter written from London to his wife March 8, 1848, Emerson answers her objections: "I do not wonder that in these late afflictions, my plans for M. looked calamitous enough to the poor invalid." He reassures Lidian that instead of asking Margaret to live with them, he will suggest that she rent Mrs. Brown's house in Concord. On April 25, 1848, he urges Fuller to take the first steamer to Marseilles, in order to meet him in Paris and return to the United States with him. Again a month later he persists in his suggestion: "But you will not wait but will come to London immediately & sail home with me!" What is significant here is not so much the invitation—his attempt to rekindle their close relationship—but the urgency of it. Urgency is the concomitant of highly charged emotion.

At the time he learned of her death, Emerson acknowledged Fuller's importance to him in his journal entry of July 21, 1850: "I have lost in her my audience." Comparing her with his Aunt Mary, he writes that unlike his favorite aunt, Margaret had "great tenderness and sympathy," and then quoting Shakespeare's famous line— — "Nor custom stale her infinite variety," he associates Margaret with Cleopatra.

Why, then, have some critics misread—or in many cases overlooked—Emerson's feelings for Fuller?[2] Perhaps because he has been "cannonized" as the "American Scholar,"—many scholars (including feminist revisionists) have accepted Emerson's judgment of Fuller, as laid down in the *Memoirs*. Fuller's reputation for lacking beauty was contributed to in large part by Emerson in the *Memoirs*—her "extreme plainness," the incessant movement of her eyelids, and her nasal voice. He added that at first impression she repelled him and this had led many biographers to relegate Emerson's feelings for Fuller to the purely intellectual plane. Early in their relationship, Emerson had praised Fuller's writing ability. But the *Memoirs*, written after her "rejection" of him, reflect a change in his attitude. While nursing his wounded pride, Emerson must have recalled his urgent letters to a pregnant woman to join him in Paris and doubtless felt foolish. Other transcendentalists, such as Samuel Ward, Anna Barker, and Caroline Sturgis engaged in lofty discussions about friendship and spiritual love, which critics equated as a manifestation of transcendentalist hyperbole with the Emerson-Fuller effusions. Emerson basked in admiration from young women. He was like a contemporary college professor who is attracted to a series of students.

Emerson's "annointed" biographer, a young disciple who would follow his hints and revisions of truth, did not question his version of reality. James Elliot Cabot mentions Fuller's "ardent somewhat masterful temperament," and that she "flung herself at him," but he fails to account for Emerson's obvious emotional response except to mention his feelings of "repulsions" which he described in his poem, "The Visit" (1:275-276). Subsequent biographers tended to follow the pattern set by Cabot. They hint that the sexually-starved spinster had more erotic interest in Emerson than she should have had, but for the most part, they fail to acknowledge that Emerson reciprocated her feelings.

Much of what has been conjectured is intended to encourage a reconsideration of Emerson's view of Margaret Fuller. At this point in time, it should be possible to recognize that, as this nineteenth century sage once wrote to Lidian during his courtship, he was after all, "a man." But this does not detract from the fact that his and Fuller's determined, desperate assertion of the ascendancy of the soul over the body was earnest, and one of literary history's most dramatic instances of an attempt to act in accordance with this ideal. And yet, their dream was a dream gone sour. Its demand, and the impossibility of its realization, predicated the fury of the thwarted. That Fuller could go on caring about a man indefinitely, in a way that could not be consummated, or if consummated, not sustained, was what Emerson must have wanted when he repeatedly insisted that she move to Concord. But Fuller, weary of playing platonic games, wanted all of love. The divine Beatrice inevitably gave way to the self-actualized feminist, Margaret Fuller. When this happened, Ralph Waldo Emerson reacted with "hatred's swift repulsions," by painting a portrait in the *Memoirs of Margaret Fuller Ossoli* of an arrogant, though charismatic woman who could not write. This canon which established the "Margaret myth," needs to be dispelled in order that Margaret Fuller may take her rightful place in the pantheon of American writers.

Notes

This essay, which has been revised, originally appeared in the *Thoreau Journal Quarterly* 10:3, 1978. Reprinted by permission.

1. Emerson was not happy to see her working for Horace Greeley. In a letter (July 31, 1846) to his friend and confidant, Thomas Carlyle, after citing the good pay, respect and benefits of her position, he wrote: "Still this employment is not satisfactory to me." *The Correspondence of Emerson and Carlyle*, ed. Joseph Slater. New York: Columbia UP, 1964.

2. Gay Wilson Allen writes in his *Waldo Emerson* that Fuller was "in love" with Emerson. When he learned of her death, "he could not get Margaret out of his mind," commenting on her on "eight separate pages of his journal." Ralph L. Rusk in *The Life of Emerson* considers Fuller's role in Emerson's life as a gadfly. On the other hand, Madeleine Stern in her *The Life of Margaret Fuller*, Joseph Jay Deiss in his *The Roman Years of Margaret Fuller* and Margaret Vanderhaar Allen in *The Achievement of Margaret Fuller* recognize Emerson's ambivalence.

Works Cited

Berkson, Dorothy. "'Born and Bred in Different Nations'": Margaret Fuller and Ralph Waldo Emerson." *Patrons and Protegees: Gender, Friendship and Writing in Nineteenth Century America*. Ed. Shirley Marchalonis. Brunswick: Rutgers UP, 1988. 3-30.

Cabot, James Elliot. *A Memoir of Ralph Waldo Emerson*. Boston, Houghton Mifflin, 1888.

Emerson, Ralph Waldo. *Journals and Miscellaneous Notebooks*. Ed. A.W. Plumstead *et al*. 9 vol. Cambridge: Belknap, 1960-1971.

Fuller, Margaret. *Art, Literature, And the Drama*. Boston: Roberts Brothers, 1874.

—. *The Letters of Margaret Fuller*. 5 vols. to date. Ed. Robert N. Hudspeth. Ithaca: Cornell UP, 1983-.

—. *Memoirs of Margaret Fuller Ossoli*. 2 vols. Ed. Ralph Waldo Emerson, William Henry Channing, and James Freeman Clarke. Boston: Phillips, Sampson and Company, 1852.

Myerson, Joel. "Margaret Fuller's 1842 Journal: At Concord with the Emersons." *Harvard Library Bulletin*, 21 July 1973: 320-340.

Sanborn, F.B. "The Women of Concord—Margaret Fuller and Her Friends." *The Critic* 2 March 1906.

Stern, Madeleine. *The Life of Margaret Fuller*. Westport: Greenwood Press, 1991.

Marie Mitchell Olesen Urbanski

Letters:
A Lady's Cameo Art

During her forty years of life, Margaret Fuller wrote thousands of letters. That around one thousand of her letters still survive attests to the value readers placed upon them. She began writing letters as a small child and continued to do so throughout her life. After she left her job teaching at the Greene Street School in Providence, she complained to her brother that she had as many as sixty correspondents, and yet, she often invited people to write. The content of her letters varied enormously, depending upon her purpose in writing them and the needs of the recipient. Fuller fits into the tradition of what is in essence a lady's literary art form that was shaped in part by the reading of epistolary novels, and in part by the necessity of writing letters as part of the social ritual. Her letters are cameos, finely etched jewels of alabaster and ivory. Wrought by careful design, they have delicacy of delineation. Like crystals, they transmit the currents of Fuller's electricity and have great power. They constitute her autobiography.

Letters were once an essential form of communication. People waited for the arrival of the mail, passed letters around, and saved them. Feeling isolated at Groton, Fuller wrote a friend the post was her "only pleasure." Exchanging letters became a solace for the legendary thwarted lovers, Eloise and Abelard. Elizabeth Barrett's *Sonnets from the Portuguese* began with a fan letter from Robert Browning. Elizabeth Hardwick's letters to Robert Lowell were used in his poetry. Perhaps to avoid writing a sequel to *Gone With The Wind*, Margaret Mitchell spent the rest of her literary life answering hundreds of letters from strangers. Vita Sackville-West corresponded with a stranger, Andrew Reiber, from Windslip, Cape Split, Maine, from 1951 to 1962. Their correspondence began when he wrote asking if the son of a friend of his could visit Sissinghurst Castle. West's correspondence with a man she never wanted to meet ripened into friendship. If she were taking a cruise, she would send her pen pal her address at ports of call, and dying, dictated a last letter to "Dearest Andrew." "Why?" I asked Nancy MacKnight, the editor of Vita Sackville-West's letters,[1] "would a busy publishing member of the Bloomsbury coterie, a British aristocrat, write for eleven years to an American actor she never met?" Nancy answered, "Vita once wrote her husband she preferred strangers to her friends," and continued, "Andrew thought she was perfect." Obliquely, this observation seems to capture the essence of the appeal of letters. Each correspondent envisions an ideal being, and projects the dream of an imaginary friendship into her letters.

Just as obliquely, the nineteenth century poet, Emily Dickinson, encapsulated the anonymity a Victorian woman felt:

> This is my letter to the World
> That never wrote to Me—

"I'm Nobody" is writing "To Whom It May Concern," and receives in reply, silence—"Return to Sender, Addressee Unknown."

Dickinson intended her audience to be self-selected as she spoke with a lady's voice, that expressed woman's feeling of marginality.

Virginia Woolf observed that letter writing was the first written mode of expression used by women who two centuries later would write novels of manners or biographies. "Had she been born in 1827, Dorothy Osborne would have written novels; had she been born in 1527 she never would have written at all. But she was born in 1627, and at that date though writing books was 'ridiculous' for a woman, there was nothing unseemly in writing a letter" ("Dorothy Osborne's 'Letters'" *Common Reader* 2:60). Letter writing could be made to fit in with the other household duties and demands of a woman's life. Written in haste amidst interruptions, time spent writing letters caused no rebuke since their purpose was useful. In her essay, "Modern Letters," Woolf sounded relieved that Aristotle had not laid down "once and for all the principles of letter-writing" (*Collected Essays* 2:260). Noting that writers of letters were anonymous, Woolf felt it was convenient that the principles were obscure. After her disavowal of the need for guidelines, Woolf delineates them conditionally:

> If the art of letter-writing consists in exciting the emotions, in bringing back the past, in reviving a day, a moment, nay a very second, of past time, then these obscure correspondents, with their hasty haphazard ways, their gibes and flings, their irreverence and mockery, their careful totting up of days and dates, their general absorption in the moment and entire carelessness what posterity will think of them, beat Cowper, Walpole, and Edward Fitzgerald hollow. (2:262)

Woolf's disguised definition garners the essence of good letter writing—spontaneity and evanescence. Woolf might well have added that there is a conversational patina to letter writing, that it is a quintessentially feminine literary art form, an outgrowth of a lady's social conditioning. Letters often begin with an apology for a delayed answer, not unlike a literary lady's conventional apology in her preface about the inadequate quality of her writing. Fragments from every woman's life—that was replete with interruptions, silence, and innuendo—letters as literary art were suggestive and empathic. As Ruth Perry noted: "Letters were the perfect vehicle for women's highly developed art of pleasing, for in writing letters it is possible to tailor a self on paper to suit the expectations and desires of the audience" (69).

Certainly Sarah Margaret Fuller's early letters to her father demonstrate her skill in the art of pleasing her audience. Of the fifty-three surviving letters she wrote from 1817 through 1825, forty-one were addressed to her father. From the age of seven when she first wrote to her father, who was in Washington as a United States Congressman for eight years, Fuller shows an acute awareness of his power over her life. Frequently, he would correct mistakes in her letters, as he had earlier corrected her Latin translations. Always deferential . . . "for I am possessed of the greatest blessing of life a good and kind father" (1:94) . . . she is occasionally provocative:

> I enclose you my composition and specimen of writing. I assure you
> I wrote the former off much better and made *almost* as many correc-
> tions as your critical self would were you at home. (1:91)

As a child, she seemed to understand with acumen psychological boundaries and she knew that the greatest humiliation for a woman was to be unmarried. In her early quest for identity, she decided at age ten to drop her first name, "Sarah," because it sounded "old maidish," and to use her second name, "Margaret." Her father did not indulge his daughter but continued to call her "Sarah," his mother's name. Frequently, she has to ask permission from her father to read novels, attend Mr. Emerson's school, obtain a Greek tutor, go to a party, or play the piano. She asks for little material for herself except for gilt-edged paper, copies of her father's speeches, books, and at age nine, for a dollar for a poor woman. Her letters reflect not only her altruism but also her impatience with her younger siblings, and her keen social observations—who was a belle at a ball, who died, who married, who called. Some constants she delineates in her letters are her interest in books and ideas, her progress in school and her desire to excel, as she sought to win Timothy Fuller's approval.

There is a strong contrast in the much less constrained letters she wrote to her mother. At eleven, she included her mother in her wish for sisterhood: "I think that we are all sisters, it is hard for me to stand unconnected . . . " (1:117). Early letters to idealized older women, Ellen Kilshaw and her former teacher, Susan Prescott, also indicate patterns of intense feeling that were later shown in some of her friendships with women. Letters, written in her youth to her parents, Ellen Kilshaw and Susan Prescott, serve as prototypes for her subsequent correspondence. Her letters to men of influence and power are much more guardedly written, whereas those to women, are more open, often displaying a less arch, more spontaneous style of humor. Timothy Fuller had taught his precocious daughter the realities of the world better than he may have realized.

At fifteen she began her quest for glory with a letter to the Marquis de Lafayette; after telling him that she loved him, admired him, she told him he had inspired her to a "noble ambition," and if glory were "possible to a female, to whom the avenues of glory are seldom accessible," she would later remind him of her gratitude (1:150). Although her letter contains the same pattern of praise and admiration she used in letters to her father, the teenaged girl would not likely have known that she might more appropriately have addressed her letter to Lafayette's travelling companion, the radical feminist, Fanny Wright. That same year—1825—she did confide her aspirations to a woman, Susan Prescott, telling her she needed genius, social polish and self-discipline to fulfill her ambition. In another revealing letter she later wrote the British writer, Anna Jameson, asking to meet her. "How I wish I was famous . . . yet I am worthy to know you"

(1:318). By the time she was thirty-one, Fuller's need for recognition had become desperate: "I must die if I do not burst forth in genius or heroism" (2:202). Speaking of the Greek concept of hell, she once noted that all of the punishments of Tartarus meted out to a Tantalus or a Sisyphus involved baffled effort. Margaret Fuller's epistles constitute her autobiography as they record her Sisyphian struggle to succeed against incalcuable odds.

Her letters reflect a youth replete with energy and optimism and maturity weary from striving and disappointment. As a defense mechanism, she had learned always to be "prepared for the worst" (1:315). She sent forth bravely scintillating sallies to her women friends, but as they got married, it is clear from her remarks that she realized she should have found a husband, too. Letters to a friend describing her vigil beside the bed of a young woman dying of a botched abortion and her dutiful call on an impoverished old mother living in poverty and isolation with her unmarried daughter, indicate she, too, feared this fate. Illness and depression weave through her life like a leitmotif, alternating with a will to hope, a willingness to keep struggling. It has never been clear what the nature of her frequently mentioned illnesses were, whether her headaches were connected to her menstrual cycle, or whether there were a bipolar syndrome in her genetic makeup.[2] It was, however, her father's death in 1835 that galvanized her to action. As Bell Gale Chevigny points out, after her father's death, Fuller "set herself to learn how to handle the family business and financial matters, for which she felt she had little skill but her mother had no capacity at all" (73). From this time on, many letters show her concern with practical financial affairs. She gives her brothers and sister detailed advice. She had to struggle with their Uncle Abraham, who had control of their father's estate, to give them an education. She wrote that she had often had reason to regret her sex, but never "more than now," as she came to understand the terrible vulnerability of a woman's legal disability. Summing up a woman's lot in 1838, she wrote to her close friend, Caroline Sturgis, "in this life, we are mutilated beings." Her problems with money continued for the rest of her life. Due to her limited inheritance, she lost her chance for an earlier trip to Europe. When she finally arranged to go to Europe as a tutor and journalist, and extended her sojourn there in Italy, she wrote desperate letters home as she sought to borrow or obtain the necessary funds to live on. Her anguish at a delayed bank draft or a lost check became her impetus to write.

She used her letters as trial balloons. In *Woman in the Nineteenth Century* she was circumspect in her comments about George Sand, but in a letter from Paris after meeting her, Fuller was unapologetically supportive. She used letters as a means of clarifying her ideas, and testing her audience's response.

Margaret Fuller's biographers have emphasized her quest for love but of equal importance was her struggle to earn a living in a way she wanted. The only job open to her was teaching school, an occupation in which she said "few persons of ability are at present engaged . . ." (1:354), and she often felt frustrated by this. Beginning in her childhood, she had been forced to tutor her younger brothers and sister. Her unpaid stint as a teacher in Bronson Alcott's Temple School in Boston was followed by a lucrative position at the Greene Street School in Providence, Rhode Island. Still, teaching did not enhance her self-esteem, as she wrote apologetically to a successful writer: "You must not get an ugly picture of me because I am a schoolmistress" (1:318). But because she had high expectations for her students and high standards for herself, her teaching required a great deal of energy. In a letter to her brother, Arthur, who was teaching school at the time and had sought her advice, she delineated her teaching philosophy saying encouragement was better than punishment. He should remember that students although imperfect, "are immortal souls," and that the teacher represents "Justice." On a final note, she warned him to "beware of over great pleasure in being popular or even beloved" (2:196). As most brilliant teachers feel at times, she was inevitably disappointed in her students. Emotionally depleted, she wrote a friend: "But I am wearied out; I have gabbled and simpered, and given my mind to the public view these two years back, till there seems to be no good left in me" (1:351). To another friend she said flatly, "I do not wish to teach again at all" (1:354), and to her brother, Richard, that she would not take a private pupil for *"any money"* (1:350). One of her students, Mary Ware Allen later wrote about Fuller's demanding teaching methods and irritation when the students were not prepared.[3] Her conversation seminars for Boston's intellectual elite women were much more satisfying to her, although they, too, often depleted her emotionally.

After quitting her lucrative job, she knew she had to return to teaching unless she were able to find time and energy to write and to publish.[4] She wrote Sturgis that she "was determined to take every precaution to ensure my having the whole time for myself" (2:58). She asked her mother to make excuses so that she did not have to socialize with the neighbors or even go downstairs for meals. She cut her time spent dressing by a quarter by wearing loose fitting robes. Her mother and sister did the mending. Nevertheless, during the first two months after her arrival home, she wrote fifty letters, worked on her German translations, and sorted through forty years of her father's papers and books. She decided what would be sold at auction and discussed their future with her mother, while at the same time, still tutoring her brother and sister two afternoons a week. She had great conflict over her duty to her family, and her duty to herself to achieve recognition as a writer. In 1840, she wrote in weariness to William H. Channing "... I can never simplify my life; always so many ties, so many claims!" (2:171).

Her mysticism and talismanic powers kept her alive. In a letter written October 21, 1838, she described her mystical experience on Thanksgiving. She learned "the secret of all things is pain" and came to understand that her own pain was insignificant in relation to the universe (1:347-8). Her merging with the cosmos, her connection with the earth, though dormant at times, never left her. Her spiritual presence attracted other people to Margaret and gave her the strength to combat adversity and to keep her vision in view. The secret of her charisma, her spiritual power, disturbed and attracted people. Fuller's intuitive understanding brought forth confessions from people who realized they had not kept faith with their best potentialities and who later were surprised they had revealed so much of themselves.

Another quality that both men and women responded to was Fuller's passionate nature. Nathaniel Hawthorne in his description of Zenobia in *The Blithedale Romance* created a character who emitted sensory vibrations, and was, according to her friends, a portrait of Margaret Fuller. Fuller's repressed sensuality fascinated and repelled timid men like Hawthorne but attracted men secure in their masculinity like James Nathan. Earlier male friends, such as George Davis, Samuel Ward, and James Freeman Clarke were attracted to Fuller but may well have been troubled by her intensity and her intellectual demands. Living with his mistress, James Nathan, on the other hand, was from an European background and responded in a direct way to Fuller's sexuality.

The love letters of Margaret Fuller to James Nathan read like the epistolary novels with which she was well acquainted. It is, however, unfortunate that only three of Nathan's letters survive. Otherwise, with multiple points of view, the reader could understand Nathan's position better if we had his responses to Fuller, letters to his mother, to the woman in Germany he later married, and his business friends, Thomas Delf and Benjamin Benson. Nevertheless, the reader can infer a lot about James Nathan from the context of over fifty letters Fuller wrote to him. Bell Gale Chevigny's astute observation that Nathan "awakened her sensuality," while "putting to sleep" her mind (137) is certainly appropriate. Unlike other men with whom Fuller had been friendly, Nathan seems to have followed Lord Chesterfield's famous advice to his son in how to manipulate women. After offending Fuller with a sexual proposition, he explained that as a man of the world, he saw *"the dame"* in her (78).

Although they needed to send short notes to arrange for their frequent meetings, Fuller still felt compelled to write at length in the tradition of romantic love about her feelings for Nathan. After falling in love with Nathan at first sight, she wrote on February 7, 1845, that their meeting was fated. Recurrently, she referred in the romantic tradition to destiny, "a divinely moved preparation for our meeting" (4:47). In her letters to Nathan, she used no coquetry or artifice, and made no effort to conceal her love for him. In her first letter she offers to bring a poem for him to read and concludes by asserting: "Tomorrow will be the first day of Spring" (4:47). Her letters continue with the rebirth of spring motif replete with descriptions of singing birds and fragrant flowers. Although she called herself "passive" in her letters to Nathan, she was aggressive in her pursuit, writing him invitations and suggestions where they could meet. As a child, Fuller was punished for reading *Romeo and Juliet* on Sunday, and like the doomed lovers, knew she faced opposition from her friends and the Greeleys with whom she was living. The forbidden character of her relationship with Nathan heightened her sense of excitement as she suggested he meet her for a walk from Dr. Leger's office. Nathan, too, played the role of a troubadour by singing and playing love ballads on his guitar. He told her he would be the cherry tree blooming outside her bedroom window, and took her on moonlit walks through the woods to sit on rocks overlooking the water. Later she retraced their footsteps, fondled the white veil he gave her, and analyzed his words in her letters.

As their relationship developed, Nathan seemed to be able to manipulate Fuller in any way he chose: "Today you put me in the dust, and a hundred miles from you, too . . ." (4:102). When she learned he had a woman living with him, he persuaded her that he was merely helping to rehabilitate her out of charity. When she felt insulted by his sexual proposition, he soon had her convinced it was her fault: "Oh dearest friend, indolent, cowardly that I am . . ."(4:86). Fuller's letters are interesting in their depiction of the psychology of someone suffering from unrequited love. She represents everyone caught in an uneven passion who does not want to accept reality. She makes excuses for Nathan when he does not come to see her; she accepts his explanations for his behavior, while at the same time desperately looking for, and even manufacturing signs of hope, while reassuring herself of his love: " . . . where I am sure of love as I am of yours . . ." (4:93). In their confrontations, Fuller usually apologized abjectly: "Your hand removes at last the veil from my eyes. It is then, indeed, myself who have caused all the ill" (4:82). She sounds childlike in her contrition: "Yet forgive if I have done amiss, forgive when I shall do amiss" (4:86). Ultimately, she comes to understand her powerlessness in their relationship: "I hear you with awe assert the power over me and feel it to be true" (4:95). Passages in her love letters are highly erotic: "Are you the guardian to domesticate me in the body, and attach it more firmly to the earth" (4:95-6). And she tells of her sleepless nights: "How can I rest when you rouse in me so many thoughts and feelings" (4:96). In a letter written just before his departure for Germany, she discusses the tears she would shed with him and then acknowledges: "You have approached me personally nearer than any other person, and have said to me words most unusual and close to which I have willingly listened" (4:110). As Julia Ward Howe wrote in her introduction to Margaret Fuller's love letters in 1903, they are "written in a tone of unreserve unusual with her," and reveal "the ardor and depth of her nature" (viii).

Fuller's letters tell her story like the epistolary novels with which she was familiar. Once she had written that George Davis resembled

Lovelace in Samuel Richardson's novel, *Clarissa*. Still, as her love story unfolded, her story turned out differently than Richardson's novels. Unlike Lovelace, Nathan did not rape her. Unlike Pamela, her virtue was not rewarded with an offer of marriage by Nathan to win her "jewel." Nor did she die of a broken heart. After learning of his engagement, she went for a long walk and became lost at night on Ben Lomond in the Scottish Highlands. She had Ossianic visions of the "spirits of heroes and white-armed maids with their blue eyes of grief" (*At Home and Abroad* 155), but used her strength and intelligence to keep moving in order to stay alive and to avoid hypothermia or drowning in the watercourse. The next morning the heather was beautiful and she knew she would have "the experience of passionate life" (4:91) with another love in the future.

Although Fuller's feelings were direct, Nathan's motives seem less clear, more complex. A "deft social climber" (Chevigny 289), Nathan was aware of ethnic and class differences. An aspiring writer himself, he was attracted to Fuller's celebrity. That she boarded at the home of Horace Greeley enhanced her desirability in the eyes of an opportunist eager to publish in the *New York Tribune*. Nathan often worried that Fuller might have confided in Mary Greeley about their relationship. Nevertheless, as a man, he was attracted to Fuller, for he could have taken advantage of her literary connections without a sexual pursuit. To his discredit, after he left the United States, he used Fuller to edit and to help publish his travel articles, and to obtain a letter of introduction to George Bancroft, Secretary of the Navy. On the other hand, since he wanted to drop her, he obviously could not continue to write the amorous letters Fuller wanted. In response to a letter from him after a four-month hiatus, she for the first time mentioned that his article on Rome was rejected by the *Tribune*. She had given him her pen and a book of Shelley's poems when he left, so he sent her a rose from Shelley's grave. All she could find were the dead leaves and stem; the flower was lost.

She was never so blind in her love that she did not understand, as she wrote Nathan on May 4, 1845, that she knew she was one of "*a few* in whose lot the meaning of that age is concentrated . . ." If Fuller represented the woman of the nineteenth century, Nathan is a precursor of the twentieth century man in his ethics and attitudes. Fuller asked him to return her letters in New York, and later demanded their return in England. Knowing they would be embarrassing to her reputation, her friends sought to retrieve them after her death.[5] Nathan kept them. In 1873 he wrote that he could not "suffer their exquisite naturalness and sweetness to sink into the grave," that "great and gifted as she was as a writer," she had "a true woman's heart" (Howe 5). Obviously, saving these letters reflects his vanity but also his recognition of their literary value. In his unorthodox courtship of Fuller, Nathan did not follow the code of a gentleman any more than he did in his refusal to return her letters. In an age in which there are no rules, contemporary readers can be grateful to Nathan for preserving these love letters. A failed writer himself, James Nathan would find his immortality only through Margaret Fuller.

There is a marked contrast between the love letters Fuller wrote to Nathan and those written to the Marchese Giovanni Angelo Ossoli. Although she was writing in a foreign language, she made no attempts to refer to Dante or other Italian witers about love. As Joseph Jay Deiss notes in his *The Roman Years of Margaret Fuller*, her letters to Ossoli had nothing in common with "the rarified romanticism" (153) of her letters to Nathan and even her handwriting changed. Although their lives are in danger, she writes nurturing and loving letters, as she tells him his coffee and her embraces will be waiting for him.

Fuller's letters from Italy are dramatic. They concern love and its consequences, a belated announcement to the folks back home of marriage and the birth of a baby, and the disinheritance of a radical son by his conservative family. They culminate in a mother's expressions of love for the baby whose arrival was so costly. This epistolary story of star-crossed love forms a counterpoint to the epic theme of a Roman revolution and its betrayal by Pope Pius IX and the French.[6]

Her letters are an archetypal expression of non-expression—a Victorian lady's silence about her sexual activity, a lady who knows full well that an illegitimate child means "ruin." Fuller's letters forge a familiar pattern for a woman trapped by an unwanted pregnancy—shocked disbelief, if not denial, of her condition, a feeling of entrapment from which only death would free her, a struggle to cope with the nausea and fatigue characteristic of the early stages of pregnancy. After the Polish poet, Adam Mickiewicz, comforts her and her lover remains supportive, her letters begin to reflect hope: "imperfect as love is, I want human beings to love, as I suffocate without" (19 May 1848). As she adjusts to her condition and begins to make plans for a furtive birth, she comes to feel in tune with nature and spring. In late May, after her escape from Rome to the villages of Aquila and Rieti, Fuller vacillates between a sense of doom and, like every pregnant woman, a wish that it would be over.

When Margaret Fuller first took Ossoli as her lover in the fall of 1847, her infrequent letters home were unequivocal in their expressions of joy. She often substituted "Rome" for "Ossoli." She wrote her mother, "My life at Rome is thus far all I hoped. I have not been so well since I was a child, nor so happy ever as during the last six weeks" (16 December 1847). Probably as she had missed her period, her mood had changed when she wrote Emerson on 20 December. She now expresses weariness with her Destiny (and perhaps prescience of her fate by drowning)—"without strength to swim." She mentions "glorious" days in Italy but fear of this "*incubus* [emphasis mine] of the future." In a letter on 11 January 1848, to a friend, it is clear Fuller knows she is pregnant, as she contrasts the intoxication of love with its aftermath: "When I arrived in Rome, I was at first intoxicated to be here . . . That is all over now, and with this year, I enter upon a sphere of my destiny so difficult, that I, at present, see no way out except through the gate of death." Her preoccupation with dying was not unrealistic, since she was in her late thirties.[7]

Fuller's letters offer multiple dimensions of meaning. Sophisticated readers will readily translate the metaphors for an unwanted pregnancy that keep cropping up in her letters: "I have known some happy hours; but they all lead to sorrow, and not only the cups of wine but of milk seem drugged with poison for me . . . I am a poor magnet with power to be wounded by the bodies I attract" (11 January 1848). Tellingly, she remembers the book of *Genesis*—"There is undoubtedly foundation for the story of a curse laid on Eve"—the curse to bring forth her children in sorrow. Another correlative image is her comparison of gestation with writing a book—when she says the book should be finished by September, she indicates the month her baby is due. Again she writes—"Apply as I may, it will take three months, at least, to finish my book. It grows upon me" (22 June 1848). Other revealing words are "issue", "trouble I am in," "*a distressed female*," and "things that invoke censure."

After the birth of their son on 5 September, the tone of her letters changes as she becomes increasingly preoccupied with the political upheaval in Rome. They reflect conflict over her multiplying re-sponsibilities—her care of the baby and for his father, her need to write for money, and her desire to support the revolution. Although Fuller's dispatches written for the *New York Tribune* give more details than her letters about the brief months of the Roman republic and the fighting in Rome, her letters do describe a battle she witnessed and a bloody wall "close to where Ossoli was." She adored the republic's charismatic leader, Guiseppe Mazzini, whom she had met in London. For her, the abortive revolution was "the glorious dream of hope," whereas Pope Pius IX was a "traitor," who used any means to recover his temporal power. Her sense of outrage and disillusionment at the sight of French troops defeating the Roman soldiers is expressed vividly. After the fall of the Roman republic, the Ossolis had to leave Rome for Florence. Nevertheless, they understood that their defeat was just an interlude, that eventually Italy would be a unified state.

The dramatic appeal of Fuller's letters never lessens. After she, Ossoli, and the baby arrived in Florence, it is clear that Fuller realized they were going to have to leave for the United States. Her letters prepare the way for future job opportunities, and she worries that Horace Greeley has not answered her. She knows well that a scandal would hurt her employment and publishing possibilities in the States, so her letters are conciliatory and guarded when she speaks of her secret marriage and baby. Occasional evidences of guilt appear, such as, "Magdalen," "unworthiness," "chastened libertine," but, mostly, she writes she has "no regrets." Her action was "not contrary to my ideas of right;" she acted out her character. She also is aware that Europeans are more tolerant of sexual impropriety than Americans, and she says it "half killed" her to write letters home with news of her "secret." Nevertheless, she is repelled by "the meddling curiosity" of people and defiantly refuses to acknowledge "the rights of the social inquisition of the U.S. to know all the details of my affairs" (30 November 1849).

Like a novel, Fuller's letters written from Italy are full of suspense. Readers are impatient to find out what happens next. Her letters show her complex response to her dilemma, her conflict between idealism and reality, reflected in her proud refusal to apologize for her actions though fully aware that adverse public opinion could hurt her. Each letter is uniquely designed for the recipient. Whenever she thought her reader would be interested, she mentioned the larger political ramifications of the Italian revolution and her dream of a more equitable society. As a consequence of their support of the revolution, Ossoli and Fuller were forced to leave Florence for the United States.

Fuller was as drawn to the sea for its healing properties as are many, and after visiting a French war ship, even wrote her brother she would like to command such a vessel. Nevertheless, her letters express fear of the sea recurrently. In a vivid letter written from Newport on August 6, 1841, Fuller described her terror of the sea:

> But the damp, cold wind came sobbing, and the waves began sobbing and wailing, too, and I was seized with a sort of terrible feeling such as I never had before, even in the darkest, most rustling wood. The moon seemed sternly to give me up to the demons of the rock, and the waves coldly to mourn, a tragic chorus, and I felt a cold grasp (2:224).

Fuller's presentiment of the manner of her death in cold water proved true. Again after realizing she was pregnant, she wrote Emerson on December 20, 1847, sounding as if her death by drowning would be a welcome escape for her. She hoped Destiny would not leave her "long in the world, for I am tired of keeping myself up in the water without corks, and without strength to swim . . ." She wished to be "born again" (4:314).

Her epistolary autobiography evolved from a novel to that of a Greek tragedy. Once they decided they had to choose a ship, Fuller became fearful: "I am absurdly fearful, and various omens have combined to give me a dark feeling . . . it seems to me that my future upon earth will soon close . . ." Again she wrote, as if certain of her impending death: "I have a vague expectation of some crisis . . . But it has long seemed, that in the year 1850, I should stand on a plateau in the ascent of life . . . Yet my life proceeds as regularly as the fates of a Greek tragedy" (*Memoirs* 2:337). Later survivors of the wreck of the ship Elizabeth said that even at the time of embarkation, she felt a dark premonition and hesitated an hour before she could go on board. A Cassandra both gifted and cursed with prescience, Fuller understood that she, her husband and baby would not survive the voyage they were about to undertake. On the Rhode Island sea shore in 1841 Fuller had a vision of her death, which she described in a letter using "a tragic chorus," to lament the fate that she knew in 1850 was inevitably a part of her own tragedy. At the same time, in her letter forecasting her death, as a seer she understood that in the future her influence would be manifest: "God will transplant the root, if he wills to rear it into fruit-bearing." Prophetic, she knew that future generations of women would be rooted into her thought.

After Fuller's death in 1850, as the nineteenth century progressed, Fuller's writing went out of print but the *Memoirs* continued to sell. Much of the appeal of the *Memoirs* is the power of Fuller's letters. The editors used many of her letters, or parts of her letters, to tell her story.

Margaret Fuller's charismatic personality is displayed in her letters. They reveal what made her so charming. Each letter is carefully designed so that the reader learns as much about the recipient as about Fuller.

Like an intricately faceted mirror over a crowded dance floor, Margaret Fuller's many letters reflect the varied movement of the society below. Each expresses a meaning uniquely designed for the recipient. Her letters create immediacy and show extraordinary empathy for the reader. Fuller's correspondence mirrors a bygone age— a society ruled by social ritual and a strong sense of community. The theme is the dazzling growth of the mind of a genius struggling to survive, in body and in spirit.

In Europe, there came a time when Fuller understood that she was writing letters for posterity. Near the end of her life—clairvoyant that she was—Fuller wrote her letters to future generations of women. At fifteen, she had written Lafayette, saying she sought glory. At thirty, she wrote she had to express her genius by heroic means or die. At forty, she fulfilled herself as a writer in a heroic struggle, which led to her death.

In 1930, Virginia Woolf wrote that the art of letter writing had been "dealt its death blow by the telephone" (*Collected Essays* 2:259).

In the 1990's the personal letter constitutes only a small percentage of the mail. Instead, there are printed messages for every occasion—death, marriage, birth—catalogs, bills, advertisements, carefully written pleas for money. Now, instead of handwriting analysis, the tone of voice gives a clue. The messages on the answering machine, fax, video phones offer a new world of connections. Today's electronic mail is faster but no more powerful than the cameos of literary art that transmitted Margaret Fuller's electricity.

Notes

1. See *Dearest Andrew: Letters From V. Sackville-West To Andrew Reiber 1951-1962* ed. Nancy MacKnight, New York: Charles Scribner's Sons, 1979, and rpt. Orono, ME: Puckerbrush Press, 1985.

2. Probably a suicide, Margaret's favorite brother, Eugene, disappeared on board a ship sailing from New Orleans to the east coast. Another brother, Arthur, who volunteered for a dangerous mission after he had fulfilled his tour of duty as a chaplain in the Civil War, also acted with reckless despair.

3. For a revealing account of Fuller's methods of teaching, see Judith Strong Albert's "Margaret Fuller and Mary Ware Allen: 'in Youth an Insatiate Student'—A Certain Kind of Friendship," *Thoreau Journal Quarterly*, 12:3, July 1980. As Fuller's student, Mary kept a journal, which was saved by her heirs.

4. Modified excerpts from my analysis of Fuller's letters written from 1817 to 1841 appeared in my review in the *Women's Studies International Forum* 7:6, London 1984. Reprinted by permission of the publisher.

5. Retrieving indiscreet love letters was considered important. Fuller accompanied Anne Lynch to Edgar Allan Poe's cottage to obtain Mrs. Frances Osgood's letters to him. Although she was acting on a friend's request, Poe who had formerly supported Fuller as a writer, never forgave her.

6. Modified excerpts from my book review of Fuller's letters written from Italy appeared in *Resources for American Literary Study* 18:2, 1992. Reprinted by permission of the publisher.

7. Background biographical material used in this study was taken from Joseph Jay Deiss's *The Roman Years of Margaret Fuller*, Paula Blanchard's *Margaret Fuller: From Transcendentalism To Revolution*, and Madeleine Stern's *The Life of Margaret Fuller*. A second edition of Stern's biography, published by Greenwood Press in 1991, contains an essay, "A Half Century of Margaret Fuller Scholarship, 1942-1990."

Works Cited

Chevigny, Bell Gale. *The Woman and the Myth: Margaret Fuller's Life and Writings.* New York: Old Westbury, Feminist Press, 1976.

Deiss, Joseph Jay. *The Roman Years of Margaret Fuller.* New York: Crowell, 1969.

Fuller, Margaret. *At Home and Abroad, Or Things and Thoughts in America and Europe.* Ed. Arthur B. Fuller. 1856. Port Washington, New York: Kennikat, 1971.

—. *The Letters of Margaret Fuller.* 5 vols. to date. Ed. Robert N. Hudspeth. Ithaca: Cornell UP, 1983-.

—. *Love-Letters of Margaret Fuller 1845-1846.* Ed. Julia Ward Howe. New York: D. Appleton and Company, 1903.

—. *Memoirs of Margaret Fuller Ossoli.* 2 vols. Ed. Ralph Waldo Emerson, William Henry Channing, and James Freeman Clark. Boston: Phillips, Sampson and Company, 1852.

—. *Woman in the Nineteenth Century.* 1845. Ed. Madeleine B. Stern. Columbia: South Carolina UP, 1980.

Perry, Ruth. *Women, Letters, and the Novel.* New York: AMS Press, 1980.

Woolf, Virginia. *Collected Essays.* vol. 2. New York: Harcourt, Brace & World, 1967.

—. *The Common Reader.* New York: Harcourt, Brace and Company, 1948.

Marie Mitchell Olesen Urbanski

The Seeress of Prevorst: The Central Jewel in *Summer on the Lakes*

PEOPLE HAVE ALWAYS TRAVELLED. A daring few who wandered from the protection of the tribe began lengthier journeys. If they returned home, they felt compelled to recount their adventures for those left behind. In the process of telling their stories over and over, they interpreted in their retrospection the meaning of the journey for themselves and for those who would listen. Margaret Fuller's *Summer on the Lakes, In 1843* concerns a circular trip she took by rail to Niagara Falls, by ship over the Great Lakes to Cleveland, Detroit, Chicago and Mackinac Island, by wagon over the Illinois and Wisconsin prairie, and back home via the lakes. After her journey's end in September, 1843, she spent several months doing research Harvard Library into the work of authorities on American Indians in the and revising her travel journal into a book. While compiling her research, editing her journal, and completing her book, the meaning of her trip west became clear to her. Fuller realized that central to her journey was the need for validation of spiritual power embodied in her text by the Seeress of Prevorst. As with other innovative works, the meaning was less clear to many of her readers.

The *Odyssey* has come to mean a quest. It features a husband and wife. During his long journey Odysseus dallies with Circe and Calypso for years, while faithful Penelope waits for him at home, rejecting many suitors. In Virgil's *Aeneid* the Fated Wanderer Aeneas enjoys the love of Dido, who kills herself when he leaves her. In these two archetypal western journeys both females stay home, whereas the males have many exciting adventures. Educated in the classical tradition, Fuller saw the need to forge a new form of narrative for a woman who wanted to travel. It is an impetus to an intensity of feeling and experience, that heightens understanding. Travel provokes new patterns of thinking as it liberates the traveller from old habits. After a safe return home while the traveller was telling her story, she took a second look at her home territory and began to examine it more thoughtfully. Inevitably the *terra incognita* once explored served as a contrast to home as did the customs of the people whom she encountered. The traveller had not only discovered a strange country, but had also rediscovered her own land. After having come to understand the nature of oppression on her journey west, Fuller applied that knowledge to the oppression of ethnic groups and women back home in the East.

Tellers of tales often embellished their stories if they saw the attention of their audience were flagging. Always of interest is the suspense of danger, with a sexual encounter, the hero's reward. If little exciting occurred romantically, a man could invent a dramatic love episode as did Captain John Smith with Pocahontas in *The*

General History of Virginia written some years after his captivity in Virginia.

When women learned to write and could contrive to travel, they wrote within the codified conventions of episodic travel literature, but modified their stories and dramatic structure to conform to the restrictions placed upon their sex. Early travel writers in North America such as Sarah Knight or Anna Jameson did not brag about sexual conquests. Fuller mentions that the ship's captain showed her the old English fort on Point St. Joseph's due to "his desire to entertain me" (147) but does not admit a flirtation. And her story about love is cautionary—not the stereotypical death from seduction—but Miranda's death from thwarted expectations in marriage. Again in her cautionary tale about the danger of drinking to excess, she reverses the reader's expectations by making the wife rather than the husband the drunkard. She devised her travel narrative to express what she called a "Lehrjahre for women" (*Letters* 3:221).

Fuller's life has itself become a legend, an archetype of Everywoman's Search for Identity. From childhood, her fantasy was that she was "an European princess" who needed transport back to her rightful kingdom. Her early dream was of a trip to Europe, which she did not realize until she was thirty-six. Her trip West was a prelude to her European sojourn. At thirty-three she still could not afford leisure travel so she accepted expenses for her journey over the Great Lakes from her friends, Sarah Shaw and James Freeman Clarke. James was artist Sarah Clarke's brother. He accompanied them as far as Chicago, but Sarah took the whole trip west with Margaret.

In *Summer* she compares her book to a necklace: "I wish I had a thread long enough to string on it all these beads that take my fancy" (148). As Susan Belasco Smith points out, this strikingly feminine image" is "an appropriate metaphor for the structure of *Summer*" (XIV)—a collection of autobiographical sketches, social criticism, conversational debates, transcendental concepts, poetry, anecdotes, and descriptions of people, the weather, and landscape. Since Fuller sought her "poetic impressions" of the West, she uses many poems written by herself and others to enrich her work. Particularly significant are her poems that begin and end *Summer.* She begins with the declaration that "those to whom a hint suffices" would be able to see the knights through dried grasses. At the same time, she recognizes her limitations. Her cup is so small in "our dwarf day" that soon it must be replenished. In her concluding poem to her reader, she uses images derived from cooking and sewing. After asking for charity from her reader who often opens a book at the end, she implies that blackberry jam is not as tasty as fresh berries, nor is *Summer* more than a diminished taste of the western experience. But for the reader who brings a "good needle with her spool of thread" there is gold to be mined. Fuller's mixed metaphor combines female and male images.

Unlike many male travel writers, Fuller does not pretend to be objective. In her impressionistic work she wishes to "woo the mighty meaning of the scene, perhaps to foresee the law by which a new order, a new poetry is to be evoked from this chaos," to call up "apparitions" of the future out of the "witch's caldron." She acknowledges her preconceived bias that she would not like the "rudeness of conquest" which she expected to see happening in the west (18). In the 1840's, immigrants, largely Northern European, were pouring into the Midwest to take possession of the land formerly inhabited by the native American.

From the time of *Summer's* publication in 1844 until the present day, this work has had mixed reviews. Her friend, James Freeman Clarke, pointed out that *Summer* is not "a pleasant book of travels," but that it needs to be read again and again, and that it conveys a "thousand suggestions and incitements to thought by every work" (*Essays* 2). Caleb Stetson proved to be a more typical reviewer than Clarke in his criticism of Fuller's digressions. In the September, 1844, issue of the *Christian Examiner*, Stetson complained of her inclusion of extraneous material, "things connected by no apparent link of association with the objects which seem to fill her eye and mind" (*Essays 4*). As with critics who followed him, Stetson singles out her inclusion of the lengthy account of the German mystic, the Seeress of Prevorst. He finds her choice "mysterious." Likewise in a review published in the fall of 1844, Orestes A. Brownson castigates Fuller for her promulgation of German writers and her "slipshod" style—"Miss Fuller seems to us to be wholly deficient in a pure, correct taste, and especially in that tidiness we always look for in woman." Moreover, Brownson, a Roman Catholic convert, dubs her a "heathen priestess" with doctrines he detested. With echoes of Socrates' infamous trial, when he was accused of corrupting the young men, Brownson asserts "no person has appeared among us whose conversations and writings have done more to corrupt the minds and hearts of our Boston community." Brownson believes Fuller's religion is Art, her Divinity, the Beautiful, her morality, Transcendentalism (*Essays 5*). Subsequent reviewers and editors were to have a more restrained but equivocal reaction to her inclusion of digressions, especially her account of the Seeress of Prevorst, which, with its dialogue-introduction, took 24 out of 156 pages of the first edition of her book.

In the first reprint of *Summer* in an anthology, *At Home and Abroad (1856)*, edited by her brother, Arthur Buckminster Fuller, extracts from works about the Indians, her translation of Kerner's account of the Seeress of Prevorst, some poetry, and her story about Mariana were all omitted. Her brother explained that, due to publishing space limitations, he made these omissions with reluctance but that he did not think they would materially diminish the value of *Summer*. In 1884 Thomas Wentworth Higginson supported her brother's decision, arguing in his biography that Fuller's inclusion of the Seeress episode lacked good judgement (197).

Twentieth century anthologists—Mason Wade, Perry Miller, and Joel Myerson—followed the lead of their predecessors and omitted the Seeress of Prevorst digression. Miller evaluated her "potpourri" in *Summer* as random and "miserably confused" so that the effect is of "an intolerable monstrosity" (116), whereas Myerson averred it was hampered by "an unconscionable padding." Myerson complained that Fuller "included large excerpts from and summaries of her reading — one extending thirty-five pages — so that less than half of the book actually dealt with the subject matter promised by its title" (13).

From the time of her brother's deletion of the Seeress episode to contemporary scholars who dismiss it, little space has been given to the content of this "digression." Her brother maintained that by his deletions, the volume gained in unity of narrative (x). Therefore, it is important to examine what the Seeress digression contains in order to understand the complexity of ideas that may seem abstruse or even threatening to readers who erase them. Fuller had just finished reading Justinus Kerner's *Die Seherin Von Prevorst* a few days prior to her departure. On May 9, 1843, she wrote Ralph Waldo Emerson that it was "a really good book." The story of the Seeress was on her mind when she started her trip and it haunted her throughout her journey. In her introductory debate to her account of the Seeress, under the persona "Free Hope", in opposition to her antagonists, "Self-Poise", "Good Sense" and "Old Church", Fuller identified with the Seeress. She acknowledges that she, too, has psychic power; as a clairvoyant, all her days "are touched by the supernatural, for I feel the pressure of hidden causes, and the presence, sometimes the communion, of unseen powers" (79). She evokes Socrates who also had a "signal" as a guide.

Although she had read about the Seeress before her trip, Fuller writes in *Summer* she read it in Milwaukee after much fatigue during her journey. She uses the visionary Seeress as a contrast to the pioneers whose lives were instinctive. The sub-title of *Die Seherin* is "Revelations concerning the inward life of man, and the projection of a world of spirits to ours." An examination of the 118-page *Seeress of*

Prevorst shows that Fuller chose to include much material about the Seeress's life and to delete many of the anecdotes about her encounters with ghosts. The author, Justinus Kerner, narrates a scientific study of his observations as the physician of the Seeress, and illustrates the work with a chart of the Spirit World and the Sunsphere. The chief physician of Weinsberg uses deductive logic in his empirical study as he describes in minute detail his observations of Frederica Hauffe. He not only describes her medical and life history but he also gives evidence from other witnesses of her psychic states. He compares observed phenomena with similar accounts from other clairvoyants. He begins as a skeptic but after numerous instances of the Seeress's encounters with spectres and of her prophetic dreams, Dr. Kerner concludes with an acknowledgement of his belief in the validity of her unseen powers. His study ends in a scientifically appropriate method with an autopsy of Frederica Hauffe's corpse. Perhaps protecting his reputation with his colleagues, he had asserted in his preface that it was annoying that a "weak silly woman should thus disturb the established system of the learned," but settled his skepticism with an appeal to Biblical authority in an Epistle from Paul: "But God hath chosen the foolish things of the world to confound the wise . . ." What Kerner does is attempt to "prove" the validity of second-sight happenings, but in her condensed summary translation, Fuller's focus in on the plight of a clairvoyant woman, living in a patriarchal society hostile to her gifts, who is forced into a marriage she does not want.[1]

In Fuller's excerpt, she writes that Dr. Kerner was a German physician who was asked to treat Frederica Hauffe near the end of her life. He learned that she was born in the hamlet of Prevorst in Wirtemberg. Her father was a gamekeeper in the forest mountains surrounding the tiny village with a population of 450 people. Even as a child, Frederica had prophetic dreams. When she was sent by her parents to study with her grandfather in Lowenstein, her grandparents discovered her susceptibility to ghosts, which they tried to repress.

After Frederica returned home, her visions and visitations of spirits increased. Still she was able to function until age nineteen when her parents betrothed her to marry Herr Hauffe, a laborer. She reacted with depression, steady tears, and sleeplessness. Nevertheless, her forced marriage took place and she had to move with her husband to Kurnbach in the valley. After seven months as a wife and house-keeper, Mrs. Hauffe became gravely ill. Although her health de-clined, her second sight and contacts with her guardian spirit, her late grandmother, continued.

"Injudicious" medical treatment, including bleeding, increased her nervousness and capacity for suffering. She began to fear all men and wished for the only escape she could envision—death. Dr. Kerner was called in for consultation after she had been in declining health for five years. Skeptical at first of clairvoyant powers, he refused to treat her when she was in her somnambulic state. When his treatment did not bring a favorable response from his patient, Dr. Kerner acknowl-edged: "It was touching to see how retiring within herself, she sought for help. The physician who had aided her so little with his drugs, must often stand abashed before this inner physician, perceiving it to be far better skilled than himself" (89). Then he permitted her to follow the magnetic treatment she had prescribed for herself so for a time she grew better. Dr. Kerner saw her living in an almost "disembodied life," as she lived only by effusions from her contact with people with whose temperament she was compatible.

She had out-of-body experiences. With her second-sight, she could see "the coffins of those about to die" (97), so people demanded to consult with her. Dr. Kerner felt she was like one arrested in the act of dying. Fuller was concerned with the Seeress as she affected people's lives, but she never forgot her overarching connection with the uni-verse of Sunspheres. As with her observation about Niagara Falls, she knew that "mutability and unchangeableness were united" (9).

She interpreted the life of the clairvoyant sybil as one whose ghosts were projections of herself but that her extrasensory perception could have been "pure facts," with which those who trust their mental impulses are familiar. Frederica's life and sun-circles, Fuller argued, were valuable in that they exemplified the position of mathematics relative to the world of creative thought and could be compared to Macaria's power and wisdom in Goethe's *Wanderjahre*. The electric fluid Frederica possessed also could pass to the spirits of metals, minerals, plants and animals. In her contact with minerals, she felt "a sense of concentrated life" (97). As with the new age interest in crystal transmitters, Fuller believed in the power of gems as talismans.

Fuller's interpretation of Frederica's observations about the left and right hemispheres of the brain has been borne out by the discoveries of contemporary scientists about the brain's fundamental dichotomy. She notes that "the Seherin ascribed different states to the right and left sides of everybody . . ." that the left side is most impressible (97). The fashioning spirit was perceived as working upward from the clod to man—who has "that immense galvanic battery that can be loaded from above, below, and around—that engine, not only of perception, but of conception and consecutive thought—whose right hand is memory, whose life is idea, the crown of nature, the platform from which spirit takes wing" (98). Fuller has uncovered in her translation of the story of the Seeress a remarkable amount of material that should be of interest to scientists and thinkers of our own time, and which in the future no doubt will merit further study. What is important for an analysis of *Summer* is that the Seeress episode is both the literal and thematic center of this book. The Seeress shines as the central jewel on Fuller's necklace; her vision illuminates what has come before and what follows it.

The Seeress was still on Fuller's mind some months after *Summer's* publication as she wrote *Woman in the Nineteenth Century* in the fall of 1844. Again she refers to the Seeress as a contemporary descendant of

Cassandra. Her "remarkable powers" were "broken and jarred into disease by an unsuitable marriage" (95), just as the enslaved Cassandra had been forced to become Agamemnon's mistress. Ralph Waldo Emerson writes of Fuller's interest in "arcana," in the *Memoirs of Margaret Fuller Ossoli* published two years after Fuller's death:

> It was soon evident that there was somewhat a little pagan about her, that she had some faith more or less distinct in a fate, and in a guardian genius; that her fancy, or her pride, had played with her religion. She had a taste for gems, ciphers, talismans, omens, coincidences, and birth-days . . . a special love for the planet Jupiter." (1:219)

She chose the carbuncle as her stone, and valued sortilege. "Coincidences, good and bad, *contretemps*, seals, ciphers, mottoes, omens, anniversaries, names, dreams, are all of a certain importance to her" (1:220).

In addition to the digression about the Seeress, other readers fault her inclusion of material about the Indians from as many as twenty other writers, such as, George Catlin, Anna Jameson, and Washington Irving. Some critics find her inclusion of this research extraneous, but Fuller apologizes for not having given more information and suggests that interested readers could find the books in the library of Harvard College. Somehow Fuller had contrived to invade Harvard's library, forbidden terriory to women. Thomas Wentworth Higginson mentions having seen her working there, "day after day, under the covert gaze of the undergraduates who had never before looked upon a woman reading within those sacred precincts . . ." (194).[2]

Everyone reading *Summer* notes Fuller's concern with the plight of the native American. She begins her journey at Niagara Falls with a feeling of "undefined dread" that compelled her to look back again and again at "images of naked savages" stealing behind her "with uplifted tomahawks" (4). She was as disturbed by Indian ghosts as was the Seeress of Prevorst by the spectres that haunted her. Throughout

Fuller's westward journey, she seems to be exorcising the spirits of the Indians whom the white man has killed. The Indians who have survived are perceived as fragmented people:

> The men of these subjugated tribes, now accustomed to drunkenness
> and every way degraded, bear but a faint impress of the lost grandeur
> of the race. (113)

Fuller understood the greatness the Indians once possessed and struggled to reconcile it to their present condition of "blanketed forms, in listless groups" (12) or to begging dances with starving Indians attempting to trade headbands for food. Her unsought communion with the unseen powers of the vanquished Indians disturbed her throughout her westward journey as she contrasted their former greatness with their broken spirits of her own day. She knew that their banishment was as inexorable as was the rattlesnake's.

Fuller considers amalgamation of the two races as a possible solution to the racial clash, but fears the Indians are fated to perish. Although she respects the American natives, she is not sentimental about them, and suggests that a national institute be established to record their history before it is obliterated.

During her sojourn on Mackinac Island, Fuller had an opportunity to observe the Indians even more closely as thousands from the Chippewa and Ottawa tribes came to receive their annual payments from the United States government. To the astonishment of her white acquaintances, she visited the women in their lodges. Fuller understood the psychology of oppression, what today is referred to as "blaming the victim," as she noted the "aversion of the injurer for him he has degraded" (72). The white men hated the Indians but the white women felt loathing and disgust. She castigated the Christian missionaries whom she thought might better preach to the "felon traders" than to the Indians ruined by the traders' rum. An example she cites of the missionaries' sacrilege is their seizure of the body of the great Indian leader Red Jacket to perform their rites over his corpse despite the fact that he had always adhered to his ancestral religion. She expresses reverence for the Indian religion that includes belief in immortality, an ethical system, and awareness of the interdependence of all life—animals, trees, humans, mountains, rivers, and plants. The Indians "were the rightful lords of a beauty they forebore to deform" (29) whereas the white settlers were the obliterating Goths. The American natives believed that once there had been a time when the animals ruled the earth and expressed their reverence for all forms of life, which were interconnected and reached the stars:

> As they loved to draw the lower forms of nature up to them divining their histories, and imitating their ways, in their wild dances and paintings; even so did they love to look upward and people the atmosphere that enfolds the earth, with fairies and manitoes. (127)

Not the ploughman but the poet could see "the meaning of the flower uprooted in the ploughed field" (79). She links the destroyed land with the loss of habitat of rapidly vanishing animals with the situation of exploited native Americans, who once lived in harmony with Nature in opposition to the destructive westward advance of the powerful pioneers. Fuller's respect for Indian myth and religion shows her as a precursor of mythic critics and environmentalists, and of the current interest in the concept of Gaea, the earth as a living being.

In a state of servitude, the American Indians live in conditions parallel to that of the pioneer women: "Has the Indian, has the white woman . . . as religious a self-respect as worthy a field of thought and action, as man?" (115). Annette Kolodny in *The Land Before Her* links the plight of the pioneer housewife to that of the earlier captivity heroine, kidnapped by the Indians. Both have been taken west against their will, although the landscape is no longer a "howling wilderness," but a promised garden which she cannot see from the "windowless cabins" that isolate her (123). Fuller finds the women unhappy and unprepared for their harsh pioneer life. Confined to a "comfortless and laborious in-door life," (72) the women went west for the love of their husbands and children, "too often in heartsickness and weariness" (38). Fuller deplores the inadequate education the women received. French and piano lessons are not helpful lessons for basic survival so she suggests more practical training for girls, such as cultivating a garden and playing the guitar. The men enjoy the hunting and outdoor life, and perhaps even war.

Fuller compares the destructive path of the pioneers to war: "The march of peaceful is scarce less wanton than that of warlike invasion" (18). At the start of her journey in Niagara Falls, she wonders how "strange" it is that men could have fought battles before a spectacle of such grandeur. Near the end of her journey at Detroit, she defends the surrender of that city by General William Hull to the British in the War of 1812. Forgotten now, General Hull was still a figure of controversy in 1843. Not a shot was fired before his surrender, so a court martial convicted him of cowardice and neglect of duty, and sentenced him to be executed by firing squad. President James Madison revoked his sentence and spared General Hull's life but not from a "despoiled old age" (155). With not atypical irony, Fuller says she is a "woman, and unlearned in such affairs; but, to a person with common sense and good eyesight, it is clear, when viewing the location, that, under the circumstances, he [General Hull] had no prospect of successful defence, and that to attempt it would have been an act of vanity, not valor" (154). In Fuller's view, then, commonsense saving of life by surrender is preferable to death with honor. On the surrender spot, she feels the presence of General Hull—"the feelings which possessed me here and now"—(155), and therefore desires justice for the memory of the disgraced general. Again Fuller posits the life of the spirit in opposition to war and violence.

In addition to finding war "strange" amidst the sublimity of Niagara Falls, Fuller finds it "no less strange" that an eagle could be chained and abused there. This captive awakens in her memory a similar episode from her childhood when she saw another eagle cruelly tormented. Were Fuller alive today, no doubt she would be a supporter of the movements for the ethical and humane treatment of animals.

At the end of her journey Fuller observes a bereaved lover seeking religious consolation in his copy of Butler's *Analogy*. It is no accident that Fuller shows him soon thereafter being consoled by "certain damsels" who board the ship at Detroit. He is linked thematically with Mariana's husband who remarries soon after her death. Women such as Mariana who could not share "the secret riches within herself" (60)—die young, and are destroyed as inexorably as are the Indians, whereas the young man on board ship takes a practical approach to his loss by looking for a replacement.

The Seeress and Mariana episodes challenge the efficacy of patriarchal medical treatment, making a direct connection between the emotions and health. When humiliated by her classmates as a schoolgirl, Mariana had convulsions and refused to eat, so her health rapidly declined. She was saved by a teacher who helped to heal her "wounded spirit," but dies after she cannot adjust to a husband who does not respond to the intensity of her love.[3] As Dr. Kerner attested, after the Seeress's forced marriage, her health began to decline. Physicians exacerbated rather than helped her condition. Her "unhappy gift" of psychic power brought her ridicule, questions by authorities, and intrusive people desperate for proof that indeed there was life after death. Obviously Fuller was interested in the Seeress's story because, psychic herself, she could identify with her. Her poor health is well-known as she had frequent illnesses and headaches. After suffering from a tooth extraction, in Paris, she went in pain to the opera and the music healed her. In her dispatch home, she exclaimed: "Ah! if physicians only understood the influence of the mind over the body, instead of treating, as they so often do, their patients like machines, and according to precedent!" (*At Home and Abroad 203*). How Margaret Fuller would shudder at medical technology today! She linked unhappiness, frustration and disappointment with illness. She understood the essential connection between body and mind, as a means of holistic healing.

Another writer from this period, Lydia Maria Child, expressed in a letter to Fuller dated August 23, 1844 the complexity of *Summer*, the "vigor and acuteness of intellect" with which it was written. At the same time, she makes an astute observation about Fuller's first original book: "you seem . . . to write with too much effort." The abundant and beautiful stream seems to be *"pumped rather than to flow"* (211). Her observation, although difficult to document, is cogent. As Fuller gained confidence and practice writing, her style seems to have become more *flowing*. Moreover, Child is cogent when she observed that Fuller's house was too full, with too much furniture for her rooms. While reading the proof sheets, Fuller, too, felt it was "desultory and ineffectual," too "rich," that she did not properly "fuse" her material (Higginson 195). *Summer* is experimental in form and in content. Multivocal, Fuller, as was her practice as editor of the *Dial*, sought to represent points of view other than her own. Her multiplicity of ideas makes it possible for different readers to find different interpretations. Those adhering to scientific rationalism expect to read a chronological travelogue and want to excise all material that seems extraneous or even threatening. A discerning critic, Susan Belasco Smith, interprets *Summer* as an expression of Fuller's search for self-discovery (x), an inward journey in which she debates her conflict with the Emersonian world view. Margaret Vanderhaar Allen perceives Fuller's theme as the interaction of nature and civilization (118), whereas Madeleine Stern believes *Summer* "was a crystallization both of the Midwest in 1843 and of Margaret Fuller" (XXVII).

Whether on the road or sitting under a tree waiting for Enlightment, those who think continue to be harassed by philosophic questions. Extrasensory perception was a phenomena of interest in Fuller's time. Male psychics, such as, Emanuel Swedenborg, the Swedish clairvoyant, were popular. In her later review of books about Swedenborg for the New York *Tribune,* she wrote that she saw no reason why holding intercourse with spirits "should not exist" (*Papers on Literature and Art 2:164*). But for women cursed with "Cassandra-power," there is an added burden of being denigrated. Although there is the possibility of illumination at the end of their quest, such women can feel very much alone amidst "hailstorms of jeers and scorn" (78). When Fuller discovered a woman with psychic affinity—the Seeress—just before her westward journey, she felt a sense of relief and a need to justify herself and to spread the "word" to other similarly afflicted women. In *Summer* she connects the Seeress's wasted gifts with the vanquished spiritual power of the American natives. She calls for the reader's intuitive thought participation; her message is for "those to whom a hint suffices." She uses indirection with a juxtaposition of episodes and ideas, so that her reader has imaginatively to make the connections. The surface *non sequitur* strung out on a string of beads becomes her structural travel guide. The Seeress's "ghostly vision" is the central carbuncle in her associative chain that connects the Unseen World of the vanquished with the incompatible world of greed and violence. She thinks the purple prairie flowers spring from the blood of the Indians as did the hyacinth from that of Adonis. In telling the myth of Muckwa, or the Bear, she suggests the kinship of all beings, and respect for animals. She wishes to be Gnome-like and recognizes Gaea's power, in ideas suggestive of the Cherokee Teachings from the Wisdom Fire by Dhyani Ywahoo so popular in the present day. What Fuller seeks in *Summer on the*

Lakes, in 1843 is a transformation of consciousness. There is a connection between body and soul. Clairvoyance is a misunderstood source of energy. In the prophetic mode, her poetic vision seeks to transcend the limitations of space and time. She knows that this task would be as difficult as mining for gold with a needle, but that a new age would follow.

Notes

[1] A translation of *The Seeress of Prevorst* was published in New York by Harper & Brothers in 1845, a year after *Summer* appeared. It was translated by Catherine Crowe (1800-1872), a British writer, and reviewed by Fuller for the *New York Tribune*.

[2] Joan von Mehren and I both searched the Harvard Archives and read the Board of Overseers Records for 1843-44, but could find no reference to permission granted to Margaret Fuller to use the library. Higginson's biography first mentions her appearance in the Harvard library.

[3] The editors of the *Memoirs* (1:42-52) republished the "Mariana" story as a true account of Fuller's experience as a school girl in Groton but deleted the part about Mariana's unhappy marriage and untimely death.

Works Cited

Allen, Margaret Vanderhaar. *The Achievement of Margaret Fuller*. University Park: Pennsylvania State UP, 1979.

Child, Lydia Maria. *Selected Letters, 1817-1880*. Ed. Milton Meltzer and Particia G. Holland. Amherst: Massachusetts UP, 1982.

Emerson, Ralph Waldo, William Henry Channing, and James Freeman Clarke, eds. *Memoirs of Margaret Fuller Ossoli*. 2 vols. Boston: Phillips, Sampson and Company, 1852.

Fuller, Margaret. *At Home and Abroad, or Things and Thoughts in America and Europe*. Ed. Arthur B. Fuller. 1856. Port Washington, New York: Kennikat, 1971.

—. *The Letters of Margaret Fuller.* Vol. 3. Ed. Robert N. Hudspeth. Ithaca: Cornell UP, 1984.

—. *Papers on Literature and Art.* 2 vols. 1846. New York: AMS Press, 1972.

—. *Summer on the Lakes, in 1843.* 1844. Ed. Susan Belasco Smith. Urbana: Illinois UP, 1991.

—. *Woman in the Nineteenth Century.* 1845. Ed. Madeleine B. Stern. Columbia: South Carolina UP, 1980.

Higginson, Thomas Wentworth. *Margaret Fuller Ossoli.* Boston: Houghton Mifflin, 1884.

Kerner, Justinus. *The Seeress of Prevorst, Being Revelations Concerning the Inner Life of Man, and the Inter-diffusion of a World of Spirits in the One We Inhabit.* Trans. Mrs. Crowe, New York: Harper & Brothers, 1845.

Kolodny, Annette. *The Land Before Her: Fantasy and Experience of the American Frontiers, 1630-1860.* Chapel Hill: North Carolina UP, 1984.

Miller, Perry. Ed. *Margaret Fuller: American Romantic.* Ithaca: Cornell UP, 1963.

Myerson, Joel. Ed. *Critical Essays on Margaret Fuller.* Boston: G. K. Hall, 1980.

—. *Margaret Fuller: Essays on American Life and Letters.* New Haven: College & UP, 1978.

Stern, Madeleine B. Introduction. *Summer on the Lakes, in 1843.* Nieuwkoop: B. De Graaf, 1972.

Wade, Mason. Ed. *The Writings of Margaret Fuller.* New York: Viking, 1941.

Marie Mitchell Olesen Urbanski

Woman in the Nineteenth Century: Genesis, Form, Tone, and Rhetorical Devices

T HE FIRST IMPRESSION a reader may get from a hasty perusal of Margaret Fuller's *Woman in the Nineteenth Century* is one of effusiveness and form-lessness. Containing a display of erudition that is impressive, it is prolix, as was the work of many transcendentalists and other writers of the past century.[1] In the April 1845 issue of his *Quarterly Review*, Orestes Brownson observed that *Woman* has "neither beginning, middle, nor end, and may be read backwards as well as forward" (*Essays* 19). In his satire, Brownson expressed aspects of the organic living quality of the work, but he did not discern its form. In the midst of its verbosity, it is still possible to see more of a pattern in *Woman* than has been maintained. Its basic structure is that of the sermon, which is appropriate, because *Woman's* message is hortatory. Its complexity and apparent lack of form are due to its dual nature. Within the sermon framework, *Woman* partakes of the major characteristics of transcendental literary art. But before analyzing *Woman* as a literary work from the standpoint of form, tone, and use of rhetorical devices, it is necessary to examine its genesis. If a study can be made of its genesis from an early draft, then some insight may be obtained as to the way in which Fuller's ideas were developing and thus a clearer perception of her composition of *Woman* is possible.

Woman developed from "The Great Lawsuit.—Man *versus* Men; Woman *versus* Women," which was published in the July, 1843 issue of the *Dial*, a year after Fuller had relinquished its editorship to Emerson. In her preface to *Woman*, she explained that she had prepared her expanded version for publication in compliance with wishes expressed from many quarters. Then she discussed her change of title. She conceded that the meaning of the original title is puzzling—"it requires some thought to see what it means." Her preference, she told her readers, was to retain the first title in her enlargement, but she was dissuaded from doing so by friends. Although awkward, her early biographer Higginson explained, the original title was intended "to avert even the suspicion of awakening antagonism between the sexes" (200). Nevertheless, this title does sound antagonistic because it suggests court action. But why is the title worded "man *versus* men" instead of "man *versus* woman," or *vice versa*, which is the usual order in the battle of the sexes? Fuller's intention was not to write a long history of woman's grievances against the tyranny of the male sex. Instead she keynoted the grievance of the individual man or woman whose aspirations were thwarted by the multitude, or by himself or herself, from becoming the developed soul he or she might become. She explained:

> I meant by that title to intimate the fact that, while it is the destiny of
> Man, in the course of the ages, to ascertain and fulfil the law of his
> being, so that his life shall be seen, as a whole, to be that of an angel
> or messenger, the action of prejudices and passions which attend, in
> the day, the growth of the individual, is continually obstructing the
> holy work that is to make the earth a part of heaven. By Man I mean
> both man and woman; these are the two halves of one thought. I lay
> no special stress on the welfare of either. I believe that the develop-
> ment of the one cannot be effected without that of the other.

She developed this concept in *Woman* by adding to "Lawsuit" her
dual epigraphs. Then, by rephrasing them, she made them applicable
to men as well. What she had to say applied to both men and women;
her message was not ambivalent but hortatory, and its significance,
again referring to her original title, was "great."

It appears at first glance that *Woman* is much longer than "Lawsuit,"
but a line-by-line examination of the content indicates that the number of words per page in "Lawsuit" is much greater than that in
Woman. The first 130 pages of the 179-page text of *Woman* are a
close adaptation of the 47 pages of "Lawsuit." In most instances,
Fuller used a verbatim transcription of "The Great Lawsuit" in
Woman. Occasionally she changed a few words to clarify or modify
the meaning of a sentence, but she did very little polishing of her
original text. For example, in the original essay she wrote, "Is it not
enough, cries the sorrowful trader," and in her second version (28)
she changed *sorrowful* to *irritated*. In the original version she wrote,
"But our doubt is whether the heart does consent with the head, or
only acquiesces its decrees." In the second version, she changed
acquiesces to *obeys* and then added to her sentence, "with a passiveness
that precludes the exercise of its natural powers, or a repugnance that
turns sweet qualities to bitter, or a doubt that lays waste the fair
occasions of life" (29-30). Another word changed to clarify meaning
is *incessant*, which in *Woman* becomes *frequent*: "Shrink not from

frequent error in this gradual, fragmentary state" (19). She deleted a phrase or a sentence a few times, but mostly she developed and elaborated on points she had already made. In her discussion of property rights for widows, she said that the wife "inherits only a part of his fortune" and then inserted in her second version the phrase "often brought him by herself" after "fortune" (31). In her treatment of illustrious old maids—"No one thinks of Michael Angelo's Persian Sibyl, or St. Theresa, or Tasso's Leonora, or the Greek Electra, as an old maid"—she added, "more than of Michael Angelo or Canova as old bachelors" (99), in order to give her sentence and idea balance. Sometimes she added discussions of writers whom she had not included before, such as Charles Fourier and Walter Savage Landor. Furthermore, she tended to add capital letters and italics for emphasis and occasionally corrected punctuation.

There are forty-nine pages of new material. The portion she added contains the most daring subject matter in the book because much of it was contemporary application of her thesis. Her new material contained some frank discussions of sex; an example of an incompatible marriage: "I have known this man come to install himself in the chamber of a woman who loathed him, and say she should never take food without his company" (32); the double standard of morality: "Let Sir Charles Grandison preach to his own sex" (151); the notorious trial of Amelia Norman; a mother's sadness when she gives birth to a daughter; the father's kidnapping of his own children as a means of coercing his wife; problems of older women—a well-preserved woman at forty who is spoken of "upholstery-wise" (99); property rights for married women; and her idea that ladies are responsible for rehabilitating prostitutes. More trenchant social criticism was used to supplement her earlier points: "Those who think the physical circumstances of Woman would make a part in the affairs of national government unsuitable, are by no means those who think it impossible for Negresses to endure field-work, even during pregnancy, or for sempstresses to go through their killing labors" (35). Also included in her enlargement was her remark about letting women be sea captains. Although she added the ancient belief that a baby's body was inherited from his mother and his soul from his father, in general her new material contained less spiritual transcendentalism until the peroration. Therefore the most controversial writing in *Woman* was that which she added to "The Great Lawsuit."[2] The importance of the earlier draft is that it gave Fuller the courage to treat inflammatory subject matter. Because the reception of "The Great Lawsuit" was on the whole favorable among the *Dial*'s small coterie of readers, she became more outspoken. One criticism she did receive about her earlier draft, as she herself explained, was that she did not make her "meaning sufficiently clear" (168). Consequently, she may have been guilty of repetition. And in order to make her meaning unmistakable, less of it is veiled in metaphor.

The residue of a trial from "The Great Lawsuit" remains. The thinking man or woman, who has not yet become the enlarged soul he or she would become, is admonished to perfect himself or herself despite all obstructions. Once this extraordinary person frees himself from ordinary frailty, then this individual could become the king or queen she seeks to lead and to inspire her waiting adversaries.

The broadest structural framework of *Woman* reflects the sermon, which she mentioned both in her introduction—"sermons preached from the text" (19)—and in her statement in the conclusion that she would retrace her design "as was done in old-fashioned sermons" (168). Closely akin to the sermon is the oration, and *Woman* contains elements of both forms. Fuller began her work with the classic *exordium* in a vague way so her thesis is not clear for several pages. Using caution, Latin and German quotations, and preliminary conciliation, she did not introduce her *proposition* until the tenth page: woman needs her turn, and improvement of her lot would aid in the reformation of men, too. Then she stated her sermon topic: "Be ye perfect." Having established her thesis at last, she proceeded with *partitio* or analysis of her subject, which is done in a debate style by raising the popular arguments men used with which to oppose women's rights, and then rebutting them. She began with her conversational method of questions and answers characteristic of the speaker who wishes to dramatize a point. A husband asks:

> "Is it not enough," cries the irritated trader, "that you have done all you could to break up the national union, and thus destroy the prosperity of our country, but now you must be trying to break up family union, to take my wife away from the cradle and the kitchen-hearth, to vote at polls, and preach from a pulpit? Of course, if she does such things, she cannot attend to those of her own sphere. She is happy enough as she is. She has more leisure than I have,—every means of improvement, every indulgence."
>
> "Have you asked her whether she was satisfied with these *indulgences?*"
>
> "No, but I know she is." (28-29)

Fuller ended this dialogue by saying that liberating measures are proposed to ascertain truth. Objectively, she continued: "Without enrolling ourselves at once on either side, let us look upon the subject from the best point of view which to-day offers" (31). She debated the issue with rebuttals that accelerated in strength until she concluded, "We would have every arbitrary barrier thrown down" (37).

Then in a long *digressio* composed of sermon-style exemplar, she considered all that is known of woman, delineating her story in myth, folklore, the Bible, poetry, fiction, history, and in her own time. Beginning with an extensive analysis of the institution of marriage, she examined the life cycle of a woman. She sought women whose lives she found inspiring such as Queen Isabella of Castile or Marina, the Native American woman who accompanied Cortez, but she evaluated the lives of other women, such as Queen Elizabeth and Mary Stuart, lauding their strengths and castigating their weaknesses. Interwoven in her examples is an attempt to buttress her argument with authority using the views of recognized authors to support her position. She conceded that women have always had some power, but they want freedom from men to learn the secrets of the universe alone. Within her narrative in a form suggestive of the *reprehension* is admonition to men, who refuse to grant women freedom and who call strong women "manly," and to women, who misuse what power they have. Scornfully she recognized that a coquette, a shrew, or a good cook could have life-long sway.

Fuller inculcated within her discussion a realistic assessment of the options open to women in various societies, ancient and modern. Reasonably enough, since most women would marry, she spent a lot of time examining the institution of marriage. She contrasted idealized concepts of courtly love in which the lady served as inspiration with the reality of arranged marriages of convenience. It is no surprise that she advocated not only a marriage of love but a spiritual union of two souls on a common pilgrimage. She also discussed other options women have, such as women who write, women who are mothers, and women who do not marry, as well as the problems of women in middle and old age. She praised women abolitionists brave enough to speak on the platform but warned that they must work for measures not only favoring slaves but also for themselves. In her all-inclusive discussion of a woman's life cycle, she discussed the child toward the end of this section, lamenting the father who stunts his daughter's education for fear she will not find a husband. Again pointing out that a woman must work alone and use her special gifts of intuition, she mentioned a crisis at hand and prophesied a New Jerusalem, which the prophets Swedenborg, Fourier, and Goethe foretell. Then her sermon became more direct as she preached about the problems of prostitutes and polygamy and warned that men must be as pure as women. In an accelerating evocative vision of the future in which both men and women rule their passions by reason, she placed her hope with the young—"harbingers and leaders of a new era" (155). Triumphantly she concluded her long narrative by proclaiming her expectation that a young "Exaltada" would serve as an "example and instruction for the rest" (156).

The structural pattern of *Woman* next takes the sermon form of an *applicatio* in a departure from the main thrust of the argument and moves from the visionary future to the prosaic present. Fuller sighed over books recently published in which the chief point was to fit a wife "to please, or, at least, not to disturb a husband" (158). She recognized the dilemmas women faced and completed this section by admonishing American women to use their moral power and not to let themselves be intimidated by aspersions on their modesty. Her application of her sermon, therefore, is that women must act to save themselves (168).

From practical application of the sermon, the form of *Woman* soars back to the sublime world of the spirit. In a *peroration*, Fuller outlined the major points of her argument and of her vision of the harmonious world that an ideal relationship between men and women would bring. then, like a minister ending a sermon, she addressed a prayer to God: "Thou, Lord of Day!" After a cold admonition to cherish hope and act, she concluded with poetry that echoed the Bible: "Persist to ask, and it will come." With an allusion to her epigraphs, she envisioned—"So shalt thou see, what few have seen,/The palace home of King and Queen"—and thus gave structural and thematic wholeness to her work.

The structure of *Woman* does seem to fit loosely the sermon-oration form. What tends to obscure its pattern is Fuller's use of writing techniques derived from transcendentalism. According to precepts generally accepted by the transcendentalists, a work of literature grows out of experience and hence is organic. As Coleridge, a romantic, wrote: "The organic form is innate; it shapes, as it develops itself from within." And Keats, using a nature metaphor, explained that good poetry grew as naturally as the leaves on a tree. Emerson later used this concept, saying a poem is "a thought so passionate and alive that like the spirit of a plant or an animal it has an architecture of its own." The basic assumption of transcendental art is of the "superiority of the spirit to the letter." Art as inspiration meant that the word became one with the thing. Ultimately, the "transcendental theory of art is a theory of knowledge and religion as well." Hence transcendental expression must coalesce the seer and spectacle into one, an organic whole (Matthiessen 24-31). Margaret Fuller, the observer, united the spectacle—her experience—with that of all other women into the final fusion of *Woman in the Nineteenth Century*.

As early as 1826 Sampson Reed published his "Observations on the Growth of the Mind," setting forth transcendental literary theory. He wrote: "Syllogistic reasoning is passing away," leaving nothing behind but a demonstration "of its own worthlessness." Both Julia Ward Howe (151) and Arthur W. Brown (127) pointed out that there was no systematic parallelism in *Woman*; however, Fuller did not intend that there should be. By not following a rigidly organized pattern of syllogistic reasoning, she was merely demonstrating that she had accepted the transcendentalist aesthetic theory that, as a member of the club, she had helped to shape. The movement of her treatise is not parallel but soaring and circular. Its dominant mode of composition is an unfolding from the subconscious in a form of spiraling thought patterns. One of her recurrent themes is an optimistic refrain that appears in a mood of confidence, disappears in a burst of admonition, and later reappears in a form of wavelike undulation characteristic of transcendental writing. Moreover, the polarities of optimistic expectation (symbolized by the epigraph, "The Earth waits for her Queen") and impatient anger (symbolized by, "Frailty, thy name is Woman") have an ebb and flow rhythm to them. She may begin in a lull with a mundane matter such as the problem of a poor widow whose husband has died leaving no will and accelerate in intensity to the sublime "ravishing harmony of the spheres," or start at the crest of the wave as it flows back to the sea. From practical application of her sermon, the thought patterns of *Woman* soar back to the world of the spirit. Instead of syllogistic reasoning, order comes from the authority that the certitude of intuition brings.

A characteristic of transcendental literature, which *Woman* reflects, is subjectivity—the individual as the center of the world. At times this method suggests a free association of ideas. One authority requires that another be included; one mythological figure suggests another. Ultimately the thought patterns lead form the conscious, to the sub-conscious mind, to the transcendental well-spring of truth, the divine intuition. Fuller used her own experience as representative of the experience of all women—that indeed the lot of woman is sad, that all women need and, in fact, should aspire to the same self-culture and fulfillment that she herself had desired. She began *Woman* by using conventional "we" but she changed to "I" after only fifteen pages. later she alternated between "we" and "I." She gave an account of her youthful education by her father under the guise of the persona, Miranda, as an example of an independent girl who was respected for being self-reliant. Fuller told this story by means of an imaginary conversation in which the "I" takes the role of the foil to Miranda's explanation of her youthful training in self-reliance, so unusual for a girl of that day (38-41). In her subjectivity there are times when she almost linked herself with the queen that the earth awaits. If not the queen directly, she associated herself in her description of Miranda with the woman of genius, possessor of the magnetic electrical element, who has a contribution to make to the world—"a strong electric nature, which repelled those who did not belong to her, and attracted those who did" (39). At another time in the discussion of woman's power of intuition, she wrote: "Women who combine this organization with creative genius are very commonly unhappy at present. They see too much to act in conformity with those around them, and their quick impulses seem folly to those who do not discern the motives" (103). By looking into her own soul, she saw reflected there the problems and the frustrated aspirations of other women: "but what concerns me now is, that my life be a beautiful, powerful, in a word, a complete life in its kind. Had I but one more moment to live I must wish the same" (177). Starting from her own angle of vision, she unfolded her hopes to the world, and she concluded her treatise as a prophet:

> I stand in the sunny noon of life. Objects no longer glitter in the dews of morning, neither are yet softened by the shadows of evening. Every spot is seen, every chasm revealed. Climbing the dusty hill, some fair effigies that once stood for symbols of human destiny have been broken; those I still have with me show defects in this broad light. Yet enough is left, even by experience, to point distinctly to the glories of that destiny; faint, but not to be mistaken streaks of the future day (178).

Thus her subjectivity became universal as she linked her own experience to that of the experience of all women and prophesied that in the future life would be better for them.

The tone of *Woman* reinforces the idea that Fuller was writing a didactic work. At times the tone admonishes the audience to act; at other times it is declamatory, but dominantly it is conversational. Although its voice patterns are conversational, the archness of Fuller's diction and tone is transcendental. Today, the mannerism of Fuller's speaking style may sound affected. Nevertheless, many people who knew Fuller said that her chief talent was as a speaker, so it is not surprising that instead of syllogisms, many phrases contain the emotive power of a conversation, of which she would have been the star. Her writing technique included both questions and answers in a debate form, but it also revealed the hallmark of the accomplished conversationalist: a flair for the dramatic. At best her conversational technique suggests breathless ejaculations rather than sentences. In a kind of accelerating excitement, she used the hortatory style: "Let us be wise, and not impeded the soul. Let her work as she will. Let us have one creative energy, one incessant revelation. Let it take what form it will, and let us not bind it by the past to man or woman, black or white. Jove sprang from Rhea, Pallas from Jove. So let it be" (117). Then her tone changes to one of intimacy. Her writing sounds as if she were talking to a small group and studying the reaction of her audience.

In the following passage, she revealed that she was a perceptive performer who could quickly adapt an argument to match the mood of her imaginary audience by modifying, explaining, and then hammering home at the proper psychological moment the point she intended to make in the first place:

> If it has been the tendency of these remarks to call Woman rather to the Minerva side,—if I, unlike the more generous writer, have spoken from society no less than the soul,—let it be pardoned! It is love that has caused this,—love for many incarcerated souls that might be freed, could the idea of religious self-dependence be established in them, could the weakening habit of dependence on others be broken up. (118)

Her excuse for her stand was love. In effect, she seemed to be anticipating objections. Her most famous suggestion combines a speaking conversational style with her flair for dramatization: "But if you ask me what offices they may fill, I reply—any. I do not care what case you put; let them be sea-captains, if you will" (174). Her frequent use of dashes suggests the pause used by accomplished speakers.

Other passages in *Woman* combine the dramatic method of composition with an aphoristic technique: "Tremble not before the free man, but before the slave who has chains to break" (63); "Whatever abuses are seen, the timid will suffer; the bold will protest" (77). In her dramatization of her thesis, she used an aphoristic method of attracting attention by reversing sex roles, beginning with her suggestion that the time had come for "Eurydice to call for an Orpheus, rather than Orpheus for Eurydice" (23).[3] Again she wrote: "Presently she [nature] will make a female Newton, and a male Syren" (116). "But Penelope is no more meant for a baker or weaver solely, than Ulysses for a cattle-herd" (44). Later she suggested, not unlike semantic changes in vogue today, that the title given to a party abroad, "Los Exaltados," be changed to "Los Exaltados, Las Exaltadas" (155). This stylistic device of sex role reversal is used to advocate one of her central ideas—that there is no "wholly masculine man, no purely feminine woman" (116)—which culminates in the "sea-captain" passage.

Whether that of a preacher, orator, or confidante, the tone of *Woman* expresses the spoken word. Hence many of Fuller's images relate to sound. Perhaps here she echoes Shelley, whom she admired: "And, if men are deaf, the angels hear. But men cannot be deaf" (26). She used music as a means of expressing the divine: "Then their sweet singing shall not be from passionate impulse, but the lyrical overflow of a divine rapture, and a new music shall be evolved from this many-chorded world" (121). Or she saw woman as a bird with clipped wings that desires to fly and sing: "no need to clip the wings of any bird that wants to soar and sing" (175). That she frequently preferred sound imagery to that of sight is again indicated by her final poem:

> For the Power to whom we bow
> Has given its pledge that, if not now,
> They of pure and steadfast mind,
> By faith exalted, truth refined,
> *Shall* hear all music loud and clear,
> Whose first notes they ventured here. (178-179)

Another type of rhetorical device that Fuller often used is imagery derived from organicism, which implies movement, growth, expansion, or fruition. Her argument rested on the "law of growth." She used phrases such as *ampler fruition, fruitful summer,* or *plants of great vigor will always struggle into blossom.* She liked movement related to the life force symbolized by the heart: "I must beat my own pulse true in the heart of the world; for *that* is virtue, excellence, health" (178). And the cycles of nature—the flowing of streams, the waxing moon, and noon-morning-dawn imagery—are favorites.

Yet despite her frequent choice of auditory and organic imagery, her work's salient characteristic is its great use of references to literature, history, religion, and mythology. These references are used primarily as an exemplar for her readers to emulate, as recognized authority to support her topic, or as allusions to Holy Writ.

Since the structure of *Woman* is sermon-like, Fuller used biblical allusions as the major support for her near-rhapsodic religious vision of the great potentialities of men and women. She derived her thematic exhortation—"Be ye perfect"—from Matthew 5:48, from which she deleted "therefore." On occasion she quoted directly from the Bible: "This is the Law and the Prophets. Knock and it shall be opened; seek and ye shall find" (19). Another way that she used biblical sources was to reshape a scriptural passage. Matthew 5:13 reads: "Ye are the light of the world. A city that is set on a hill cannot be hid. Neither do men light a candle, and put it under a bushel, but on a candlestick; and it giveth light into all that are in the house." Fuller changed the meaning: "The candlestick set in a low place has given light as faithfully, where it was needed, as that upon the hill" (17). In this passage, she incorporated biblical allusions and Christian concepts: "Love has already been expressed, that made all things new, that gave the worm its place and ministry as well as the eagle; a love to which it was alike to descend into the depths of hell, or to sit at the right hand of the Father" (20). She used a clause, such as, *a love that cannot be crucified* or commonly used biblical terms, as *future Eden, lamb, green pastures, Prince of Peace,* and *Holy Child* to symbolize hope and renewal. From traditional Christian theology she derived a reference to the deadly sin of sloth. Phrases that connote Calvinism, such as "doomed in future stages of his own being to deadly penance," can be found in *Woman.* Elements of the providential doctrine appear: "Yet, by men in this country, as by the Jews, when Moses was leading them to the promised land, everything has been done that inherited depravity could do, to hinder the promise of Heaven from its fulfillment" (25).

She found inspiration in the figure of the Madonna, whom she mentioned several times: "No figure that has ever arisen to greet our eyes has been received with more fervent reverence than that of the Madonna" (56). She referred to the Virgin Mary's powerful influence to reinforce her idea that women are born not only to nurture and alleviate the loneliness of men but also are possessors of immortal souls.

But it was to the Old Testament that she turned for the woman who would redeem mankind. Adam, she wrote somewhat ironically, "is not ashamed to write that he could be drawn from heaven by one beneath him,—one made, he says, from but a small part of himself" (56). Adam "accuses" Woman—through her "Man was lost, so through woman must Man be redeemed" by "Immortal Eve" (156).

Fuller employed biblical and religious allusions in the usual way to clarify meaning and as the wellsprings of her treatise. In addition, she cited contemporary writers—feminists, socialists, and transcendental-ists—to buttress her argument that women could play a broader role in society. Her use of allusions to outstanding women from all recorded time, however, was complex. Their use is not an affectation but an intrinsic part of her way of thinking and the rhetorical method she adopted in order to make her point. Her allusions not only clarify her meaning but also serve as models of conduct to inspire or instruct women. Examples used as affirmations are taken from poetry, such as Britomart; from history, such as Aspasia; from mythology, such as Isis and Iduna or Sita in the *Ramayana*; from folklore, such as Cinderella; or from more contemporary life, such as the Polish Countess Emily Plater. Instead of cataloging lists of words, as Emerson suggested and Whitman did, her technique was to catalog women. She barely escaped creating an encyclopedic effect because she appears not to have wanted to leave anyone out. She admitted she "may have been guilty of much repetition" (168). It could be argued that Fuller should have been more selective,[4] but on the other hand,[5] through sheer weight of numbers, the women cited from the ages become a catalog that is an evocation, a challenge to men to remove "arbitrary barriers" through proof that women can succeed. Thus she explained her use of her numerous examples: "I have aimed to show that no age was left entirely without a witness of the equality of the sexes in function, duty, and hope" (172). As Fuller said, the function of her examples is to serve as a witness. Her citation of women from history and women from fiction finally blends into women from mythology. Her search led her to delve beyond patriarchal Hebrew-Christian society to the prototype mythic woman—an earth mother who was recognized as a powerful figure, a priestess with powers of intuition and serving as a medium to the divine. Fuller's figures become in themselves the incarnation of concepts. Cassandra and Iphigenia serve as witnesses to her argument that not only are women enslaved in Western civilization but that they are not allowed to use their special gifts of "electric or magnetic powers" with which they could be enriching the world. She cited the Seeress of Prevorst and "a friend" as examples of contemporary women whose gift of psychic power was wasted. Summarizing this concept, she asked: "grant her, then, for a while, the armor and the javelin. Let her put from her the press of other minds, and meditate in virgin loneliness. The same idea shall reappear in due time as Muse, or Cereas, the all-kindly, patient Earth-

Spirit" (121). It was to classical mythology that Fuller turned for models to illustrate her ideas of the possibilities of the feminine principle.

In her search for an ideal of feminine virtue, she considered many of Shakespeare's heroines. She preferred his portrait of Cordelia, whose virtue she greatly admired. She also discussed the quality of the marriages he portrayed and found the marriage of Portia and Brutus superior to those in *Cymbeline* and *Othello*. Nevertheless, she used the relationship between Portia and Brutus as an example of the way women were neglected in ancient Rome. She thought Shakespeare was a genius with greater poetic power than John Ford and Philip Massinger, whom she also cited, but believed he did not portray women as heroic as they did or as did Spenser.

> Shakespeare's range is also great; but he has left out the heroic characters, such as the Macaria of Greece, the Britomart of Spenser. Ford and Massinger have, in this respect, soared to a higher flight of feeling than he. It was the holy and heroic Woman they most loved, and if they could not paint an Imogen, a Desdemona, a Rosalind, yet, in those of a strong mould, they showed a higher ideal, though with so much less poetic power to embody it, than we see in Portia or Isabella. (66-67)

Her main interest in her evaluation of Shakespeare's female characters was whether their images were heroic.

Of all of the authors in British literature, Fuller chose Edmund Spenser as the one who gave the best portraits of female characters: "The range of female character in Spenser alone might content us for one period" (66). Britomart was her choice for an ideal woman not only because she was virtuous but also because she was strong and independent. Having mentioned Britomart several times, Fuller eventually began to compare her with contemporary women. She believed that Madame Roland was as valiant as Britomart and that

Mary Wollstonecraft and George Sand would not have become out-laws had there been "as much room in the world for such, as in Spenser's poem for Britomart" (75). When a character like Britomart satisfied her expectations, Fuller sounded as if she were speaking of a real person and began to mix fictional with historical women.

According to Fuller, having a woman monarch (whatever Elizabeth's quality as a ruler) had its value in inspiring Spenser's creation of epic women characters: "Unlike as was the English queen to a fairy queen, we may yet conceive that it was the image of *a* queen before the poet's mind that called up this splendid court of women" (66). If Queen Elizabeth helped to inspire Spenser, any strong woman inspired Fuller. She used her outstanding women—dead or alive, literary or historical or mythical—to witness the capabilities within women when they rely on themselves. Figures as disparate as Lady Godiva, Cinderella, George Sand, Anne Hutchinson, Cassandra, Eve, Hagar, and Venus served as testimonials in her sermons on the power within women.

This plethora of examples represents a remarkable amount of schol-arship and Fuller delved into countless sources in her search for answers. Although written in nineteenth-century language with some words as outmoded as *purity* and *delicacy* and a conversational style that might be considered affected, her work is surprisingly modern in its concepts. Her brilliant treatise presents and prefigures such modern ideas as the need for role models. Fuller searched beyond Judeo-Christian patriarchy for the feminine principle and the earth mother. She posited an androgenic quality in all people, a need to do away with sexual stereotyping. In essence, Fuller's creation becomes the archetype of woman, of "The Woman in the Nineteenth Century," and of any woman who has aspired, who has wondered and been thwarted but who has still refused to compromise. Fuller's archetypal woman knows that in any compromise, she compromises not only herself but everyone else as well; and that men who become exploiters suffer and lose their humanity themselves.[6]

As with all scholarly and complex literature, reading *Woman* calls for active participation from readers. Also, since *Woman* is a highly suggestive work, readers must be receptive to its message. Both Edgar Allan Poe and Henry David Thoreau said that Fuller's writing and speaking voice were one. A careful scrutiny of *Woman* reveals the dynamism and insights that Fuller's conversation praised, and readers who are willing to become engaged in the profundity of her thought processes will be amply rewarded.

Essentially *Woman* is an affirmation, a witness to the possibilities within women and men who discover within themselves their spirituality and permit it to grow. It is a call for excellence. The first obstruction, the self, is on trial. beginning with the individual, who must take responsibility for her or his own life, *Woman* envisions a world that would correspondingly reflect this changed self. Ultimately, *Woman* transcends the issue of woman's rights. Paradoxically, after preaching self-reliance for women, it becomes a philosophic message on the interdependence of all people.

Woman in the Nineteenth Century's philosophic framework is predicated on universals; principles of right and wrong do indeed exist. Margaret Fuller was not ashamed to preach because she believed an individual could reshape her or his life—in fact, could approach perfection. And her sermon had effect. Early feminists were inspired to action by *Woman in the Nineteenth Century*. Three years after its publication, they called the first woman's rights convention in Seneca Falls, New York.

Woman in the Nineteenth Century: *Genesis, Form, etc.*

Notes

This essay was originally published in *Margaret Fuller's Woman in the Nineteenth Century: A Literary Study of Form and Content, of Sources and Influence*, Greenwood Press, 1980. Reprinted by permission of the publisher.

1. See Vivian C. Hopkins, "Margaret Fuller: Pioneer Women's Liberationist, *American Transcendental Quarterly*, 18, Spring 1973. She writes: "profusely illustrated and somewhat over-written, the book nevertheless has the effect of bringing the real closer to the ideal."

2. Another factor to consider in this discussion is that she wrote *Summer on the Lakes* between the publication of the earlier and later work. It served as a journey of self-discovery for Fuller, a means of crystallizing her thinking. Observing Indian and pioneer women in the West enlarged Fuller's perspective as to the hardships women had to endure.

3. In a letter (1841) that Alexander H. Everett wrote to Orestes A. Brownson, Everett referred to her as "Eurydice Fuller." George Willis Cooke, *An Historical and Biographical Introduction to Accompany the Dial* (1902; rpt., New York: Russell & Russell, 1961), 1:79.

4. See Francis Edward Kearns, "Margaret Fuller's Social Criticism" (Ph.D. diss., University of North Carolina, 1960), p. 148: "As Edmund Berry has pointed out, 'some of the extracts from her reading look suspiciously like padding. . . .' Moreover, one detects a faint aroma of pedantry about these long extracts. Frequently they appear to be totally out of context and to be dragged in merely to illustrate Margaret's erudition. And not only is the style inflated, but it is annoyingly repetitious."

5. Poe pointed out flaws in her style but concluded: "the style of Miss Fuller is one of the very best with which I am acquainted. In general effect, I know no style which surpasses it. It is singularly piquant, vivid, terse, bold, luminous; leaving details out of sight, it is everything that a style need be." *The Works of Edgar Allen Poe.* ed. Edmund Clarence Stedman and George Edward Woodberry (New York: Appleton-Crofts, 1951, 8:81.

6. Additional information can be obtained in Marie Urbanski's "Margaret Fuller's *Woman in the Nineteenth Century*: The Feminist Manifesto," *Nineteenth-Century Women Writers of the English Speaking World.* ed. Rhoda B. Nathan, Westport, Connecticut: Greenwood Press, 1986. Also informative

is Urbanski's "Margaret Fuller: Feminist Writer and Revolutionary," *Feminist Theorists*, ed. Dale Spender, New York: Pantheon, 1983.

Works Cited

Brown, Arthur W. *Margaret Fuller*. New York: Twayne Publishers, 1964.

Fuller, Margaret. "The Great Lawsuit.—Man *versus* Men; Woman *versus* Women," *The Dial: A Magazine for Literature, Philosophy, and Religion*. July 1943. Rpt., New York: Russell & Russell, 1961.

—. *Woman in the Nineteenth Century and Kindred Papers Relating to the Sphere, Condition, and Duties of Women*. ed. Arthur B. Fuller. Boston: John P. Jewett, 1855.

Higginson, Thomas Wentworth. *Margaret Fuller Ossoli*. Boston: Lee & Shepard, 1882.

Howe, Julia Ward. *Margaret Fuller (Marchesa Ossoli)*. Boston: Roberts, 1883.

Matthiessen, F.O. *American Renaissance*. London: Oxford University Press, 1941.

Myerson, Joel. *Critical Essays on Margaret Fuller*. Boston: G.K. Hall, 1980.

Margaret A. Lukens

The Awakening of a
Margaret Fuller Scholar

I ARRIVED AT HARVARD in the fall of 1973, just a few years after the time of student activism and unrest. The campuses of Harvard and Radcliffe were becoming coeducational in most ways, and change was perceptible in some classrooms. However, if Professor Heimert lectured on the works of Margaret Fuller in his American literature survey course, his remarks left only a vague impression and characterized her as an ancillary figure to the great men of the American Romantic period.

Again, when I entered graduate school in Boulder, Colorado in 1984, I encountered a course, this time entitled "American Symbolists," in which Fuller's work would have made interesting reading but was not included. Somehow, though, the vague impression from undergraduate days had grown in me so that when I came to teach my own survey of American literature, I made certain to assign my students some reading from "The Great Lawsuit" or *Woman in the Nineteenth Century*—Fuller was by 1985 prominent in the *Norton*

Anthology of American Literature. However, I felt myself at first to be at a loss and unprepared to teach about her; that feeling sent me on further investigations.

Eventually I discovered a nexus of women writers from the nineteenth century whose works seemed to indicate a particular pattern of struggle for cultural change through authorship; a very unspecialized group of them—Margaret Fuller, Harriet Jacobs, Sarah Winnemucca, and Zitkala-Sa—became the focus of my dissertation which I called, "Creating Cultural Spaces." Ironically, Fuller's name was the only one most people recognized when I told them what I was writing about!

Life has a way of making sense down the road, and I find myself at the University of Maine where one of the most liberating Fuller critics I encountered in my dissertation research, Marie Olesen Urbanski, is now my colleague. I am grateful for this occasion to add to the present scholarship on Fuller, and to have the opportunity to meditate on Fuller's time in New York, where, in some ways, things were just beginning to get interesting for her.

Margaret A. Lukens

Columnist of Conscience: Margaret Fuller's New York Years

I

N THE FALL OF 1844 Margaret Fuller was living in Jamaica Plain, Massachusetts, a few miles from the Cambridgeport home where she had been born thirty-four years earlier. Only two and a half years later, however, she had taken up residence in Italy, formed personal connections with several Italians who were patriots and radicals, and immersed herself in the brewing revolution. Her apparent "sea-change" from conversation leader and feminist theorist in the Transcendentalist circles of Boston, Cambridge, and Concord to war correspondent and revolutionary in Italy has led critics in the past to surmise about her motivations. The most misogynist of these tried to account for her radical shift by painting Fuller in hot pursuit of an elusive European boyfriend who "was fleeing for his life" (Miller 202), while more friendly critics have cited her romantic involvement with James Nathan as *"the most significant catalyst behind her decision to travel abroad"* [italics mine] (Steele xl). However, Fuller had cherished the dream of touring Europe since her early youth (Chevigny 73), and had been prevented from making an earlier journey by the financial difficulties attendant upon her father's death. A careful look at the often-neglected social criticism Fuller wrote for the *New York Tribune* between December, 1844, and August, 1846, provides a clearer and more complete picture of the range of her motivations. Fuller's social criticism from her New York years depicts her increasing desire to put her theories of social equality into practice, and to lead her own life according to the radical reforming urges of her conscience. In the light of these lesser-known journalistic writings, her relationship with James Nathan falls into place as an *exemplum* of her willingness to cross social and physical boundaries, and her move to Rome appears as the full bloom of the budding New York radical.

Fuller's move to New York City in December, 1844, to accept the post of book reviewer and columnist offered her by Horace Greeley represented a logical step in her career beyond the completion of *Summer on the Lakes* and *Woman in the Nineteenth Century*; it was an opportunity to move conscience and philosophy to action. Her trip to the West in the summer of 1843 had begun "to break the spell of New England elitism"(Chevigny 286) because of the opportunities it provided for her to observe and associate with white settlers of various classes and Native American people. What she saw was that the chaotic, violent, and greed-driven colonization of the frontier degraded not only the indigenous people, but the Anglo-European whites as well, particularly the women. In Chicago she remarked, "I like not the petty intellectualities, cant, and bloodless theory there at home, but this merely instinctive existence . . . pleases me no better." Eventually, however, the experiences of her "summer on the lakes" brought her to warm appreciation of "the unwritten poetry which common life presents" and its "great contrast to the subtleties of analysis, the philosophical strainings of which [she] had seen so much."

Travel in the West exposed Fuller to varieties of life and humanity she had only imagined before. This experience certainly encouraged her to expand the concepts contained in her essay "The Great Law Suit" and from it to bring forth her most famous work, *Woman in the Nineteenth Century*. *Woman* was a full exposition of the feminist thought she had been developing during her years of participation in the Transcendentalist circles of Boston and Cambridge, but it went beyond the social and intellectual boundaries inscribed around her work in those years that led her to avoid consideration of such issues as abolition and local politics. *Woman in the Nineteenth Century* was an outgrowth, too, of her experience as a teacher of young women at the Greene Street School in Providence and leader of intellectual "Conversations" for adult women of her own social class in Cambridge. Fuller's decision to move away from New England was to provide her with a wider spectrum of social acquaintances, and, in her capacity as a newspaper reporter, with the chance to scrutinize society's ills and institutions at close range.

New York began to offer opportunities for direct contact with other kinds of women, "the so-called worst," even before Fuller took up residence with the Greeleys. She paid two visits to the female inmates at Sing Sing Prison, in October, and again in December, 1844. Eliza Farnham had recently been appointed to the post of matron there, and Farnham's refusal to accept the popular dogma that "fallen" women were impossible to rehabilitate appealed to Fuller. Fuller's physical entry into the prison space to share the day with these women indicated her growing desire and willingness to put her body where her mind had already been; she was beginning to include in her own experience contact with women outcast from society.

For Fuller, initially the prison visit was an opportunity to do some research at first hand; in a letter to Elizabeth Hoar she wrote, "I told them I was writing about Woman; and, as my path had been a favoured one, I wanted to gain information of those who had been tempted to pollution and sorrow." When some of the women responded with the desire to speak privately to her "as they could then say *all*," Fuller expressed her own wish "to go there again, and take time for this" (Chevigny 335.) Her return at Christmas perhaps fulfilled the wish, although the only record of the day that survives is a version, by William Channing, of Fuller's address to the prisoners in which she says ". . . the world said:—'Women once lost are far worse than abandoned men, and cannot be restored.' But, no! It is not so! . . . for the great improvement so rapidly wrought here gives us all warm hopes" (*Memoirs* 2:146-48.) This experience of "hands-on" work with the women imprisoned at Sing Sing and the example of Eliza Farnham's "gentle and intelligent treatment" of them stayed with Fuller throughout her investigations of social conditions in New York, and led her to seek out opportunities to assist in the rehabilitation of women on an individual basis. In a literary biography written thirty-four years after her death, Thomas Wentworth Higginson recognized the strength of her urge for involvement in reform:

> Her sympathy was strong for these women, betrayed into a life of crime by the sins of others; and Mr. Greeley expresses confidently his belief that "if she had been born to large fortune, a house of refuge for all female outcasts desiring to return to the ways of virtue would have been one of her most cherished and first realized conceptions." (214)

Greeley, as might be expected, knew and valued Fuller's individual commitment to reform, but he was able to imagine the effect she had upon society only by translating her generosity of energy into monetary terms.

No doubt, though, Fuller's personal development and political inclinations were fostered and encouraged during her employment at the *Tribune*. In an unpublished article from 1979, Madeline Stern crystallized the characteristics of the newspaper: from its beginnings in April, 1841, as "a one-cent Whig daily directed principally to labor," Horace Greeley had tried to make his paper, as he said, "a journal removed alike from servile partisanship on the one hand and from gagged, mincing neutrality on the other." With an estimated circulation of 11,000, the *Tribune*'s influence was wide and its content evidently characterized by strong ethical messages; its nickname was "The Great Moral Organ." Stern cites Frank Luther Mott's summation of the *Tribune*'s achievement: "In the *Tribune* the cheap-paper movement reaches its highest point in democratic ideals and reformatory zeal" (Mott 271-78); Stern asserts that the two hundred and fifty articles contributed by Fuller "did much toward establishing that reputation" (2-3). Evidently a symbiotic relationship had been established between the growing reformer in Fuller and the reputation of the print "organ" that was her medium in New York.

Although Fuller's *Tribune* articles published between December, 1844, and August, 1846, seem to be of two kinds—literary reviews and social criticism—it is difficult to draw the line when one begins to read them. In her articles on social issues she often refers to, quotes liberally from, and incisively appraises contemporary books and articles on the topic. Conversely, in what appear to be book reviews, Fuller frequently injects her opinion on the social issues suggested by the work being reviewed. For example, in a review of Thomas L. McKenney's *Memoirs, Official and Personal* (8 July 1846, 1:1-3), she meditates on the "burning pain of shame and indignation" in the relationship between mainstream American society and Native American tribes. She takes the opportunity to urge her readers that

> "the time to attend to the subject, get information and act, is NOW, or never. A very short time and it will be too late to release ourselves . . . from the weight of ill doing, or preserve any vestigies [sic] of a race . . . whose life and capacities ought . . . to be held infinitely precious . . ."

The thrust of her review is to ignite a sense of urgency in her readers, and to hope for the "general circulation" of McKenney's book, not for the author's sake, but for the sake of Native American people.

Fuller published her first regular column in the *Tribune* on December 7, 1844. It was a review of Emerson's *Essays: Second Series*; in it she lauded Emerson's career as a philosopher and chided the American public for being slower to purchase and digest copies of Emerson's works than their counterparts in Great Britain. However, she took the opportunity to levy against Emerson a charge he would not have refuted, but that told clearly the concerns of the reviewer herself:

> The human heart complains of inadequacy, either in the nature or experience of the writer, to represent its full vocation and its deeper needs. . . . Here is, undoubtedly, the man of ideas, but we want the ideal man also; want the heart and genius of human life to interpret it, and here our satisfaction is not so perfect. We doubt this friend raised himself too early to the perpendicular and did not lie along the ground long enough to hear the secret whispers of our parent life. We could wish he might be thrown by conflicts on the lap of mother earth, to see if he would not rise again with added powers. (1:1)

By implication, Fuller's method was beginning to differ from Emerson's, in that it was informed by her own emotional response and by the "experience" she ironically found wanting in him. Certainly Fuller's convictions about the influence a "good" woman's presence could have on the rehabilitation of female criminals illustrate this widening gulf between herself and Emerson and bear out her increasing need to "get involved."

On December 12, 1844, less than a week after her column had begun to appear in the *Tribune*, the installment entitled "Thanksgiving" appeared. It is a relatively conventional moral meditation on the holiday, and moves from the contemplation of Thanksgiving as the characteristic New England celebration to calling upon her individual readers to examine their own contributions to the betterment of society. However, it is evident that her mind is on the prisoners at Sing Sing when she attempts to define how a person might perform practical service to the world:

> In the present complex state of human affairs, you cannot be kind unless you are wise. . . . It would, indeed, seem to be a simple matter at first glance. "Lovest thou me?"—"Feed my lambs." But now we have not only to find pasture, but to detect the lambs under the disguise of wolves, and restore them by a spell, like that the Shepherd used, to their natural form and whiteness. (2:1)

The detection of "lambs under the disguise of wolves" is only possible in close proximity, such as Fuller had achieved in her first visit to Sing Sing. Further on in the article she mentions that she has attended an organizational meeting of a prison reform group and voices the hope that she and her fellow philanthropists might not prove "wholly Pharisees." She registers her optimism about the cause thus:

> [t]he prisoner, too, may become a man. Neither his open nor our secret faults, must utterly dismay us. We will treat him as if he had a soul. . . . and perhaps, he will recover from these ghastly ulcers that deform him now. (2:1)

At the end of the article Fuller reports directly on her first visit to Sing Sing, offering her own testimony as to the effectiveness of humane treatment. She reports having witnessed a choral concert given by the women prisoners as evidence of the power of "[t]he good spirit that dwelt in the music [to make] them its own. And," she asks, "shall not the good spirit of religious sympathy make them its own also, and more permanently? . . . And will any man dare take the risk of opposing plans that afford even a chance of such a result?" Fuller's belief in the efficacy of personal intercourse to rehabilitate women convicts is borne out in her own actions during the months following her visit to Sing Sing. Evidently she had taken a particular interest in the case of one woman, Honora Shepherd, whom she had met in the prison.

Her correspondence from the early spring of 1845 shows that she had occasional meetings with Honora Shepherd and eventually, with the help of Fuller's friend from Brook Farm, Georgiana Bruce, who was by then working with Farnham at Sing Sing, Shepherd obtained pardon from the Governor of New York and release from prison. In a letter to James Nathan on or about April 25, 1845, Fuller says "I brought Honora out with me to-day and had a full talk as we were walking. The love and trust shown by many seem to have given a new development to her mental history" (4:89). Earlier that month, in a letter to Nathan dated April 6, 1845, Fuller appeared to be working out her feelings about the recent surprising revelation that Nathan had been living with an English woman whom he represented as a fallen woman he was trying to assist. Fuller asked,

> Could the heart of woman refuse its sympathy to this earnestness in behalf of an injured woman? Could a human heart refuse its faith to such a sincerity, even if it had accompanied the avowal of error! (4:68).

Her words indicate the desire to forgive and provide aid to the "injured woman," but also show her desire to excuse Nathan from any imputation of guilt on the basis of his "earnestness" and "sincerity." Critics have persisted in regarding this as a moment of willful blindness on Fuller's part, induced solely by her infatuation with Nathan. However, the complexity of Fuller's feelings at that moment becomes evident when one realizes the extent to which her own belief in women's capacity for "rehabilitation" and her drive to have personal associations with women in need of such help were being challenged. This was a chance to put principles into action in an intensely personal situation, in Fuller's own words, to show herself not to be "wholly [a] Pharisee." Perhaps, in the very intensity of her attachment to Nathan, it became clear to her how quickly and irrevocably a woman's reputation might be judged as lost, and how easily she herself might "fall" to the level of the women incarcerated at Sing Sing.

Fuller's relationship with James Nathan has been analyzed variously by critics and biographers, but none has advanced a theory that he was anything but an aberration in her emotional career and a distraction that proved her womanly weakness in spite of her feminist principles. It is difficult to discount the question of "which of the effects Nathan had on Fuller was stronger: the awakening of her sensuality or the putting to sleep of her mind" (Chevigny 137). Doubtless a certain amount of love's blindness shaped Fuller's relationship with the European businessman, but another look at her writings from the spring of 1845 casts another light. In her first letter to Nathan, dated 7 February 1845, Fuller wrote,

> I have long had a presentiment that *I should meet, nearly, one of your race,* who would show me how the sun of to-day shines upon the ancient Temple,—but I did not expect so gentle and civilized an apparition and with blue eyes! [Italics mine] (4:47).

Evidently, one of Nathan's appealing features in Fuller's mind was his being a Jew; it seems from her language in the letter that he was the first Jewish person with whom she had close social contact, whom she had met "nearly," and that she was eager to expand her horizon by including him in her life. For Fuller and her contemporary New England intellectuals Jews probably seemed exotic "others;" most of what they knew of Jewish people would have been from what they had read, and likewise, their anti-Semitism was derived from literary sources. Although one might presume such "literary" racism to be bloodless and therefore benign, literature tends to reinscribe the forms and assumptions of the dominant paradigm unless the writer embarks upon conscious resistance to the attitude of the "powers that be." Fuller and her contemporaries, therefore, imbibed the influence of centuries of hatred in their reading of Shakespeare and other European authors who distilled a stereotyped Jewish "essence" from the attitudes of their own societies. Fuller's flirtatious admission of surprise at first meeting Nathan—"I did not expect so gentle and civilized an apparition"—plays off against the anti-Semitism of her day, which suggested that "gentle and civilized" behavior was not to be expected from Jews. Despite her obvious warmth, Fuller's orientation towards Nathan is from an ethnocentric perspective; important, however, is her inclination to refute that ethnocentrism by engaging in direct experience of the "other." In other words, while Fuller's attraction to Nathan gave a particular impetus to her interest in his ethnicity, the converse is also true: his ethnicity might have been, in Fuller's mind, a justification for the strength of her interest in him.

Further evidence of this complex dynamic appears in a column Fuller wrote for the *Tribune* of April 21, 1845, two and a half months into her relationship with Nathan, entitled "The Modern Jews." In three long columns on the front page of the newspaper she cited authorities ranging from writers in the *North American Review* to "Mr. Ridley H. Herschell, a converted Jew of London" and editor of a periodical called *The Voice of Israel*, on the subject of the historical and contemporary oppression of Jews. Much of the second half of the column consists of Fuller's English translation of Markgraff's *Latest Epochs of the Literature and Culture of Germany*, which she introduces by saying,

> There are excellent accounts of the situation of the Jews in Germany, of an old-fashioned Rabbinical education, and of the influence exerted by Mendelssohn on the culture and growth of his nation; for there is now culture and growth among them. (1:2)

It is possible that Fuller identified James Nathan with the highly cultivated Jewish intelligentsia in Germany, and added this supposed cultivation to her stock of reasons for being attracted to him, but beyond this, her article figures forth another image of "the Jewish man" no doubt highly prized by her:

> The girdle which so tightly repressed the vital energies of the nation is broken, and the form and proportions of the Jewish man are expanding and approximating to the modern European standard.—Nay, more! the Jew who is throroughly 'emancipated', inclines to join or even to head the extreme radical party . . . . A movement party is, to be sure, necessarily a Reform party, but has no right to assume so noble a name, unless its leaders, . . . are intelligent or prophetic of the principles which must animate the next development of organic life. (1:2)

Just when it seems Fuller has fallen again into the trap of ethnocentrism with the implication that it was progress for Jews to attain "the modern European standard," she pulls the reader back with her exclamation, "Nay, more!" The "emancipated" Jew, Fuller asserts, will naturally be, like herself, a radical, and even has the potential to lead the party of reform. For Fuller, such a natural inclination towards reform as she attributes to "the emancipated Jew" would have been the greatest good; in fact, the words she uses at the end of the passage could as well be applied to herself, and seem to echo what others said about her: that she was "intelligent or prophetic of the principles which must animate the next development of organic life." Her evaluation of Jewish people in this day's column probably is a good indication of the high opinion she held of James Nathan at that time, and of the hopes she might have entertained for their future together.

Her open-mindedness on the subject of "others" extended to another group of social pariahs of her day, the Irish. In a short, evocative, and passionate column entitled "The Irish Character" Fuller attempted to prick the consciences of her natural-born American readers on behalf of Irish immigrants, who at the time were suffering extreme prejudice in employment practices and the attendant ills of poverty, poor education, and alcoholism. Again, she speaks fervently in defense of the humanity of Irish people, and the special qualities of national character that she says should be valued for their difference, not condemned.

Fuller enumerates in a conventionally sentimental way the positive traits of character she associates with the Irish, such as loyalty to "intense family affections" and naturally eloquent expressions of grief. But she turns the mirror towards the reader from the dominant culture when she writes of how the Irish are blamed not only for the ills of their own lives but for major problems of American society: "by their ready service to do all the hard work they make it easier for the rest of the population to grow effeminate and help the country to grow too fast" (28 June 1845, 2:2). Her documentation of the willingness among Anglo-Americans to "rank among [their faults] what others would not" turns this sentimental piece into a critique of the ethnic stereotyping and scapegoating prevalent in American society.

Like the reform of prisons and outreach across cultural and racial boundaries, the radical socialist movement captured Fuller's interest. What had begun for her at Brook Farm had echoes and outgrowths across the Atlantic in "Communism, Socialism, and Humanism." She translated an article from the *Deutsche Schnellpost* on the subject of "the social movement in Europe" in which the writer reacts negatively to radical theories of revolution:

> I hold the absolute theories of Communism to be as despotically hostile to freedom as old Absolutism. . . . I want what the new humanitarian school wants, a harmonious improvement of the human race by means of harmonious culture, material comfort and satisfaction of the common natural instincts for all. (5 August 1845 1:1-4)

In the body of the article the writer refers to Marx and to Engels, as well as other political theorists of the day, now less well known to us; Fuller's adroit presentation of the relationships among them indicates her currency with the topic. The writer offers the example of the way the journeymen carpenters of Paris were asserting their right to fair wages and equal opportunity in the face of hard-hearted opposition from the master carpenters and the French government. Fuller translated the description of their strike thus:

> the last eighteen days all the works are deserted, and in Tours, Blois, Amboise and St. Germain en Laye, the journeymen carpenters have followed the example of their comrades at Paris. If they persist in their present course, if all of their trade throughout France follow their example, if other trades are emboldened by their example to adopt a similar course, . . . if in this way a Fourth Estate, the Estate of the Workmen, break an entrance to the privileges of social life, will not that be a revolution? (1:3)

The writer claims that whether such a revolution *will* happen, "it *can* happen, and that is enough." The column ends with an assertion that "the new era, when the laborer shall be thought worthy of his hire, and every man entitled to express the wants that consume him" is not far in the future (1:4). Not only her familiarity with theories of social revolution, but also Fuller's choice to translate this particular story of a revolution in progress, shows her growing attention to the mechanisms of social change.

This writer for the *Schnellpost* characterized himself as "a light *chasseur* to the army of Reform, constantly in the field against our ancient enemy." Half a year later Fuller counted herself among "the 'extreme left' of the army of Progress" (*Tribune* 17 January 1846, 1:1), and in another half year she was sailing for Europe, heading for the greatest risk and the greatest commitment of her life in the Roman revolution. In the years she had spent as columnist at the *New York Tribune* she had widened her view of the world and confirmed her will to be instrumental in its process of change for the benefit of people in greatest need. She was now fully ready, both intellectually and emotionally, to engage in the revolutions of the world.

Works Cited

Chevigny, Bell Gale. *The Woman and the Myth: Margaret Fuller's Life and Writings.* Old Westbury, NY: The Feminist Press, 1976.

Fuller, Sarah Margaret. *Memoirs.* James Freeman Clarke, Ralph Waldo Emerson, and William H. Channing, eds. 2 vols. Boston: Phillips Sampson, 1852.

—. *Summer on the Lakes, in 1843.* 1844. Introd. Susan Belasco Smith. Urbana and Chicago: University of Illinois Press, 1991.

—. *Woman in the Nineteenth Century.* New York: Greeley & McElrath, 1845.

Higginson, Thomas Wentworth. *Margaret Fuller Ossoli.* Boston: Houghton Mifflin Co., 1885.

Hudspeth, Robert N., ed. *The Letters of Margaret Fuller.* 5 vols. Ithaca: Cornell University Press, 1983-92.

Kearns, Francis Edward. *Margaret Fuller's Social Criticism.* Diss. University of North Carolina, 1961. Ann Arbor, UMI, 1971.

Miller, Perry, ed. *Margaret Fuller, American Romantic.* Ithaca: Cornell University Press, 1963.

Mott, Frank Luther. *American Journalism, A History of Newspapers in the United States through 250 Years, 1690 to 1940.* New York: Macmillan, 1941.

Myerson, Joel. *Margaret Fuller: A Descriptive Bibliography.* Pittsburgh: University of Pittsburgh Press, 1978.

New York Daily Tribune, 7 December 1844 through 12 August 1846.

Reynolds, Larry J. and Susan Belasco Smith. *These Sad but Glorious Days.* New Haven: Yale University Press, 1991.

Steele, Jeffrey. *The Essential Margaret Fuller.* New Brunswick: Rutgers University Press, 1992.

Stern, Madeline B. "Margaret Fuller: Journalist." Unpublished essay, 1979.

Judith Strong Albert

Encountering
Margaret Fuller

"She not only did not speak lies after our foolish social customs, but she met you fairly . . . Encountering her glance, something like an electric shock was felt. Her eyes pierced through your disguise. Your outworks fell before her first assault, and you were at her mercy. And then began the delight of true intercourse... She demanded our best, and she gave us her best. (Sarah Clarke, in Higginson,118)

M Y MEETING MARGARET FULLER now seems inevitable. In 1976, however, pursuing my doctorate at St. Louis University, her name was unfamiliar to me whereas that of Ralph Waldo Emerson, frequently praised by my advisor John Jacob O'Brien ("JJ"), was commonplace. In that ecumenical learning atmosphere where things empirical lived side by side with intangible ideas concerning American philosophies of education, I studied *Transcendentalism* and Emerson, Spiritual Culture and Bronson Alcott, and the rise of the American Kindergarten and Elizabeth

Peabody, without considerations of their link to women's development per se, and without seeing their potent ties to feminist thought—which were, unbeknownst to me, being forged in those same explosive years.

For Professor O'Brien, Emerson represented all that epitomized nineteenth century American self-reliance and individualism among mankind. The questions of whether these attributes extended to women or whether *mankind* include *womankind*, were unposed. But as it came time to select a dissertation topic, and having come across Fuller's name in Emerson's letters as well as debating her merits in an unforgettable evening with her great-grand nephew, Buckminster Fuller, I decided to respond to JJs challenge that Emerson was the apogee of nineteenth century thought. Fuller became my subject in part because she was as important a figure as Emerson regardless of her sex, and because she was a woman.

Imagine my delight when I discovered any number of living women who already were well-acquainted with her, including Madeleine Stern, Susan Conrad, Bell Gale Chevigny, Paula Blanchard, and Marie Olesen Urbanski! The "electrical, intuitive and magnetic" qualities Fuller possessed and had spoken of in her Conversations were vitally alive and present. I joined Margaret Fuller's Women.

Believing that she is a gift to generations of mothers and daughters writing, I have brought drafts of my own reflections on Fuller and friends to my mother, editor and friend, Jean Jacobson Strong for criticism and intellectual honing. Fuller keeps introducing me to the joy of being a woman among women, those related by blood and by thought.

Judith Strong Albert

Currents of Influence: "The electrical, the magnetic element in woman . . ."

In the nineteenth century a woman was not encouraged to be an artist. On the contrary, she was snubbed, slapped, lectured and exhorted" (Woolf, 56).

HY IS MARGARET FULLER important to-day? In what ways were her Boston Conversations of 1839 to 1844 influential then and in what ways are they now, as we near the twenty-first century? These questions touch upon the multiple facets of her thinking and the ever-changing interpretations succeeding generations have applied to it. The range of human qualities Fuller sought to understand encompass philosophy, the arts,

history, education, mythology, and perhaps foremost of all, psychology. She melded these disciplines without separating subject matter into categories. She avoided artificial boundaries. In this very avoidance lay one of the fundamental beauties of her contribution.

The resilience and plasticity of her Conversations appealed to a select circle of women in her own era and has shown itself open to the inevitable ebb and flow of new generations, new times. Rather than having offered a rigid set of doctrines, Fuller put forward queries and axioms each of which have engendered new corollaries. Grappled with by members of her first conversational circle including Elizabeth Palmer Peabody (1804-1894)—promoter of the American kindergarten; Lydia Maria Child (1802-1880)—advocate of civil rights and parity for women and children; and Caroline Wells Healey Dall (1822-1912)—defender of women's equality, in the late twentieth century many of her original propositions concerning education, human rights and women's rights have taken on new meanings which were obscure if not absent during her own era. This holds especially true when applied to her concepts regarding the nature and character of Woman.

During her lifetime, Fuller's insights were ill-understood. Even the brightest Boston minds resisted comprehending just what she was talking about. When she volunteered to "supply a point of union to well-educated and thinking women, in a city which . . . boasts, at present, nothing of the kind" (*Memoirs* 325), there was confusion over what she meant by "union." Her lecture series, held weekly over six successive winter seasons in Peabody's bookshop on West Street or in the home of George and Sophia Ripley—Unitarians turned Utopian Transcendentalists—stressed as constant theme and undertone the concept that women must "name themselves." Women then and now have had difficulty with that phrase.

Fuller did most of the conversing at her talks, drawing the sort of paying audience now found in university courses on women's studies and history, in lectures and adult education classes, and in libraries which women of all ages call their own. Economic and social independence was rare in the eighteen forties. The audience at Fuller's conversations had read books from the libraries of their fathers, their brothers and their husbands. But many had done so without imagining possible future applications to a larger set of choices. Probably all were well-versed in the Scriptures and some had been tutored in classical literature and language, Shakespeare's and Molière's plays, Montaigne's essays, Kant's philosophical treatises, and the works of Goethe. These women were from literate and free-thinking Unitarian households, and most if not all had grown up in respectable circumstances. Their younger siblings were, to some extent, tutored by these same usually older sisters. They were all Caucasian and representatives of the solid families of descendants of the American revolution in an era when the village rather than the city was the normal scale. They were exceptional in that they were capable of acting upon the life of the mind. But whereas a great many women today have grown accustomed to possessing the emotional equivalent of five hundred pounds a year and "rooms of their own," as Woolf argued they must in 1929 (4), Fuller's circle did not often find themselves in books *by* women, or among the few books that they thought of as their own.

It is appropriate and acceptable now to use the term "loner" in describing the sort of women in Fuller's circle. It was a liability then. Among Fuller's seniors, Child was a public figure who had published several successful children's books including a highly original story of a Native American, *Hobomok* (1824); a series of American "how to" domestic handbooks for women including *The Frugal Housewife* (1829); and an extremely controversial abolitionist essay on civil rights, *An Appeal in Favor of that Class of Americans Called Africans* (1833). Comparably, Peabody was an established teacher, the author of two allegorical children's stories, and co-author of a definitive study of an important progressive educational experiment before the establishment of pre-schools or public schools, *The Record of a School* (1835). We now recognize that these works of Child's and Peabody's were among those laying the groundwork for the American civil rights and progressive education movements. But while these two women, almost a decade older than Fuller and at the talks with ideas of their own, brought critical judgment to the conversations, they could hardly afford to think of themselves at all either literally or metaphorically.

Similarly, a certain lack of self-sufficiency characterizes Fuller's younger students in the circle including Caroline Wells Healey [Dall], who was virtually unknown although she had managed to publish a few essays in the Boston *Observer and Register* in her teens. Healey's initial resistance to Fuller's ideas of women's independence made her uncomfortable at the talks. Arguing in a school newspaper essay a few years earlier with a friend who was also present at Fuller's Conversations, Ednah Dow Littlehale [Cheney], Healey observed in 1837 that the "political rights" of women were potentially ruinous to women:

> Are you a friend of Harriet Martineau's? Would you wish your
> husband to stay at home, and take care of your children? for you to go
> to Caucus? . . . . I think you are a *ninny* to call yourself a slave (Healey
> to Littlehale, Cheney Papers).

Ironically, Healey's chippy sensitivity, coupled with her habitual self-doubt, would at a later period lend strength to the intense introspection and loneliness required to internalize and react to Fuller's difficult demands for self-sufficiency in females. Healy's preoccupation with herself would be necessary in the subjective struggle for autonomy that followed. She longed for the security of wifely and motherly womanhood that was still, as Woolf stated in 1929, "a protected occupation" (41). But Healy's life would force her to examine the terms of obtaining women's independence at agonizingly close range. She deliberated women's condition in exposing the wrenching results of having to straddle both a need for dependence and a yearning for independence

What ideas did Fuller convey when she spoke of naming, or union, or fluidity? Above all, she forced those present in the circle to think for themselves, a concept we take for granted in the nineteen nineties because she asserted it in the eighteen forties. A few of them were prodded into analyzing and expressing who they were as individuals rather than as wives, mothers, sisters and daughters. Fuller stated that action would be required to make changes in their lives, that self-reliance is hard won, a path historically almost impossible for women. She implied they would need to do battle within themselves if they were to remain true to themselves without necessarily joining an organization or accepting a marriage of convenience. She warned that their new understanding of "Woman's nature" would make their lives difficult in the process of making it different. She suggested that the fluidity she was talking about applied to each individual life, especially the quality of Woman's life:

> In so far as soul is in her completely developed, all soul is the same; but as far as it is modified in her as woman, it flows, it breathes, it sings. . . . Such may be the especially femine element, spoken of as Femality ("The Great Lawsuit" 43).

Despite the difficulties of her vocabulary and her messages with their convoluted and mysterious layers of meaning, and despite her own personal limitations—she had neither money of her own nor public recognition—Fuller set the intellectual foundations for major future breakthroughs for her sex. Something in her nature touched and matched corresponding parts in the make-up of the characters of her listeners. She angered some, a form of provocative influence; she overwhelmed others. Elizabeth Peabody's two younger sisters—Mary (who would marry Horace Mann), and Sophia (who would marry

Nathaniel Hawthorne)—referred to Fuller as "Queen Margaret"; Lidian Emerson, the wife of Ralph Waldo Emerson, may have reported home that certain stances taken by Margaret Fuller defied conventional wisdom. Caroline Healey, who "loved and admired Miss Fuller," objected that the talks were sometimes obscure and confusing, that mixing Greek and Roman gods and goddesses was troublesome, that Miss Fuller was too partial to some students and too demanding for most. For all in the audience, however, vibrations between the lines were everywhere in the room, perhaps more real than specific issues could be.

Each of that small, receptive audience came away from the talks aware of having become less susceptible to feminine limitations, less insufficient within themselves. They could see as never before that their disappointment in themselves and their prospects was not unique to them but was felt by other women of their station, class and upbringing. Discontent and agitation became theirs; criticism of the disparate relationship between a man and a woman became theirs. Their attention was turned to questions about the nature of love and the institution of marriage, and the uneasy belief that genuine, equal relationships barely existed. The relevance and depth of female education, the kind that would bring all women greater intellectual and economic parity, became their concern. Further, they would begin to be able to identify the inner conflicts resulting from pursuing Fuller's course: A woman's well-being had been rooted in silence and in conformity, the very traits she insisted they acknowledge, question, and leave behind.

The key figures, Peabody, who never married; Child, who had married David Lee Child in 1824; and Healey, who married Charles Dall in 1844, made an impression on the age that would influence succeeding generations. They were exposed to a range of Fuller's ideas in the Conversations, not only her outward views but her inward motivations. These touched upon her awareness of what are now recognized as "fictions that echo and extend previous fictions" concerning motherhood and wifehood (Fort 11); changes in human rights; in women's educational opportunities, and in determining new physical and intellectual horizons. Each woman in the circle must decide how to act upon these perceptions, for until the Conversations there were few referents and virtually no vocabulary to support or bolster women's reactions.

Fuller proposed that union should guide their development and surround their lives. It is this unrestricted teaching that appeals to twentieth century followers with ever-increasing meaning, and this word, union, that serves as the foundation of both Fuller's signal essay, "The Great Lawsuit: Man vs. Men, Woman vs. Women" (1843) and her major work stemming from it, *Woman in the Nineteenth Century* (1845). In these, Fuller cryptically proposes that "Union is only possible to those who are units" ("The Great Lawsuit" 44, and *Woman in the Nineteenth Century* 106). Like her teachers in philosophy and the humanities (her teachers were primarily her father and his books), Fuller was more committed to a quest for inner implications of the term than to the specific outlets arising from having experienced it.

Fuller's death in 1850 did not end the quest for a lasting definition of union; if anything, it accelerated the range of specific tasks that women knew they faced in achieving it. The views of the first circle were instrumental in establishing human rights, civil rights, women's rights, and a woman's personal rights to herself. But little of this was clear when Fuller concluded in "The Great Lawsuit," that woman "herself must teach us to give her the fitting name":

> And will she not soon appear? The woman who shall vindicate their birthright for all women; who shall teach them what to claim, and how to use what they obtain? . . . [Woman] herself must teach us to give her the fitting name (47).

It was not clear when, looking through the various discrepant and disconnected elements that composed a woman's existence in the nineteenth century, Fuller spoke of a "great radical dualism" between the sexes and within Woman herself, and described a complete being in whom self-love and other-love, a sense of proportion, and character were joined. Our present ability to focus on the terms of what constitutes union in women's history is a luxury borne in part of Fuller's and her circle's struggle with the concept.

There has been enormous improvement in the personal and professional status of American women since the eighteen forties, any number of rights obtained along with a great deal of self-reliance. Yet many of the same private restrictions and public social and economic limitations that hindered women more than a century and a half ago are still with us. We are still defining the dimensions of Fuller's naming through union, which I trace here with respect to her far-reaching influences on Child, Peabody and Dall. Their activities were expressions of Fuller's thought, of views raised initially in her Boston Conversations, refined as editor of *The Dial* from 1840 to 1842, sharpened as translator and as critic of art, literature and drama at Horace Greeley's *New York Tribune* between 1844 and 1846, and lived in her Italian years, 1846 to 1850. In all aspects of her career she personally tested the meaning of union whether applied to marital symmetry, gender equity, socio-economic equality or psychological wholeness. For her, the recognition of her own unity was the essence of all Women's Rights, all elements of a "Unit Self" woman's name.

Fuller's Transcendentally formed construct of self-reliance in the eighteen thirties and forties, gave way to the demand for women's autonomy called for in the first American Woman's Rights Conference 1848 in Seneca Falls, New York; it anticipated an end to human slavery fought for in the Civil War a dozen years later. It precipitated widening continual shifts between individual and group values, and rifts between self and community norms, intellectual agitations that in

Fuller's day were more a matter of discussion than of actual confrontation. After 1850, these revolutionary movements were no longer considered parlor room and lecture hall abstractions. They erupted into angry gatherings, riots, and culminated in a murderous war. The United States was home to unceasing racial, class and societal foment.

For Maria Child after 1850, calls for the total and immediate abolition of slavery and the right of self-sovereignty, which she had advocated in the eighteen twenties, became imperative. Child would focus her influential career in journalism on exposing the sources of and remedies for Native American and African American socio-economic injustice that she had first articulated in *Hobomok*, in her antislavery treatises and anti-establishment tracts including *An Appeal in Favor of Americans Called Africans*, *The Oasis*, and *An Anti-Slavery Catechism*. Her later writing would extend her views on injustice to women's subordination, including her *Memoirs of Madame De Stael and of Madame Roland* (1854), to supremacist concepts of the world's religions in *The Progress of Religious Ideas Through Successive Ages* (1855), toward still-indentured freed slaves in *The Freedmen's Book* (1865), and toward Native Americans in "An Appeal for the Indians" (1868).

After 1860, Peabody, whose expertise in the field of children's education antedated Fuller's, applied new views on women's and children's educations to the creation of a public Kindergarten and the concept of a kindergarten "Mother" through a philosophy based on the confluence of individuality and citizenship:

> Love and the sense of individuality are correlative creations. . . . Later, the sense of individuality becomes a positive self-love . . . and the perception of otherness of person becomes the basis of the self-forgetting generosity of mankind (*Lectures* 59).

From the Civil War years, Dall's response to Fuller's call for woman's self-awareness, which she initially resisted and qualified, became firmly allied with the Women's Rights movement through her articles in *The Una*, an early feminist journal, and in critical essays written during the Civil War years and published in 1867 as *The College, the Marketplace, and The Court.* Reconciliation with Fuller's views for Dall would involve reappraising Fuller's contribution to Women's Rights and linking her with her past eighteenth century European predecessors including Mary Wollstonecraft, De Stael (Germaine Necker), and Madame Dudevant (George Sand), and with current leaders in the Woman's Right movement including Paulina Wright Davis, Susan B. Anthony and Elizabeth Cady Stanton. Dall saw herself as carrying a synthesis of Fuller's ideas forward.

Over the course of the second half of the nineteenth century "good works" evolved into sciences in fields such as home economics, classroom curriculum development, and in educational fields dedicated to definitions of women's legal, economic, and personal rights. Any number of abstract relationships between women became fastened to specific organizations dealing with health, education and welfare. Fuller's views found substantive application in Child's, Peabody's, and Dall's hands, which were by no means replicas of Fuller's views but prototypes of their own. Child's efforts at setting ethnic and gender houses in order was more pragmatic than her colleague's call for equality between races had been. Peabody's stress on the importance of early childhood education with respect to the integrity and effectiveness of future citizenship would insist that a woman was above all, "in the maternal relation to society," a position countering Fuller's emphasis on female autonomy of and in itself (*Letters* 349). And Dall's search for the new American woman, while based on Fuller's claim for self-reliance, would include her own claims for a woman's "place" in educated surroundings, in businesses, and in courtroom decisions where quantitative and qualitative legal changes in women's existence would be deliberated.

Fuller's first circle extended and broadened her views on women's personal identity, their role in civil rights, their influence on children's educational reform, and their impact on social and economic conditions. A few further crossed lines separating women by station, economic circumstance, and skin color which Fuller had crossed as well. Where Fuller observed and wrote about prostitution and poverty, her circle took real steps to elevate disadvantaged and minority women, identifying themselves with a more diversified and multicultural nation than had existed either in Boston in 1840 or the world experienced by Fuller in Europe in 1848 when she fought in the Italian uprising. They moved into wider and more global networks of women.

Child's association with Harriet Jacobs, an escaped slave who wrote about her condition in the early eighteen sixties at the start of the Civil War, became a working partnership between women of different races. Peabody's friendship in the eighteen eighties with the Piute Native American, Sarah Winnemucca, an educator with spiritual views on children and women much like Peabody's, unified native American education with that of white America. Dall's identification with the Indian physician, Anandabai Joshee in the eighteen sixties, was a sharing of views of women from completely different backgrounds. These transcultural relationships were the "consequence of a natural following out of principles," which Fuller had observed would be achieved by "women [who] have been prominent in the cause" of human rights ("The Great Lawsuit" 9). It was her belief that among like-minded people of all races, conditions and backgrounds, "It is inevitable that an external freedom, such as has been achieved for the nation, should be also for every member of it" ("The Great Lawsuit" 8).

Civil Rights

> Of all [Women's Rights] banners, none has been more steadily up-
> held . . . than that of the champions of the enslaved African. And this
> band it is, which . . . makes just now, the warmest appeal on behalf of
> woman. (Fuller, "The Great Lawsuit" 9-10).

The professional friendship between Maria Child and Harriet Jacobs
became more than a collaboration on a slave narrative, of which a
good number were published during the Civil War years. *Incidents in
the Life of a Slave Girl* (1861) was Jacobs's autobiography of her own
personal subjugation, an account Child took a personal stake in
getting published. Jacobs wrote it, and Child acted as editor and
agent, following in the footsteps of agitators like Fuller, the Grimke
sisters, and Abby Kelly, who had raised the issues of women's demo-
tion and emphasized that all women were in bondage by virtue of
being born female. Fuller had pointed out that there were primary
parallels between women's condition in general and black African
slavery in particular:

> [Woman] does not hold property on equal terms with men . . . if a
> husband dies without a will, the wife, instead of stepping at once into
> his place as head of the family, inherits only a part of his fortune, as if
> she were a child, or a ward only, not an equal partner ("The Great
> Lawsuit" 11).

Armed with this insight, which bolstered views she already held,
Child's support of Jacobs was not merely one more slave account but
a highly visible and acclaimed woman's recounting of sexual and racial
exploitation in which a slave's word had heretofore counted for
nothing.

Child's and Jacobs' goals for women were identical. Both believed
that women required freedom and a home. Aware that discussions of
rape and physical abuse were considered too delicate for most ears in

that Victorian era, Child encouraged Jacobs to speak in her own way. She conscientiously kept her editing minimal, commenting that it was of utmost importance for readers to hear Jacobs' voice; she had not "altered fifty words in the whole volume" (*Incidents* xxii). In identifying herself with Jacobs, Child forged visible ties between slave and free women, black and white women, and poor and privileged women. She advanced the idea that enslavement was an elemental aspect of woman's condition. This understanding, broadly expressed in Fuller's writing and more precisely shaped in Child's, was essential to the future of feminist thought. In *The Creation of Patriarchy*, Gerda Lerner observes that "[t]he domestic subordination of women provides the model out of which slavery developed as a social institution" (99). Lerner states that "sexual exploitation is the very mark of class exploitation" for *all* women (215). Fuller, Child and Jacobs are prominent examples of Lerner's nineteenth century teachers.

Child's lifelong identification with African Americans and Native Americans, central to almost everything she ever penned, reflected an abiding commitment to a multinational perspective. Her belief that a better relationship between women and men of different races and social backgrounds would only become possible when the basic understanding in America was shifted from artificial and often hypocritical assumptions to greater multicultural outlooks, paralleled Fuller's. They both revolted against what they saw as an inherent imbalance characterizing American life, against restricted relationships between people of different origins and backgrounds. Both women were criticized for defending disadvantaged and minority peoples. Child felt alieneated from the impact of white dominant society and asked to be buried "in some ground belonging to the colored people" (*Selected Letters* 356). Even more decisively than Fuller, who remained an outsider to religious and social groups by choice during her American years, Child's aversion to joining any organization prevented her from becoming a member of one, whether it were the American

Antislavery Society, the Garrisonian abolitionist camp, or in due course the Women's Rights movement. Child's definition of fundamental human rights was firmly fastened to the lonely principle of self-determination; like Fuller's, it rested on self-sovereignty.

Today, Angela Davis and Alice Walker are among a growing number of American writers maintaining, as did Child, that black women's voices are central to the expression of African American thought. Davis asserts that "Black women could hardly strive for weakness; they had to be strong, for their families and their communities needed their strength to survive" (231). Walker observes that black female creativity survives and endures through terrible conditions that have historically maintained that it is a "punishable crime for a black person to read or write" (234). The setting for this awareness has included Fuller's and Child's demands for women's freedom of self-expression a century and a half ago.

Women's & Children's Rights

> So much is said of women being better educated that they may be better companions and mothers of men. . . . But a being of infinite scope must not be treated with an exclusive view to any one relation (Fuller, "The Great Lawsuit" 35).

Elizabeth Peabody's life and educational career started long before her friendship with Fuller began. Peabody was absorbed in how children learn, in what she and Bronson Alcott identified as "Spiritual Culture" in the mid-eighteen thirties. Her ideas gained form and strength in response to Fuller's talks; her views of women's uniquely maternal function were opposed to Fuller's idea that there was "no wholly masculine man, no purely feminine woman" ("The Great Lawsuit" 43). Peabody elevated woman's role as Mother and Kindergartner. She stated that it was "[woman's] instinct and method, clearly understood in all its bearings and acted out," that created her importance. "To be a kindergartner is the perfect development of womanliness . .

the highest finish that can be given to a woman's education," she asserted. "One who *could not* be educated to become a kindergartner should never dare to become a mother," she maintained in the eighteen eighties (*Lectures* 5, 13).

This contrast between Fuller and Peabody represents a much debated point in late twentieth century feminist thought. Adrienne Rich, whose work *Of Woman Born* deliberates distinctions between being a woman and a mother, has defined mothering as "both an institution and an experience" (19), suggesting that while each is part of the totality of women's multiple being, mothering has historically consumed female identity and confined woman's growth as an individual. Rich is restating Fuller's claim that women's self-image has always been bound up with male definition and that now, as in the past, "in a majority of instances, the man looks upon his wife as an adopted child, and places her to the other children in the relation of nurse or governess, rather than of parent" (*Woman* 58). Rich's views are fortified by Fuller's reflections on the subject of women's assumed inferiority within a hierarchical, male-centered family structure.

In "The Great Lawsuit," and amplified in *Woman in the Nineteenth Century*, Fuller commented that the circle of domesticity surrounding most women was, "if the duller, is not the quieter," and that "if kept from excitement, [a woman] is not from drudgery" ("The Great Lawsuit" 12). Her insistence on woman's self-dependence was one Peabody countered by elevating the nature of the relationship between a mother and child. For Peabody, this was the most essential and important of all human ties and the key to woman's identity. Peabody correlated spheres of female biology and spirituality. In her deliberations she anticipated John Dewey's twentieth century term, "the whole child," recognizing the natural (her word was "organic") links that existed between home and school, parents and teachers, mothers and children. She saw imagination and psyche as inseparable from physiology. In her view, mothering expressed woman's function throughout human existence.

Elements of Peabody's arguments are found today in Nancy Chodorow's assertion in *The Reproduction of Mothering*, that women mother because they have been "mothered" by women. Chodorow maintains that women "not only bear children," they "take primary responsibility for infant care, spend more time with infants and children than do men, and sustain primary emotional ties with infants" (3). Chodorow is restating the heart of Peabody's beliefs when she states that "women's mothering is a central and defining feature of the social organization of gender" (9). But her views rely on Fuller's thoughts as well when she observes that, "Because of their child-care responsibilities, women's primary social location is domestic. . . . Men's location in the public sphere, then, defines society itself as masculine" (9). Chodorow ultimately finds, as did Fuller in her era, that definitions of male and female tend to polarize, that "Being a mother, then, is not only bearing a child—it is being a person who socializes and nurtures" (11).

Peabody's quest for the meeting point between physiology and the psychology of mothering is manifest in a debate that began with Fuller and has gone on to include Rich and Chodorow. Spheres labeled "domestic," "motherly," and "womanly," reflect Peabody's emphases. The restrictions that limited her views of woman's entirety are still prevalent among women. Peabody neither could nor would challenge theories and attitudes bolstering male dominance, insisting that men support their families while women raise them, that men do the world's business while women rock cradles at home. Peabody offered progressive coeducational tenets and theories of reformed classroom strategies and educational attitudes revolutionizing twentieth century schools, but she left dual-track gender divisions intact. These still preoccupy our century's mindset.

Peabody's limitations prevented her from redefining woman as daringly as did Fuller. But her insistence on inherent female spirituality transcended her age's dualistic cultural and religious outlooks. Like Child, her views were non-denominational, multiethnic, and multicultural by commitment and inclination. At the height of her kindergarten reform movement in the eighteen eighties, she sided with Sarah Winnemucca's views on bilingual teaching in Piute and English languages at Winnemucca's Indian reservation schools, stating that their integration "rends the veil that has been hanging between the two races from the beginning" (*Letters* 397). While maintaining her century's religious distinctions between heaven and earth, social and psychological divisions between the spheres of women and men, operational differences in the realms of home and business, Peabody's multicultural insights on educational practices and bilingual perspectives anticipated our own. Her views on women's nurturing and nature are essential matters of discussion in an expanding view of women's identity.

Women's Rights

> The especial genius of Woman I believe to be electrical in movement, intuitive in function, spiritual in tendency. She is great not so easily in classification, or re-creation, as in an instinctive seizure of causes, and a simple breathing out of what she receives that has the singleness of life, rather than the selecting or energizing of art (Fuller, "The Great Lawsuit" 43).

Caroline Healey Dall held views embodying her own physical turmoil and emotional pain. Her perspective on Women's Rights was a precursor of feminist ideology. Reaching into and articulating deep recesses within her own psyche, she struck a nerve. She uncovered some little-understood conflicts which must be faced by women undertaking emancipation. She did this despite her youthful insistence on 'womanly' and 'manly' spheres, which she discussed in essays published in her mid-teens and which seemed in line with Peabody's strict delineation of a woman's maternal role. A latent wish for gender difference was never to fully disappear from her professional writing.

Dall wrestled privately and publicly with her formative years: "From the age of thirteen I was my father's housekeeper, for my mother's health had failed . . . ," she reveals in *Alongside*, her autobiography published in 1900 (31). Acknowledging that she "was little more than a child in experience, when my father's unexpected reverses . . . sent me down [to the District of Columbia] to teach" (*Alongside* 47), Dall began to build a career for herself based upon calls for women's self-determination in spite of admitted emotional stunting during her early childhood and her own adolescent resistance to concepts of women's independence. She analyzed the events that had limited her growth—her mother's impaired physical health and morbid state of mind, her father's catastrophic financial ups and downs which were coupled with his authoritarian domination of his daughter, the death of a favorite brother, her convoluted feelings of romantic love and a zealous religious conversion at sixteen which she described as her salvation—and turned them into generic examples of a great many women's restricted chances for growth. She posited that her own confined education was a mirror of other women's diminished training, her own meager economic resources typical of other women's blocked entry into business, her own tortuous marital path an example of how women were kept enthralled through legal and social means. She viewed her own private failures as sources of women's inability to become whole persons.

Following Fuller's death, Dall began redefining the grounds of the naming process that her mentor had tantalizingly and only partially explored. She wrote autobiographically about herself and biographically about Fuller in studies resembling similar portraits executed on Wollstonecraft, De Stael, Recamier, Anne Hutchinson, Mary Astell, George Eliot and George Sand. Dall probed her own identity in these characterizations. In contrast to Fuller's ideal Woman, who had withdrawn into herself to locate her own uniqueness, Dall's was "taught from the first to regard herself as the equal of men, [and was] totally incapable of considering the question of sex so far as it concerned the fulness of thought, speech, or deed" (*Historical Pictures* 260). Dall's Woman was a combination of having become "self-sufficing" (Fuller's term), and at home in the world of men, women and children. She was neither Minerva nor an invincible goddess, but was like Dall herself, flawed, vulnerable, and dissatisfied. Society scorned her as it had Margaret Fuller; Dall suggested that she and Fuller were perhaps the two "most misunderstood women in New England" of their respective eras:

> To Margaret's estimate of me, to my self-assertion in her presence, I owe much of the misunderstanding and superficial condemnation which has made my public life unnecessarily painful and severe ("Remembrances" 417).

In her public writings Dall examined intricate shades of her own and women's character through educational, economic and legal frameworks, clarifying the elements that would enable women to travel further along a speculative path staked by Fuller—who had obliquely observed that "[m]any women are considering within themselves what they need that they have not, and what they can have, if they find they need it" ("The Great Lawsuit" 11). Fuller's elusive goal for her sex had been the philosophical accomplishment of "inward and outward freedom," the attainment of liberty "not yielded as a concession but acknowledged as a right" ("The Great Lawsuit" 11). How that goal was to be achieved had been left open-ended, in part because Fuller's role models were few and her own opportunities scattered. She had been among a rarified handful of women who claimed selfhood from almost invisible roots.

With more unrestrained exposure of herself than Fuller had ever shown, Dall compared her development with Fuller's. She had received less education, had come from a less loving family, and had experienced a less fulfilling future than Fuller had known. In naming herself, Dall chose to uncover and reveal her own insecurities, her own deficiencies. Her anxieties and neuroses, discussed in her journals in great detail, revealed distorted senses of self-love and self-loathing. These may be more realistic indicators of how a woman's character developed a century ago than were Fuller's sometimes abstruse and lofty exhortations. Dall's journals, which she did not destroy at the end of her life but rather reread, revised and rewrote, portrayed an often agonized, psychologically torn and discontented woman aware of her torment and, perhaps more important, a woman carefully documenting it. *The College, the Marketplace, and the Court* emerged as a conscious sequel to Fuller's *Woman in the Nineteenth Century*.

Feminist historians will recognize a critical twentieth century level of understanding in Dall's undertaking. Here was a diarist trying to remain within an historic tradition which would urge women to portray themselves as content with domesticity and conjugal life, and to think of themselves as appendages to men. But unable to see herself in this figure, Dall knowingly revealed her failure to *be* such a woman. Sadness and loss marked her private outpourings; they pervaded the text in her sketches and studies of other women. Recognition and exposure of her own entrapment is the stuff of feminist history. For better or worse, Caroline Healey Dall herself wanted her own predicament to represent a woman's life at the crossroads of change in the latter part of the last century. She was living proof that the terms of Fuller's naming were not easy.

In writing herself into her sketches of other strong-willed women, Dall further strengthened the bonds that Fuller had discovered linked autobiography and biography. Dall's friendship in the eighteen eighties with Anandabai Joshee, whose biography she wrote, was in good part a self-study. Describing Joshee's background, Dall paralled her life with the young Indian woman's despite national and personal differences, finding that like herself, Joshee was a favorite daughter of a wealthy father who had withheld financial support when it was most critically needed, refusing to support his daughter's development; that like herself, Joshee was forced to marry a man she did not love, a man who became a millstone around her neck when her own desire for a career surfaced. In the face of grave social opposition, Dall related that Joshee had come to America without her husband. Alone, she had endured "the necessity of repression" and experienced "a desire to escape from the influences around her" (*Life of Dr. Anandabai Joshee* 32). Incorporating a phrenologist's description of Joshee's character into her biography, one sees Caroline Dall's idealized portrait of herself in Joshee:

> This is an intellectual well-balanced mind, cultivated with great care. . . . The writer is a lady of more than ordinary brain power, very independent, but neither egotistical . . . [nor] afraid to investigate any subject no matter how unpopular (*Life of Dr. Anandabai Joshee* 121).

Most of Dall's studies were of brilliant, maligned women defying society, self-portraits executed in the process of self-definition. In biographical sketches of two eighteenth century figures, Charlotte Temple and Eliza Wharton, for example, Dall remarks that "their tale, as I tell it, seems almost like a bit of autobiography, I am well aware: I make no apology for it. Psychologically the whole train of events forms a curious study" (*Romance of the Association*, viii). All of Dall's work may be viewed as composite pieces of a self-study of a woman nearing self-realization at the approach of a new century.

The Terms of Self & Other Love

"We would have every arbitrary barrier thrown down! We would have every path laid open to woman as freely as to man" (Fuller, "The Great Lawsuit" 14).

The opening path for women that Fuller had created led to an immeasurable private world within each woman and to an inner self who was the other half of a public and professional self:

If you ask me what offices [women] may fill, I reply, any. I do not care what case you put; let them be sea captains, if you will (Fuller, *Woman* 174).

This "sea captain" metaphor embodied a figure possessing "infinite scope," a woman without "mediators" able

to pass in review the depths of thought and knowledge, and to place them in due relation to one another—To systematize thought, and give [it] precision and clearness; to ascertain what pursuits are best suited to us, in our time and state of society (Fuller, *Memoirs* 325).

One of Fuller's major contributions was her intention to eradicate false perceptions of Woman's constricted identity. She rejected the century's philosophical and religious insistence on dual spheres with their implications of greater and lesser gender worth—on the one hand, earth; on the other heaven; on the one hand substance, on the other idea; on the one hand flesh, on the other spirit. In this equation women had historically been evaluated by a male standard and found wanting. Fuller stated that "[t]here is no wholly masculine man, no purely feminine woman" (*Woman* 116). Her challenge to women was her definition of feminine infinite scope, a range of being she called for women to assimilate into themselves. Her personal exploration arose from her desire to experience the power of self and other love within herself. She felt she could only love another being as much as she could love herself:

> The time is come when Eurydice is to call for an Orpheus, rather than Orpheus for Eurydice; that the idea of Man, however imperfectly brought out, has been far more so than that of Woman, that she, the other half of the same thought, the other chamber of the heart of life, needs now to take her turn to the full pulsation, and that improvement of the daughters will best aid in the reformation of the sons of this age (*Woman* 13).

Fuller offered that for this Woman, marriage might become a mutual "pilgrimage towards a common shrine" (*Woman* 69), but only if it took place between wholly independent individuals. For women, this union meant having overcome a sense of inherent inferiority, and upon both sexes' ability to move to relationships beyond "mutual idolatry" or "intellectual companionship":

> It is not the transient breath of poetic incense that women want; each can receive that from a lover. It is not life long sway; it needs but to become a coquette, a shrew, or a good cook, to be sure of that. It is not for money, nor notoriety. . . . It is for that which at once includes these and precludes them. It is for that which is the birthright of every being capable to receive it,—the freedom, the religious, the intelligent freedom of the universe, to use its means; to learn its secret as far as nature has enabled them, with God alone for their guide and their judge (*Woman* 50-51).

For women past and present, this view of the self and its identity in an independent partnership has been extremely difficult to conceptualize, let alone achieve. Women's economic, social and psychological dependencies have been and are still pronounced; feelings of inferiority have chained women to themselves. As Adrienne Rich has put it, "[t]his is what women have always done" (6). The results of the insistence on gender difference are still with us; that which we cannot easily label we reject. That which approaches an inner knowledge we resist; that which we cannot readily classify we denounce.

For Fuller, an elemental prerequisite of marriage was the prior union that had to occur between a woman and herself. A unified "[w]oman, self-centered, would never be absorbed by any relation," she asserted ("The Great Lawsuit" 47). Having publicly maintained this, Fuller's private anguish and frustration in acknowledging her attraction to Ralph Waldo Emerson, a man she wrote she could "never meet . . . while one atom of our proper identity & individuality remains" (Rusk 455), must have tortured and disappointed her. If, as Marie Olesen Urbanski has noted, "during this highly creative time of their lives, it is clear that Fuller was the major inspiration for Emerson's ideas and the writings of them, as he was for hers" (29), then how could she allow herself to be absorbed by him?

Fuller invented an Emerson who could be her matching self; but the Sage of Concord's granite walls never came down. From the start of their fitful relationship he complained that he could not "see into you & have not arrived at your law" (Rusk 336), while she admitted that "[w]hen I come to yourself, I cannot receive you, & you cannot give yourself; it does not profit . . ." (Rusk 336). After an almost two year encounter, she may well have put a layer of defense between herself and her heart, a layer that moved her from a position of dependency to one of independence.

In Italy in 1847, Giovanni Angelo D'Ossoli may have finally satisfied Fuller's unvictorian search for a mate. But D'Ossoli would not be necessary for her completion. They were different persons, with separate lives that came together as components of a whole. Lois Banner suggests in her book, *In Full Flower*, that in taking up with the marchese D'Ossoli, who was nearly a decade younger than she, Fuller consciously contemplated a "positive role for aging unmarried women as social reformers and as exemplars of human self-realization" (238). This perspective does not adequately describe a relationship that was both passionate and compassionate. Fuller loved D'Ossoli from the fullness rather than the poverty of her being; he fit her long-cherished image of the "ideal man" perfectly:

> No thin Idealist, no coarse Realist, [he is] a man whose eye reads the heavens while his feet step firmly on the ground, and his hands are strong and dexterous for the use of human implements . . . a man who knows the region of emotion, though he is not its slave; a man to whom this world is no mere spectacle . . . but a great solemn game to be played with good head, for its stakes are of eternal value (*Summer on the Lakes* 103).

Having sounded the depths of her being, Fuller observed her existence in Italy as an emancipated female. Bearing her own child and participating in the civil war, at the front and surviving in the midst of death and dying, she had become united with herself. Her commitment to living on the edge of events, including her decision to return to America in 1850 with a foreign mate and an infant son, were decisions beyond the set of New England constraints that had bound her American life. Aware of what she was doing, she had arrived at herself. It was not a marriage of convenience or of intellectual detachment Fuller made, but a union composed of self-and-other love.

For Maria Child, the concept of an enduring marriage arose out of the early republic's emphases on solid family life. Child recognized that the pattern was undergoing dramatic change during her lifetime; much of her writing was in response to this recognition. Child clung to the true values of pioneer America and saw dangers arising from altering patterns which diminished and devalued women's strength and purpose. Glenna Matthews has recently suggested in her history of domesticity, *Just a Housewife*, that in all eras and for all time, "[a]ll of us need home, whatever our particular household arrangements might be" (225). This understanding lies at the heart of Child's life, explaining her unique attitudes toward the value and necessity of women's work, and perhaps explaining why she chose to remain married to David Lee Child, a man she came to know to be daring if quixotic, liberal if too impulsive, generous but irresponsible where money was concerned. Child venerated the institution of marriage itself and believed that men and women must honor it to honor themselves.

On the one hand, Child needed a home and intended to keep it. She believed that all women did. When being courted, Maria Francis had loved her fiancé's chivalry and gallant ways. She hoped his visions might be more than mere dreams, that she might be the "little partridge drumming its feathers" at her own hearth. On the other hand, however, she sensed that the national ideal did not apply to her mate, that there were distinct flaws in her marriage not resembling the traditional picture. Early on, a reversal of the dependency pattern occurred. In the Child household it would be Maria who earned their keep. She wanted fervently to respect David, to follow the path he might set. But there seemed to be no path. She tried for years to keep them both financially and emotionally afloat. Her early house-keeping books were her own domestic tips to herself on keeping a home on a shoestring budget, on sharing moderate needs and raising wholesome families.

The Childs' long separation after almost a decade of married life came after dashed efforts at housewifely frugality and practicality, of diminished hopes and prospects. Divorce was out of the question; her letters from New York to her mate were loving while they were lonely. The rationale for their separation was financial; living away from him she could at least direct her fortunes and remain intact. Child's pragmatism kept her alive. It kept three meals on the table. Yet buried inside this self-disciplined and utilitarian woman, one whose Franklinesque moderation in all things was lifelong, was a being whose inner difficulties were not to be addressed directly. After the Boston Conversations in 1843, en route to New York where she would live without her husband for more than half a decade, Child wrote a brief essay for *The Dial* on the question of "What is Beauty?" It was both a Transcendental and a Victorian essay in which were feelings far beyond the common sense she was famous for:

> The two creative principles of the universe are LOVE and WISDOM. Their union, and perfect proportion, constitutes BEAUTY. . . . Wherever the soul catches a glimpse . . . of a perfect union of Love and Truth, it rejoices in the radiant marriage-vesture, and names it Beauty (491-2).

Her reconciliation with David at the end of the eighteen forties began her most unified writing years, from her *Progress of Religious Ideas through Successive Ages* (1855), which drew together her view of the world's religions, to her call for unity among blacks and whites in her antislavery tracts, echoed in *Incidents in the Life of a Slave Girl*, and in pragmatically grounded manuals on the terms and methods of integration, including *The Freedmen's Book* (1865). These would be followed by an uncompromising denunciation of white supremacy in *An Appeal for the Indians* (1868), and concluded with a reflective look backward at her own spiritual unification in *Aspirations of the World* (1878). Each dealt with the terms of autonomy and self-sovereignty, for herself as a citizen and as a woman. These continued the pattern she had set into motion with her early work, from her children's story of the American Indian, *Hobomok*, to her founding and editing of *Juvenile Miscellany*, America's first children's journal in 1825. Her popular and perennially useful look at housewifery in *The Frugal Housewife* (1829), and her books on childrearing practices which included *The Little Girl's Own Book* (1833) and *The Mother's Book* (1844), were outgrowths of her cherished views on woman's self sufficiency, on her capacity to embody other-love as part of self-love.

Like Fuller, Child tapped into herself to find the model of an ideal and completed Woman. But Child's model, quite different from Fuller's, was a figure whose existence depended upon meeting moderate expectations and making only modest demands, a woman selflessly contributing to society's well-being by exemplifying a simple existence of 'not-too-much,' whether this applied to cooking recipes or comfortable clothing, to saving scraps of paper or keeping one's cupboards well scrubbed. Child's view depended upon self-determination and moderation in all things:

> Rise early. Eat simple food. Take plenty of exercise. Never fear a little fatigue. Avoid the necessity of a physician. . . . Pay careful attention to your diet. . . . Wear shoes that are large enough. (*Frugal Housewife* 87).

She considered marriage every woman's work. The meaning of a woman's life was embedded in the doing of it. By definition, self-love meant giving oneself to another to become whole. Likening each sex by itself to "half a pair of scissors," Child's marriage turned out to be an exception to wholesome rules she had hoped to set for the nation's and women's well-being. Writing to David, she asked:

> In all that relates to external circumstances, our married life has been a stormy journey. But in all other respects, my dear husband, have we not realized *more* than we hoped? . . . I love you. Do you love me? (*Collected Correspondence* 1979).

Maintaining that "[s]ociety will never come truly into order until there is perfect equality and co-partnership between men and women in every department of human life" (*Letters* 245), Child never stopped applying the principle that what was good for the one must be good for the many, that within herself was the model for the frugal housewife. In *In Search of Our Mothers' Gardens*, Alice Walker likens the fabric of hardworking women's lives like Child's in the last century to the craft those women undertook so matter-of-factly to do without thinking about it, quilt-making:

> though it is made of bits and pieces of worthless rags, it is obviously the work of person[s] of powerful imagination and deep spiritual feeling (239).

Elizabeth Peabody remained single by choice although she had loved five men whose imprint on her life profoundly shaped it. William Ellery Channing, the father of American Unitarianism, provided her with transcendent religious certainty. Bronson Alcott, the father of Spiritual Culture, gave her an educational commitment to children. Horace Mann, the father of progressive public education, imparted his views of a child's daily development to her, while Nathaniel Hawthorne, the father of historical symbolism, sensitized her to the benefits of rejecting puritanical thought in raising a child. Friedrich Froebel, the father of the European kindergarten, planted the seeds of teaching as mothering in her. To each, Peabody may have seen herself as "Mother" and "Wife." With each she maintained distinct connections to mothering without having children of her own. From each she added to her belief in the divine goodness of children and the power of maternal love.

Peabody's younger sisters were her first pupils; her favorite girlhood pastime was playing the real game of school, held in the Peabody parlor window seat with herself as teacher. She grew up in a household in which her mother was the dominant figure, the one making practical decisions and supplementing the family's income by running a boarding house, while her father, a sometimes-practicing dentist whose love of teaching had begun when he was a preceptor at Andover Academy, was content to mend broken crockery and run domestic errands. Elizabeth would associate with gentle rather than authoritarian men.

Born into a Unitarian household, she gravitated toward Transcendental educational attitudes which combined sensate physical reality with tenets of spiritual indoctrination. While her mother had prided herself on her strong Calvinist background, in 1817 she took her eldest daughter, then thirteen, to hear the great orator, William Ellery Channing. The event was decisive: Elizabeth wrote decades later that the sermon had 'thrilled' her. She had witnessed "a man communing with God face to face" (*Remembrances* 13). Inspired by this momentous occasion, she later recalled being "[o]n the eve of entering upon the vocation for which I had been educated from childhood," teaching (*Remembrances* 40). It was more than a profession; it was the completion of herself. Peabody opened a school of her own at the age of sixteen in Lancaster, Massachusetts, with her two sisters among her earliest students. This was followed by a girls' school in Brookline, Massacchusetts, which she ran with Mary. In 1826, involved in a school in Boston, she appeared in Channing's study "to announce that she was going to copy out his sermons," convincing him that she should "be allowed to serve as his unpaid personal secretary" (*Letters* 18). By 1828 she was thoroughly admitted to the Channing household; his only daughter became one of her earliest students.

In the next decade, Peabody threw herself into religious and secular teaching, the zenith of which was Bronson Alcott's Temple School. In 1839 she initiated and hosted Fuller's Conversations, one of many similar projects. She felt chosen. Other women might follow a path of courtship, wifehood and motherhood. Not she, for Channing had convinced her that "[t]he book of Nature and the soul are the ultimate standards" (Peabody, *Remembrances* 124), that her call to teaching was motivated not from earthly but from heavenly origins. Peabody dedicated herself during her twenties to seek what Channing called "the great thought of our times—the education to freedom of individual action" (Peabody, *Remembrances* 97). In those years when other young women got married, she wed Ideals. As Bruce Ronda, editor of Peabody's letters, has commented recently, Channing "seems never to have inquired about her marriage prospects" (Peabody, *Letters* 19). Perhaps Channing preempted them.

Sustained by an image of herself as both "Lady and Christian," a phrase from her letters, Peabody's association with Bronson Alcott, a self-educated Connecticut farm boy turned language specialist and spiritual educator, began in the mid-eighteen thirties. The two educators established themselves as co-principals of Alcott's Temple School in Boston in 1834. In this venture, which liberal Boston first acclaimed and later disowned, he played the part of the pupils' father, holding hours-long talks with the children (who were ages five through eight or nine) on the meaning of words and thoughts, and stressing self-analysis. Maternally, Elizabeth sat close by and recorded the children's responses. She edited these records and published her notes as *Record of a School* the following year.

The homelike quality of the Temple School classroom helped to initiate Peabody's lifelong interest in changing stark schoolrooms into homelike, pleasant settings where children could feel comfortable. It was one of several experiments in which she saw herself as both teacher and mother. Her union with Alcott, however, became an intellectual estrangement in the months that followed. She would later claim that "Peculiarities of Mr. Alcott's own mind" were at fault. She wrote:

> He is not able to keep practically to his idea of letting the instincts of the children's minds lead him . . . he prefers abstraction to the natural form of ideas ("A Review" 260).

When their relationship worsened, Peabody left the school and found educational reaffirmation in the ideas of Horace Mann, the future Massachusetts superintendent of public coeducation who would push forward the concept of universal free schooling in the next decades. Living in a Boston boarding house with Mary, where

Mann was also housed, Elizabeth was drawn to her fellow boarder in a way reminiscent of her attachments to Channing and Alcott. She was spiritually attracted to educational ideals matching her own. Mann fell in love with and married Mary. A subsequent shortlived attraction to childhood friend Nathaniel Hawthorne, whose children's stories, *Twice Told Tales*, Elizabeth discovered and promoted, ended in his proposal of marriage to Sophia. Elizabeth returned to Education.

Peabody's last soul mate was Friedrich Froebel, the Swiss educator whose kindergarten movement swept through Europe after his death in 1852. Traveling abroad, Peabody searched for Froebel's philosophical ideals and teaching practices in Kindergarten classrooms, far more excited by them than in seeing European capitals. She returned to America to establish what she called "the true American kindergarten" in the early eighteen sixties, an effort that consumed her time and energy, and which permanently influenced the development of early childhood education in this country. For the Mother of the American Kindergarten, this career was the "one relation" of her life. Peabody's writing, from her early children's stories to her midlife essays on Brook Farm and communal living arrangements, to countless articles on the development of the Kindergarten and her late autobiographical reminiscence of William Ellery Channing, exemplifies her commitment to strengthen the early education of youngsters and reflects her commitment to the concept that mothers and children are joined. She later observed that her love of Mann and Hawthorne were less meaningful to her than a lifelong commitment to the idea of marriage:

> There is generally conjured up some romantic story about any woman who is never married. . . . I have known and understood married love in the persons of my sisters, and also of several other friends. I believe matches are made in Heaven. . . . It is because I believe marriage is a sacrament, and nothing less, that I am dying as an old Maid (*Letters* 432).

Love and marriage permeated Caroline Wells Healey Dall's thoughts. As a child she adored her Unitarian pastor, Charles Lowell, to whom she confessed a desire to "open my whole heart—that you may judge of its fitness for the reception of the blessing which it craves" (*Transcendentalism* 35), an attraction which was followed in her twenties by her confessional friendship with the fiery Transcendentalist orator, Theodore Parker. When it came time to marry, however, she chose a weak-willed Unitarian minister, Charles Appleton Dall, perhaps because there was no other choice on the horizon and perhaps because, like Peabody, she gravitated to gentle men—in her case the antithesis of her overbearing father. Conventionally raised to believe that a woman grew up, married, and had children, her union with Dall at twenty-two may have been an attempt to wed what she always sought in men, approbation and praise. The match would prove a lifelong disaster for both of them.

In 1855, when Dall was thirty-three and the mother of two young children, her husband left her and moved to India where he remained as a Unitarian missionary until his death in 1886. Their infrequent visits together in the United States over that thirty year period were bitter and rancorous. He was, to her way of thinking, mentally unstable and perpetually vacillating, and she was self-professedly a woman misunderstood and battered by overwhelming emotional and financial circumstances. In her care, her children grew up by fits and starts, never fully receiving her attention or her love. A single mother, Dall was distracted and often distraught, insecure and obsessively concerned with herself, traits that were hardly the approved home-body character that women were supposed to possess. Dall dwelled on her worries, successes and failures in her journals. With very little money to cushion her vulnerable position, she managed to make ends meet, frequently in poor health and almost always in a despondent mood. Her journals became her therapy, a major vent for airing her private and professional conflicts.

Having attended Fuller's Conversations as a disappointed teen age debutante whose father's income had evaporated with the depression of 1837, over the next seven decades Dall never forgot either her anger and fear of her father's financial failure, her husband's personal weakness and instability, her children's apparent ingratitude, or her attraction and repulsion for Margaret Fuller. These became sources of a love/hate relationship with herself that were to characterize her adult life. With her husband thousands of miles from her, and battling her father for his financial support, she joined the gathering women's movement in the eighteen fifties as Paulina Wright Davis's associate at *The Una*, an early feminist journal.

Perhaps more than any other woman in the circle, Dall's wish was to see herself as Fuller's representative in the second half of the century. Noting at the close of her life that it would be "hopeless to convey to those who never saw her any idea of Margaret Fuller, to give to those who never lived in the circle that she inspired any impression of her being and influence" (*Transcendentalism* 32), she allied herself with Fuller as both a nineteenth century Transcendentalist—"I am a Transcendentalist of the old New England sort," she wrote (*Transcendentalism* 35)—and a harbinger of twentieth century feminist thought. Her commitment ensured Fuller's passage into a new age. Dall reexamined Fuller's views with fresh eyes and with new levels of meaning. She intended to vault herself and Fuller into the present.

Dall's contribution to women's history is still being evaluated. Her major work, *The College, the Marketplace, and the Court*, is complemented by a handful of biographical portraits, as well as by a series of studies on Fuller which reveal a great deal about Dall herself as well. These works gain stature when they are read in the context of her daily journals, where she exhibited an unending need to vindicate herself, and in conjunction with her pioneering efforts in the American Social Science Association, promotion of the women's crafts guild, the New England Women's Hospital, and in classes on women's history which she conducted over the decades ahead.

Dall's self-adulation and self-pity were twin products of late nineteenth century changes taking place in women's lives. She was both insecure in her successes and defensive about her failures. Her honest self-evaluation casts a direct light on the worst effects of woman's self-abnegation. But in the process of this exploration, Dall advanced Fuller's demand that each woman find her own fitting name. *The College, the Marketplace and the Court* deserves more recognition than it has received. Dall's uneven lack of an easily defined position within the Woman's Rights movement, like her too candid observations on her own failed marriage and uneven prospects and friendships, jar our expectations of her strength and unsettle our certainty in her balance. They seem out of phase with the level-headed symmetry that characterizes her appraisal of woman's condition vis-à-vis her education, her opportunities to earn a living, and her legal rights. Comparably, Dall's efforts to bring Margaret Fuller's name to prominence were erratic; she zigzagged between revering and criticizing her mentor. The unevenness of Dall's mixed messages, her dubious efforts in marriage, motherhood, and an uncharted career, make her a challenging study of the complex and driven results of early trials in women's liberation.

Conclusion

> I know that I, a daughter, live through the life of man; but what concerns me now is, that my life be a beautiful, powerful, in a word, a complete life of its kind" (Fuller, *Woman* 163).

Margaret Fuller's diligence and honesty in the quest to discover herself may be a key to the longevity of her ideas. Anne C. Rose states in *Transcendentalism as a Social Movement* that "the transition from sisterhood" in the last century, "to feminism" in the late twentieth, "has been extremely difficult" (184). Rose notes that "Margaret Fuller's contribution to Transcendentalism" and to the rise of twentieth century feminism and values, "was her balanced respect for woman's individual identity" (184), which she notes elementally influenced the social development of both sexes: "Men as well as women . . . suffered from the bonds of womanhood that kept humanity as a whole from its destiny" (184). On the one hand, Margaret Fuller never forgot that she was a woman. On the other, she never wanted that reality to dictate her choices or limit her opportunities.

Extending the boundaries of Woman's sphere, Fuller included in it the properties of masculinity which she insisted belonged naturally and immutably as well to women. By 'Man' she "meant both man and woman:

> These are the two halves of one thought. . . . I believe that the development of the one cannot be effected without that of the other (*Woman* xiii).

In defining the new woman, Fuller faced several dangers with open eyes. She worried about the distribution of weight existing between men and women, speaking of their proportion as a balance between "Energy and Harmony, Power and Beauty, Intellect and Love" (*Woman* 169). Fuller saw that male traits were too frequently stated as the first of each of these pairs. Energy, power and intellect were considered masculine, while harmony, beauty and love were feminine. The lopsided interpretation putting the male half at the beginning, still happens. Fuller sought to define the parity of pairs carrying equal value, if not in advocating that humanity must rise above constructs of pairing altogether.

Another danger was silence. Women were accustomed to being quiet observers; their voices were assumed to be private rather than public, gentle rather than powerful, and submissive rather than assertive. Most women of the generations before Fuller's considered themselves, as Xaviere Gauthier noted, "outside the historical process" (Smith 18). But the "double bind" women experienced was that if they entered too aggressively, and began "to speak out and write *as men do,* they might enter history subdued and alienated" (Smith 18). Fuller was conscious of trying to think and write as a woman, but not as a protected woman, one whose sex constricted her. To use Woolf's later description, Fuller "wrote as a woman, but as a woman who has forgotten that she is a woman" (96).

She predicted a change and enlargement of women's education. She impressed on Elizabeth Peabody the point that schools must be established so that "girls be given as fair a field as boys" (Fuller, *Woman* 94), so that methods and topics in the classroom be offered by women, for they "had experienced the same wants" as their young female charges. She challenged Peabody to rethink a home circle in which the adage, "Her mother did so before" might "no longer [be] a sufficient excuse" for continuing an education based on a confining female outlook (*Woman* 95).

Comparably, Fuller knew that civil rights must be seized by women. They silently suffered many of the same indignities as slaves and were too often considered chattels belonging to their husbands. Maria Child understood Fuller's charge that "If the negro be a soul, if the woman be a soul, apparelled in flesh, to one Master only are they accountable" (*Woman* 37). Fuller's thought, that "[i]t may well be an antislavery party that pleads for Woman" (*Woman* 31), was a resounding one. Child would be governed by the need for all people to take a personal interest in all people long after Fuller's death:

> It is salutary, both for mind and heart, to take an interest in . . . slavery, or war, or intemperance, or the elevation of woman, or righting the wrongs of the Indians, or the progress of education, or the regulation of prisons, or improvements in architecture, or investigations into the natural sciences. . . . Nothing is more healthy for the

soul than to go out of ourselves, and stay out of ourselves (*Toward Sunset* 175-76).

Lastly, Fuller knew that only by finding themselves in women models who had left their mark on the world would her sex be able to move forward. She emphasized that mythological Woman, "Sita in the Ramayana . . . the Egyptian Isis . . . in Greece Ceres and Proserpine, in Rome Diana, Minerva, and Vesta" (*Woman* 51), had offered early examples of woman's capacity to be self-sufficing. In her era, she rejoiced that "the female Greek of our day is as much in the street as the male, to cry, What News?" ("The Great Lawsuit" 13). Wollstonecraft had been a useful model for women, for among other qualities having made a marriage in which "minds are linked" (Fuller, "The Great Lawsuit" 28). De Stael was worth emulating because "[s]he could not forget the woman in the thought, while she was instructing you as a mind" (Fuller, "The Great Lawsuit" 34). George Sand "did not care whether she were brother or sister." Sand was one "who will speak now and cannot be silenced." These were figures who had made it "easier [for women] to lead true lives" (Fuller, *Woman* 76-7).

Caroline Healey Dall may have acquired strength when she heard Fuller speak of the fact that "the electrical, the magnetic element in Woman has not been fairly brought out at any period," and that "[e]verything might be expected from it" (Fuller, *Woman* 103). She took heart when Fuller maintained that despite taking pride in their history, "[w]omen who combine this organization with creative genius are very commonly unhappy at present" (Fuller, *Woman* 103). It seemed to Caroline that Fuller saw into her and the dilemmas crushing her spirit. It became her destiny to keep the Fuller courage alive and to reintroduce Fuller's name so that in the new century she would be among those whose names were familiar to women. Dall would assure that Fuller's work "has gone steadily on" (Dall, *Historical Pictures* 212).

This work continues. Margaret Fuller and her representative women remind us forcefully of it: Their shortcomings and insecurities, their successes and failures as individuals, tell us that our own grapplings are not restricted to ourselves alone or to this time, that self-doubt and friction mark the course of women's progressive growth and development. Their inquiry into woman's nature and place is ours. Fuller's circle includes all of us.

Works Cited

Banner, Lois. *In Full Flower: Aging Women, Power, and Sexuality*. New York: Alfred Knopf, 1992.

Child, Lydia Maria. *The American Frugal Housewife*. 1829. Revised ed. Boston: Carter, Hendee & Co., 1835.

—. *An Appeal in Favor of Americans Called Africans*. 1833. New York: Arno Press, 1968.

—. *The Collected Correspondence of Lydia Maria Child*. Eds. Patricia Holland and Milton Meltzer. Millwood, New York: N.p., 1979.

—, ed. *Incidents in the Life of a Slave Girl, Written by Herself*. By Harriet Jacobs. 1861. Cambridge: Harvard UP, 1987.

—. *Lydia Maria Child: Selected Letters, 1817-1880*. Eds. Milton Meltzer and Patricia Holland. Amherst: U of Massachusetts P, 1982.

—. *Toward Sunset: Essays & Stories*. Boston: Ticknor and Fields, 1866.

—. "What is Beauty?" *The Dial*. 3.4 (April 1843).

Chodorow, Nancy. *The Reproduction of Mothering: Psychological Analysis and the Sociology of Gender*. Berkeley: UCP, 1978.

Dall, Caroline Healey. "To Ednah Dow Littlehale Cheney." 13 Nov. 1837. In Folder 7, Ednah Dow Littlehale Cheney Papers. Boston Public Library.

—. *Historical Pictures Retouched*. Boston: Walker, Wise & Co., 1860.

—. *Life of Dr. Anandabai Joshee*. Boston: Roberts Bros., 1888.

—. *Romance of the Association, or One Last Glimpse of Charlotte Temple and Eliza Wharton*. Cambridge: John Wilson & Son, 1875.

—. *Transcendentalism in New England, A Lecture*. Boston: Roberts Bros., 1897.

Davis, Angela. *Women, Race and Class*. New York: Random House, 1983.

Fort, Bernadette. *Fictions of the French Revolution*. Illinois: Northwestern UP, 1991.

Fuller, Margaret Ossoli. *Memoirs*. Eds. W. H. Channing, J. F. Clarke, F. H. Hedge, R. W. Emerson. Vol. I. Boston: Phillips, Sampson and Co., 1852.

—. *Summer on the Lakes in 1843*. 1844. N.p.: Nieuwkoop B. DeGraaf, 1972.

—. "The Great Lawsuit: Man vs. Men, Woman vs. Women." *The Dial*. 4.1. (July 1843).

—. *Woman in the Nineteenth Century*. 1845. Ed. Madeleine Stern. Columbia: U of South Carolina P, 1980.

Lerner, Gerda. *The Creation of Patriarchy*. New York: Oxford UP, 1986.

Matthews, Glenna. *Just a Housewife: The Rise and Fall of Domesticity in America*. New York: Oxford UP, 1987.

Joel Myerson. "Remembrances of Margaret Fuller by Caroline Healey Dall." *Harvard Library Bulletin*. 22.4. (Fall 1974).

Peabody, Elizabeth Palmer. *Lectures to Kindergartners*. Boston: D. C. Heath and Co., 1888.

—. *Letters of Elizabeth Palmer Peabody, American Renaissance Woman*. Ed. Bruce Ronda. Wesleyan, Ct: Wesleyan UP, 1984.

—. *Remembrances of William Ellery Channing*. Boston: Roberts Bros., 1880.

—. "A Review of Alcott's Conversations." *The Register and Observer*, n.d.

Rich, Adrienne. *Of Woman Born: Motherhood as Experience and Institution*. New York: Bantam Books, 1976.

Rose, Anne C. *Transcendentalism as a Social Movement, 1830-1850.* New Haven: Yale UP, 1981.

Rusk, Ralph. *The Letters of Ralph Waldo Emerson.* New York: Columbia UP, 1939.

Smith, Sidonie. *A Poetics of Women's Autobiography.* Bloomington: Indiana UP, 1987.

Urbanski, Marie Olesen. "The Ambivalence of Ralph Waldo Emerson Towards Margaret Fuller." *Thoreau Journal Quarterly.* 10.3 (July 1978).

Walker, Alice. *In Search of Our Mothers' Gardens.* New York: Harvest, 1984.

Woolf, Virginia. *A Room of One's Own.* New York: Harcourt, Brace, Jovanovich, Inc., 1929.

Marie Mitchell Olesen Urbanski

Afterword
Woman in the
Nineteenth Century

A FTER HAVING BEGUN my study of *Woman in the Nineteenth Century* more than twenty years ago, I still conclude that Margaret Fuller's treatise is a work of genius. I can write now—what I did not feel free to write then—that similar problems of *audience* confronted Fuller as confronted me. Adrienne Rich in "When We Dead Awaken" hopes for a time of "awakening consciousness" when women no longer would be haunted "by internalized fears of being and saying themselves." She discusses problems a woman writer has to overcome with her anxiety about "male judgment," explaining that "no male writer has written primarily for women" but every female writer writes for men, even when ostensibly addressing women. Obviously, a woman like Fuller trained in "lady-like" deference and decorum, skilled at serving as a "looking-glass" with, as Virginia Woolf expressed it, "the magic" to reflect "the figure of man at twice its natural size," faces a dilemma. She has a conflict which any woman speaking out against the injustice of men faces since acknowledging male oppression diminishes rather than magnifies their stature. Therefore, Fuller in *Woman* uses a pattern of conciliation followed by a radical idea and then reassurance as to the implications of her suggestion.

As Dale Spender so lucidly explained in *Man Made Language*, women writers had to confront the contradictions of a dual male/female reality. Fuller used woman's speaking style, at times writing with qualifiers, at times writing obliquely, while at the same time, she transcended her own self-doubt in *Woman*.

An interesting connection that now can be made is that the transcendental organic theory of literary art is very much like that which contemporary theorists consider feminine style, with its subjective, autobiographical voice. Rather than adhering to syllogisms, women write impressionistically in patchwork; rather than adhering to authority, they listen to their intuition. So, too, did the transcendentalists, with a theory of literary art in the prophetic mode that Margaret Fuller and Ralph Waldo Emerson created.

Elizabeth Hardwick in *Seductions and Betrayals* and Dale Spender in *The Writing or the Sex?* pointed out the double bind women writers felt. Fuller knew she had not only to meet the publishing rules laid down by men but also to give freely of her intellectual energy and writing skills to men. Emerson was not the only writer of his era to avail himself of Fuller's genius. Although this has not been acknowledged by most Thoreau scholars, Henry David Thoreau is very much in Fuller's debt. She saw him in Staten Island, New York, when she stopped there on her way back from her Great Lakes tour that engendered *Summer on the Lakes*. Even the title of *A Week on the Concord and Merrimack Rivers* which he wrote soon afterwards echoes *Summer*. Thoreau's work about a river camping trip is similar to

Fuller's travel piece as it contains many digressions, historical and scientific notes, Indian legends, anecdotes, poetry, and even an oblique reference to her—"I know a woman who possesses a restless and intelligent mind . . ." (296). Moreover, in *Walden* he writes his spiritual autobiography as did Fuller in *Woman in the Nineteenth Century*. He shows how a man could live cheaply while meditating, reading, and writing. And in *Walden*, he develops as a major theme her observation: "He presented a striking instance how men, for the sake of getting, forget to live" (*Summer* 240), and also adopts "Jonathan" as the generic American as she did in *Summer*.

Edgar Allan Poe, who was acquainted with her in New York literary salons, quoted from *Summer* in a discussion of her prose style, and applied some of her concepts from the "Seeress of Prevorst" account to his cosmological prose poem *Eureka*. Poe uses the word "electrical," in the way Fuller interpreted it as a feminine attribute, opposite the male "gravitational." According to Poe, the two ruling principles of the universe were *attraction* and *repulsion*. He equated attraction with gravity and the material, and repulsion with electricity and the spiritual. In *Eureka*, Poe travels within the Sunsphere to a universe diffused into black holes awaiting another Big Bang.

Herman Melville, too, was well aware of Margaret Fuller. As a columnist for the *New York Tribune*, Fuller reviewed his *Typee* favorably. Melville, too, decried the exploitation of native people by "Christian" missionaries, and showed respect for non-Caucasian races. He begins *Moby Dick* with the subjective—"Call me Ishmael"—and catalogues whales whereas Fuller catalogues women. In *Moby Dick* he challenges Manifest Destiny, by extending Americans' exploitation of the natural world from the prairies to the oceans. Melville had an intense relationship with Nathaniel Hawthorne who profited from his friendship with Fuller. Her writings were a source of inspiration to Hawthorne. He was so fascinated with Fuller and her feminist ideas that he devoted much of the two romance novels—*The Scarlet Letter* and *The Blithedale Romance*—to crusading against independent, sensuous women personified by Margaret Fuller. Although I have discussed this subject in my book, *Margaret Fuller's Woman in the Nineteenth Century* much more study needs to be devoted to ways in which the major writers of the American Renaissance adapted Fuller's ideas and literary style to their own ends. She was not a "whetstone of genius" but a wellspring which sated the thirst of male writers.

Woman in the Nineteenth Century so long considered obscure has today as it had twenty-five years ago, as it had one hundred and fifty years ago, inspiration for the discerning eye.

Appendix

Margaret Fuller's Translations from Goethe

Johann Wolfgang von Goethe
(Translation by Margaret Fuller)

The New Paris

THE NIGHT BEFORE WHITSUNDAY I dreamed that I stood before a mirror, examining the new summer clothes which my kind parents had ordered to be made for me to wear on that occasion. This dress consisted, as you know, in handsome leather shoes, with large silver buckles, fine cotton stockings, black sarsnet trowsers, and a green coat with gold trimmings. The vest of gold stuff was cut out of the vest my father wore at his wedding. My hair was curled and powdered, so that the locks stood out from my head like wings. But I could not manage to finish dressing myself, for always one thing would fall off as I put on another. While I was in this dilemma came up a handsome young man and accosted me in the most friendly manner. "Ey, you are welcome," said I, "I am delighted to see you here." "You know me then," said he with a smile. "Why not," said I, smiling also, "you are Mercury; I have often seen your picture." "Yes," said he, "that is my name, and the gods have sent me to you with an important commission. Do you see these three apples?" He stretched out his hand and showed me the three apples, so large that he could hardly hold them, and very beautiful, one red, one green, and one yellow. I thought them jewels to which the form of those fruits had been given. I wished to take hold of them, but he drew back, saying, "you must first understand that they are not intended for yourself. You must give them to the three handsomest young men in the city, who then, each according to his lot, shall find consorts such as they would wish. Take them and do well what I ask of you." So saying he put the apples into my hands and went away. They seemed to me to have grown larger; I held them up to the light and found that they were transparent. As I looked at them they lengthened out into three beautiful, beautiful ladies, not larger than dolls, whose clothes were each of the color of her apple. They glided gently up my fingers, and, as I tried to grasp them, or at least to hold fast some one of the three, floated up into the air. I stood astonished, holding up my hands and looking at my fingers as if there were still somewhat to be seen there. Suddenly appeared dancing on the points of my fingers a lovely maiden, smaller than the others, but elegantly shaped and very lively. She did not fly away like the others, but kept dancing up and down while I stood looking at her. But at last she pleased me so much that I tried to lay hold of her, when I received a blow on the head which felled me to the earth, where I lay senseless till the hour came to get ready for church.

During the service, and at my grandfather's, where I dined, I thought over again and again what I had seen. In the afternoon I went to a friend's house, partly to show myself in my new dress, my hat under my arm, and my sword by my side, partly because I owed a visit there. I did not find the family at home, and hearing that they had gone to their garden, I thought I would follow and enjoy the afternoon with them. My way led past the prison to that place which is justly named that of the bad wall, for it is never quite safe there. I walked slowly, thinking of my three goddesses, and still more of the little nymph; often, indeed, I held up my finger, hoping she would have the politeness to balance herself on it. While engaged with these thoughts, my attention was arrested by a little door in the wall, which I could not recollect ever to have seen before. It looked very low, but the tallest man could have passed through the arch above it. Both arch and wall were most elegantly ornamented with carving and sculpture, but the door especially attracted my attention. It was of an ancient brown wood, very little adorned, but girt with broad bands of iron, on whose metal foliage sat the most natural seeming birds. But what struck me most was that I saw neither key-hole, latch, nor knocker; and I thought the door could be opened only from within. I was right, for as I drew nearer and put my hand upon the ornaments, it opened, and a man appeared, whose dress was very long, wide, and of singular fashion. A venerable beard flowed on his breast, which made me fancy he might be a Jew. But he, as if he guessed my thought, made the sign of the holy cross, thus giving me to understand that he was a good Catholic. "How came you here, young gentleman, and what do you want?" said he with friendly voice and gesture. "I am admiring," said I, "the workmanship of this door; I have never seen anything like it, though there must be specimens in the cabinets of amateurs." "I am glad," said he, "that you like the work. But the door is much more beautiful on the inner side; come in and examine it, if you like." I did not feel particularly easy as to this invitation. The singular dress of the porter, my solitary disposition, and a certain something in the atmosphere disturbed me. I delayed therefore, under the pretext of looking a little longer at the outside, and stole a glance into the garden, for it was a garden which lay behind the wall. Immediately opposite the door I saw a square, so overshadowed by ancient lindens, planted at regular distances one from another that a very numerous company could have been sheltered there. Already I was upon the threshold, and the old man easily allured me a step farther. Indeed I did not resist, for I had always understood that a prince or sultan would not in such a situation inquire whether he was in any danger. And had I not a sword by my

Johann Wolfgang von Goethe

side, and should I not easily be even with the old man, if he should manifest a hostile disposition? So I went confidently in, and he put to the door, which fastened so easily that I scarcely observed it. He then showed me the delicate workmanship of the door within, and seemed really very kind. Quite set at ease by this, I went yet farther to look at the leaf-work of the wall, and admired it very much. I saw many niches adorned with shells, corals, and minerals, also Tritons spouting water into marble basins, cages with birds and squirrels, Guinea pigs running up and down, and all sorts of such pretty creatures. The birds kept calling and singing to us as we walked, especially the starlings said the oddest things; one would call Paris, Paris, and the other Narciss, Narciss, as plain as any schoolboy could speak. I thought the old man looked earnestly at me whenever the birds called him these names, but I pretended not to observe him; indeed I was too busy with other matters to think much about it, for I perceived that we were going round and that the lindens inclosed a circle, probably much more interesting. We reached the door, and the old man seemed inclined to let me out, but my eyes were fixed on a golden lattice which I now saw surrounded the middle of this marvellous garden, though the old man had tried to hide it by keeping me next the wall. As he was about to open the door, I said to him with a low reverence, "you have been so very polite to me, that I venture on asking one other favor before I go. Might I look nearer at the golden grate which seems to surround the centre of the garden?" "Certainly," he replied, "if you will submit to the conditions." "What are they?" I asked hastily. "You must leave behind your hat and sword, and I must keep hold of your hand all the while." "Willingly," cried I, laying my hat and sword on the nearest stone bench. He then seized my right hand and drew me forward with force. When we came near the grate, my admiration was changed into astonishment; nothing like it had I ever seen! On a high ledge of marble stood innumerable spears and partizans arranged side by side, whose singularly ornamented upper ends formed a fence. I looked through the interstices, and saw water flowing gently in a marble channel, in whose clear current I saw many gold and silver fishes, which sometimes singly, sometimes in numbers, sometimes slow, and sometimes quickly, moved hither and thither. Now I wanted to look beyond this canal and see what was going on in the heart of the garden; but I found to my great trouble, that there was on the opposite side a similar grate, and so made, that there was a spear or a partizan opposite to every interstice of the one at which I stood, so that, look what way I would, I could see nothing beyond it. Beside, the old man held me so fast that I could not move with any freedom. But the more I saw the more curious I grew, and I summoned up courage to ask if I could not pass the grates. "Why not?" said he, "yet are there new conditions." When I asked what they were, he gave me to understand that I must change my dress. I consented, and he conducted me to a neat little room near the wall, on whose walls hung many dresses, in fashion very like the oriental costume. I was soon drest in one, and my guide to my horror, shook all the powder out of my hair, and stroked it back under a variegated net. I looked in a large mirror and was well pleased with my new apparel, which, I thought, became me far more than my stiff Sunday dress. I made some gestures and leaps, like what I had seen at the theatre at the time of that fair. Looking in the glass as I did this, I saw behind me a niche, where on a white ground with some green cords, wound up in a way I did not understand. I asked the old man about it, and he very politely took down a cord and showed it to me. It was a green silk cord of some strength, whose ends drawn through two cuts in a piece of green morocco, gave it the air of being intended for no very agreeable purpose. This disturbed me, and I asked the old man what it meant. He answered in a kind and sedate manner, "It is intended for those who abuse the trust that is here shown them." So saying, he hung the noose up again and desired me to follow him. This time he did not take my hand, but left me free.

Johann Wolfgang von Goethe

I was most of all curious to see where the door or bridge might be, by which I was to cross the canal, for I had not been able to find anything of the sort. I therefore looked earnestly at the golden grate as we went up to it, but I almost lost the power of sight, when suddenly spears, halberds, and partizans began to rattle and shake, and at last all their points sank downwards, just as if two squadrons, armed in the old-fashioned way with pikes, were to rush upon one another. Eyes and ears could scarcely endure the clash and confusion. But when they were all lowered, they covered the canal, making the finest of bridges, and the gayest garden lay before me. It was divided into many beds, which formed a labyrinth of ornaments, all set in green borders of a low, woolly plant, which I never saw before. Each bed was of some particular sort of flower, and all of kinds that grow but little way from the ground, so that the eye could pass with ease over the whole parterre and take in its design. This beautiful scene, now lying in full sunshine, completely captivated my eyes. The winding paths were of a pure blue sand, which seemed to represent on earth a darker sky, or a sky in the water. In these I walked, my eyes cast downwards, sometimes by the side of the old man, till at last I perceived in the midst of this flower garden a circle of cypresses or poplar-shaped trees, through which the eye could not penetrate, because their lower branches seemed to come directly from the ground. My guide led me into this circle, and how was I surprised to find there a pavilion supported by pillars, with entrances on every side. Even more than the sight of this beautiful building enchanted me the celestial music that proceeded from it. Sometimes I seemed to hear a harp, sometimes a lute, sometimes a guitar, and at intervals a tinkling unlike any of these instruments. We went to one of the doors, which opened at a slight touch from the old man. How astonished was I to see in the portress a perfect likeness of the pretty little maiden, who in the dream had danced on my fingers. She greeted me with the air of an acquaintance, and asked me to come in. The old man remained

without, and I went with her through an arched and highly ornamented passage, into the saloon, whose fine, lofty dome immediately
excited my attention and wonder. Yet my eyes were soon diverted
by a charming spectacle. On a carpet spread directly underneath the
cupola, sat three women in the three corners, drest in the three different colors, one red, the second yellow, the third green; the seats were
gilt, the carpet a perfect flower-bed. They held the three instruments
which I had been able to distinguish from without, but had stopped
playing on my entrance. "You are welcome," said she who sat in the
middle facing the door, drest in red, and holding the harp. "Sit down
beside Alerte and listen, if you love music. Now I saw a rather long
bench placed obliquely, on which lay a mandolin. The little maiden
took it, sat down, and called me to her side. The I looked at the lady
on my right, she wore the yellow dress, and had a guitar in her hand.
And as the harp player was of a stately shape, dignified aspect, and
majestic mien, so was the guitar player gay, light, and attractive in her
appearance and manner. She was slender and flaxen haired, the other
had dark chestnut tresses. But the variety and harmony of their music
could not prevent my fixing my attention on the beauty in green,
whose performance on the lute seemed to me peculiarly admirable
and moving. She it was also, who seemed to pay most heed to me,
and to direct her playing to me, yet I knew not what to make of her,
for she seemed sometimes tender, sometimes whimsical, sometimes
frank, and then again capricious, according as she varied her playing
and her gestures. Sometimes she seemed desirous to move me, sometimes as if she made a jest of me. But do what she would she won
little on me, for my little neighbor, by whom I sat elbow to elbow,
charmed me, and seeing in the three ladies the sylphides of my dream,
and the colors of the three apples, I well understood, that they were
not to be obtained by me. I should willingly have laid hold of the
little one, had I not too well remembered the box of the ear with
which she had repulsed me in the dream. Hitherto she had not used

her mandolin, but when her mistresses had finished, they bid her play some lively air. Scarcely had she begun the merry dancing tune, than she jumped up. I did the same. She played and danced. I imitated her steps, and we performed a sort of little ballet, with which the ladies seemed to be well pleased; for when we had finished, they bade the little maid give me something good, to refresh me until supper should be prepared. Alerte led me back into the passage through which I had come. It had at the sides two well arranged room, in one in which she lived she set before me oranges, figs, peaches, and grapes, and I enjoyed with keen appetite the fruits of foreign lands and of this season. There was also confectionery in abundance, and she filled for me a crystal cup of foaming wine, but I had sufficiently refreshed myself with the fruit, and did not need it. "Now let us go and play," said she, and led me into the other room. Here it looked like a Christmas market, yet at none did you ever see such splendid, elegant things. There were all sorts of dolls, doll's clothes and furniture, kitchens, parlors, and shops, and single playthings innumerable. She led me about to all the glass cases in which these fine things were kept. But the first one she soon shut, saying, I know you will not care for these matters. From this next we might take building blocks, and make a great city of walls and towers, houses, palaces, and churches. But I don't like that; we must find something which may entertain us both." She then brought some boxes, full of the prettiest little soldiers that ever were seen. She took one of these and gave me the other. "We will go to the golden bridge," Said she, "that is the best place to play with soldiers, the spears make lines on which it is easy to arrange the armies." When we reached the golden floor, I heard the water ripple, and the fishes plash beneath me, as I knelt down to arranges my lines. All the soldiers were on horseback. She boasted of the Queen of the Amazons with her host of female troopers, while I had Achilles, and a squadron of stately Greek horsemen. The armies stood opposite one another. Never was seen anything finer. These were not flat, leaden

horsemen, like ours, but both man and horse round and with perfect
bodies, worked out in the most delicate manner. It was not easy to
understand how they kept their balance so perfectly, for each stood by
itself without the aid of a foot-board.

After we had surveyed them for a while with great satisfaction, she
gave the signal for the attack. We had found artillery in the chests,
namely, boxes full of polished agate balls. With these we were to fight
at a given distance, but under the express condition, that no ball was
to be thrown with force enough to hurt a figure, only to throw it
down. For a while, the cannonade went on agreeably enough. But,
when my antagonist observed that I aimed truer than she, and was
likely to beat her, she drew nearer, and then her girlish way of
throwing the balls was very successful. She threw down my best men
in crowds, and the more I protested, the more zealously she threw her
balls. This vexed me, and I declared I would do the same. Then I not
only went nearer, but in my anger threw my balls so violently, that
two of her little centauresses were snapt in pieces. In her eagerness
she, at first, did not remark this; but I stood petrified, as the broken
figures, joining together again, and becoming a living whole, left the
golden bridge at full gallop, and after running to and fro as in the lists,
were lost, I knew not how, against the wall. My pretty antagonist no
sooner was aware of this, than she broke out into loud weeping and
wailing. She cried, that I had been to her the cause of an irreparable
loss, far greater than she could say. But I, who was in a passion, was
rejoiced to vex her, and threw a couple more balls with blind fury
into her army. Unluckily I hit the Queen, who was not engaged in
our regular play. She fell in pieces, and her adjutants were also
shattered, but they recovered themselves like the others, galloped
through the lindens, and were lost against the wall.

My antagonist scolded and abused me, while I stooped to pick up
other balls, which were rolling about on the golden spears. In my
anger, I should have destroyed her army, but she sprang upon me, and

Johann Wolfgang von Goethe
gave my ears a box which made my head resound. I, who had always
heard, that when a maiden boxes your ears, a good kiss to follow,
seized her head in my hands and kissed her again and again. But she
screamed so loudly, that she frightened me, and luckily I let her go,
for at that moment the flooring began to quake and rattle. I observed
the grate was rising, and was fearful of being spitted on one of the
spears, as indeed the partizans and lances, as they rose up, did tear my
clothes. I scarcely know how I got away. I lost my sight and hearing.
When I recovered, I found myself at the foot of a linden, against
which the now erected barricade had thrown me. My anger was
again aroused by the jests and laughter of my antagonist, who probably had fallen more gently on the other side of the grate. I jumped
up, and seeing my little army had been thrown down with me, seized
Achilles, and threw him against a tree. His recovery and flight pleased
me doubly, as gratifying my resentment, and giving me the prettiest
sight in the world, and I should have sent all his Greeks after him, but
that at once water began to spout and sprinkle from the wall, stones,
branches, and ground, wetting me on every side. My light robe was
soon wet through; it was torn before, and I did not hesitate to cast it
from me. Then I threw off my slippers, and piece by piece all the rest
of my apparel, and began to think it very pleasant to have a shower
bath on so warm a day.

I then walked up and down with a grave, dignified mien, amid this
welcome water, and enjoyed myself highly. As my anger cooled I
wished nothing more than to make peace with the pretty maiden.
But now in an instant the water ceased to spout, and I stood dripping
on the wet ground. The presence of the old man, who now approached me, was far from welcome. I wished I could, if not hide,
yet at least cover myself. Ashamed, shivering, trying in some way to
cover myself, I made but a pitiful figure; and the old man took the
occasion to reproach me severely. "What hinders me," cried he,

"from using the green cord if not upon your neck, at least upon your back?" I was much incensed by this threat. "You had best," cried I, "avoid such words, or even such thoughts, if you would not ruin yourself and your mistresses. "Who are you," said he, contemptuously, "that you should presume to speak thus?" "A darling of the gods," said I, "on whom it depends, whether those ladies shall find proper bridegrooms, or whether they shall languish away and grow old in this magical cloister." The old man drew back several steps. "Who has revealed this to thee?" asked he, astonished and thoughtful. "Three apples," said I, "three jewels." "And what dost thou ask as a reward?" said he. "Above all things, I replied, "the little creature who has brought me into this annoying situation." The old man threw himself on his knees before me, without regarding the wet and mud; then he rose, quite dry, and taking me affectionately by the hand, led me into the dressing room, and assisted me to put on my Sunday clothes, and dress my hair. He said no word more, but as he let me out, directed my attention by signs to the opposite wall, and then again to the little door. I understood well that he wished I should impress these objects on my memory, in order that I might be able again to find the door, which shut suddenly behind me. I now looked attentively at the opposite side. Above a high wall rose the boughs of some ancient walnut trees, partly covering the cornice which finished it. They reached to a stone tablet, whose ornamental border I could perceive, but could not read what was inscribed upon it. It rested on the projection of a niche into which an artificially wrought fountain poured its waters from cup to cup, into a basin, as large as a little pond, imbedded in the earth. Fountain, tablet, walnut-trees, stood directly one above the other. I could paint the spot just as I saw it.

You may imagine how I passed this evening, and many following days, and how often I repeated to myself the particulars of this history, which I myself can hardly believe. As soon as possible I went in search of the place, in order at least to refresh my memory, and look once more at the wonderful door. But, to my astonishment, I found things much changed. Walnuts rose indeed above the wall, but not near one another. There was a tablet, but far to the right of the trees, and with a legible inscription. A niche on the left hand contains a fountain, but one not to be compared with that I saw the other time, so that I was ready to believe the second adventure as much a dream as the first, for of the door I found no trace. The only thing that comforts me is to observe, that these three objects seem constantly to be changing place, for in my frequent visits I think I see that trees, tablet and fountain seem to be drawing nearer together. Probably when they get into their places, the door will once more be visible, and I will then attempt to take up again the thread of the adventures. I cannot say whether it may be in my power to tell you the sequel, or whether it may not expressly be forbidden me.

This tale, of whose truth my companions were passionately desirous to convince themselves, was greatly applauded. They visited singly, without confiding their intention to me or to each other, the spot I had indicated, found the walnuts, the tablet and the fountain, but at a distance from one another. They at last confessed it, for at that age, it is not easy to keep a secret. But here was the beginning of strife. One declared the objects never changed their places, but preserved always the same distance from one another. The second, that they changed, and the third agreed that they moved, but thought they approached one another. A fourth had seen something still more remarkable, the walnut-trees in the midst, and tablet and fountain on the sides oppo-site the spot where I had seen them. About the door they varied as much in their impression. And thus I had an early example how men, in cases quite simple and easy of decision, form and maintain the most contrary opinions. As I obstinately refused a sequel to the adventure, a repetition of this first part was frequently solicited. I took care never materially to vary the circumstances, and the uniformity of the narration converted fable into truth for my hearers. (*Dial* 2: 8-17)

Margaret Fuller

[On Goethe's *Iphigenie auf Tauris*]

HERE IS AN ENGLISH TRANSLATION (I know not how good) of Goethe's Iphigenia. But as it may not be generally known, I will give a sketch of the drama. Iphigenia, saved at the moment of the sacrifice made by Agamemmnon in behalf of the Greeks, by the goddess, and transferred to the temple at Tauris, appears alone in the consecrated grove. Many years have passed since she was severed from the home of such a tragic fate, the palace of Mycenae. Troy had fallen, Agamemmnon been murdered, Orestes had grown up to avenge his death. All these events were unknown to the exiled Iphigenia. The priestess of Diana in a barbarous land, she had passed the years in the duties of the sanctuary, and in acts of beneficence. She had acquired great power over the mind of Thoas, king of Tauris, and used it to protect strangers, whom it had previously been the custom of the country to sacrifice to the goddess.

She salutes us with a soliloquy, of which this is a rude translation.

On Goethe's Iphigenie auf Tauris

Beneath your shade, living summits
Of this ancient, holy, thick-leaved grove,
    As in the silent sanctuary of the Goddess,
Still I walk with those same shuddering feelings
    As when I trod these walks for the first time.
My spirit cannot accustom itself to these places,
    Many years now has kept me here concealed
A higher will to which I am submissive;
    Yet ever am I, as at first, the stranger
For ah! the sea divides me from the beloved ones;
    And on the shore whole days I stand,
Seeking with my soul the land of the Greeks,
    And to my sighs brings the rushing wave only
Its hollow tones in answer.
    Woe to him who, far from parents, and brothers, and sisters,
Drags on a lonely life. Grief consumes
    The nearest happiness away from his lips;
His thoughts crowd downwards—
    Seeking the hall of his fathers, where the Sun
First opened heaven to him, and kindred-born
    In the first plays knit daily firmer and firmer
The bond from heart to heart.—I question not the Gods,
    Only the lot of woman is one for sorrow;
In the house and in the war man rules,
    Knows how to help himself in foreign lands.
Possessions gladden and victory crowns him,
    And an honorable death stands ready to end his days.
Within what narrow limits is bounded the luck of woman!
    To obey a rude husband even is duty and comfort;—how sad
When, instead, a hostile fate drives her out of her sphere.
    So holds me Thoas, indeed a noble man, fast
In solemn, sacred, but slavish bonds.
    O with shame I confess that with secret reluctance
I serve thee, Goddess, thee, my deliverer;

My life should freely have been dedicate to thee,
But I have always been hoping in thee, O Diana,
   Who didst take in they soft arms me, the rejected daughter
Of the greatest king; yes, daughter of Zeus,
   I thought if thou gavest such anguish to him, the high hero,
The godlike Agamemmnon;
   Since he brought his dearest, a victim to thy altar,
That, when he should return, crowned with glory, from Ilium,
   At the same time thou shouldst give to his arms his other treasures,
His spouse, Electra, and the princely son,
   Me also thou wouldst restore to mine own,
Saving a second time me, whom from death thou didst save,
   From this worse death, the life of exile here.

These are the words and thoughts, but how give an idea of the sweet simplicity of expression in the original, where every word has the grace and softness of a flower petal.

She is interrupted by a messenger from the king, who prepares her for a visit from himself of a sort she has dreaded. Thoas, who has always loved her, now left childless by the calamities of war, can no longer resist his desire to reanimate by her presence his desert house. He begins by urging her to tell him the story of her race, which she does in a way that makes us feel as if that most famous tragedy had never before found a voice, so simple, so fresh in its naiveté is the recital.

Thoas urges his suit undismayed by the fate that hangs over the race of Tantalus.

   Was it the same Tantalus,
Whom Jupiter called to his council and banquets,
   In whose talk so deeply experienced, full of various learning,
The Gods delighted as in the speech of oracles?

On Goethe's Iphigenie auf Tauris

IPHIGENIA

It is the same, but the Gods should not
   Converse with men, as with their equals.
The mortal race is much too weak
   Not to turn giddy on unaccustomed heights.
He was not ignoble, neither a traitor,
   But for a servant too great, and as a companion
Of the great Thunderer only a man. So was
   His fault also that of a man, its penalty
Severe, and poets sing-Presumption
   And faithlessness cast him down from the throne of Jove
Into the anguish of ancient Tartarus;
   Ah, and all his race bore their hate.

THOAS

Bore it the blame of its ancestor or its own?

IPHIGENIA

Truly the vehement breast and powerful life of the Titan
Were the assured inheritance of son and grandchild,
   But the Gods bound their brows with a brazen band,
Moderation, counsel, wisdom, and patience
   Were his from their wild, gloomy glance,
Each desire grew to fury,
   And limitless ranged their passionate thoughts.

Iphigenia refuses with gentle firmness to give to gratitude what was undue. Thoas leaves her in anger, and, to make her feel it, orders that the old barbarous custom be renewed, and two strangers just arrived be immolated at Diana's altar.

Iphigenia, though distressed, is not shaken by this piece of tyranny. She trusts her heavenly protectress will find some way for her to save these unfortunates without violating her truth.

The strangers are Orestes and Pylades, sent thither by the oracle of Apollo, who bade them go to Tauris and bring back "the Sister," thus shall the heaven-ordained parricide of Orestes be expiated, and the Furies cease to pursue him.

The Sister they interpret to be Diana, Apollo's sister, but Iphigenia, sister to Orestes, is really meant.

The next act contains scenes of most delicate workmanship, first between the light-hearted Pylades, full of worldly resource and ready tenderness, and the suffering Orestes, of far nobler, indeed heroic nature, but less fit for the day, and more for the ages. In the first scene the characters of both are brought out with great skill, and the nature of the bond between "the butterfly and the dark flower" distinctly shown in few words.

The next scene is between Iphigenia and Pylades. Pylades, though he truly answers the questions of the priestess about the fate of Troy and the house of Agamemmnon, does not hesitate to conceal from her who Orestes really is, and manufactures a tissue of useless falsehoods with the same readiness that the wise Ulysses showed in exercising his ingenuity on similar occasions.

It is said, I know not how truly, that the modern Greeks are Ulyssean in this respect, never telling straight-forward truth, when deceit will answer the purpose; and if they tell any truth, practising the economy of the king of Ithaca, in always reserving a part for their own use. The character which this denotes is admirably hit off with few strokes in Pylades, the fair side of whom Iphigenia thus paints in a later scene.

> Bless, ye Gods, our Pylades,
>   and whatever he may undertake!
> He is the arm of the youth in battle,
>   The light-giving eye of the aged man in the council.
> For his soul is still; it preserves
>   The holy possession of Repose unexhausted,
> And from its depths still reaches
>   Help and advice to those tossed to and fro

On Goethe's Iphigenie auf Tauris

Iphigenia leaves him in sudden agitation, when informed of the death of Agamemmnon. Returning, she finds in his place Orestes, whom she had not before seen, and draws from him by her artless questions the sequel to this terrible drama wrought by his hand. After he has concluded his narrative in the deep tones of cold anguish; she cries,

Immortals, you who your bright days through
Live in bliss throned on clouds ever renewed,
Only for this have you all these years
Kept me separate from men, and so near yourselves,
Given me the childlike employment to cherish the fires on your altars
That my soul might, in like pious clearness,
Be ever aspiring towards your abodes,
That only later and deeper I might feel
The anguish and horror that have darkened my house
O, Stranger
speak to me of the unhappy one, tell me of Orestes.

ORESTES

O might I speak of his death!
Vehement flew up from the reeking blood
His Mother's Soul!
And called to the ancient daughters of Night,
Let not the parricide escape;
Pursue that man of crime. He is yours.
They obey, their hollow eyes
Darting about with vulture eagerness,
They stir themselves in their black dens,
From corners their companions
Doubt and Remorse steal out to join them,
Before them roll the mists of Acheron,
In its cloudy volumes rolls
The eternal contemplation of the irrevocable,
Bewildering round the head of the guilty.

Permitted now in their love of ruin they tread
    The beautiful fields of a God-planted earth,
From which they had long been banished by an early curse.
    Their swift feet follow the fugitive,
They pause never except to gather more power to dismay.

IPHIGENIA

Unhappy man, thou art in like manner tortured,
    And feelest truly what he, the poor fugitive, suffers!

ORESTES

What sayest thou, what meanest of "like manner."

IPHIGENIA

Thee, too, the weight of fratricide crushes to earth; the tale
    I had from thy younger brother.

ORESTES

I cannot suffer that thou, great soul,
    Shouldst be deceived by a false tale,
A web of lies let stranger weave for stranger,
    Subtle with many thoughts, accustomed to craft,
Guarding his feet against a trap;
    But between us
Be Truth;————
    I am Orestes;—and this guilty head
Bent downward to the grave seeks death,
    In any shape were he welcome.
Whoever thou art, I wish thou mightst be saved,
    Thou and my friend; for myself I wish it not.
Thou seem'st against thy will here to remain;
    Invent a way to fly and leave me here, &c.

Like all productions of genius, this may be injured by the slightest change, and I dare not flatter myself that the English words give an idea of the heroic dignity expressed in the cadence of the original by the words

On Goethe's Iphigenie auf Tauris

> "zwischen uns
>
> Sey Wahrheit!
> ICH BIN OREST!"

Where the Greek seems to fold his robe around him in the full strength of classic manhood, prepared for worst and best, not like a cold Stoic, but a hero, who can feel all, know all, and endure all. The name of two syllables in the German is much more forcible for the pause than the three syllable Orestes.

> "between us
>
> Be Truth!"

is fine to my ear, on which our word Truth also pause, with a large dignity.

The scenes go on more and more full of breathing beauty. The lovely joy of Iphigenia, the meditative softness with which the religiously educated mind perpetually draws the inference from the most agitating event, impress us more and more. At last the hour of trial comes. She is to keep off Thoas by a cunningly devised tale, while her brother and Pylades contrive their escape. Orestes has received to his heart the sister long lost, divinely restored, and in the embrace the curse falls from him, he is well, and Pylades more than happy. The ship waits to carry her to the palace home she is to free from a century's weight of pollution, and already the blue heavens of her adored Greece gleam before her fancy.

But oh! the step before all this can be obtained. To deceive Thoas, a savage and a tyrant indeed, but long her protector,–in his barbarous fashion her benefactor. How can she buy life, happiness, or even the safety of those dear ones at such a price!

> "Woe,
>
> O Woe upon the lie. It frees not the breast,

Like the true-spoken word; it comforts not, but tortures
   Him who devised it, and returns,
An arrow once let fly, God-repelled, back
   On the bosom of the Archer!"

   O must I then resign the silent hope
Which gave a beauty to my loneliness?
   Must the curse dwell forever, and our race
Never be raised to life by a new blessing?
   All things decay, the fairest bliss is transient,
The powers most full of life grow faint at last,
   And shall a curse alone boast an incessant life?
Then have I idly hoped that here kept pure,
   So strangely severed from my kindred's lot,
I was designed to come at the right moment,
   And with pure hand and heart to expiate
The many sins that spot my native home.

   To lie, to steal the sacred image!
Olympians, let not these vulture talons
   Seize on the tender breast. O save me,
And save your image in my soul.

   Within my ears resounds the ancient lay,
I had forgotten it, and would so gladly;
   The lay of the Parcae, which they awful sang,
As Tantalus fell from his golden seat
   They suffered with the noble friend, wrathful
Was their heart, and fearful was the song.
   In our childhood the nurse was wont to sing it
To me and the brother and sister. I marked it well.

Then follows the sublime song of the Parcae, well known through translations.

But Iphigenia is not a victim of fate, for she listens steadfastly to the god in her breast. Her lips are incapable of subterfuge. She obeys her own heart, tells all to the king, calls up his better nature, wins, hallows, and purifies all around her, till the heaven-prepared way is cleared by the obedient child of heaven, and the great trespass of Tantalus cancelled by a woman's reliance on the voice of her innocent soul.

If it be not possible to enhance the beauty with which such ideal figures as the Iphigenia and the Antigone appeared to the Greek mind, yet Goethe has unfolded a part of the life of this being, unknown elsewhere in the records of literature. The character of the priestess, the full beauty of virgin womanhood, solitary but tender, wise and innocent, sensitive and self-collected, sweet as spring, dignified as becomes the chosen servant of God, each gesture and word of deep and delicate significance;—where else is such a picture to be found?

It was not the courtier, nor the man of the world, nor the connoisseur, nor the friend of Mephistopheles, nor Wilhelm the Master, nor Egmont the generous free liver, that saw Iphigenia in the world of spirits, but Goethe in his first-born glory, Goethe the poet, Goethe designed to be the keenest star in a new constellation. Let us not in surveying his works and life abide with him too much in the suburbs and outskirts of himself. Let us enter into his higher tendency, thank him for such angels as Iphigenia, whose simple truth mocks at all his wise "Beschrankungen," and hope the hour when, girt about with many such, he will confess, contrary to his opinion, given in his latest days, that it *is* well worth while to live seventy years, if only to find that they are nothing in the light of God. (*Dial* 2:34-41)

Johann Wolfgang von Goethe
(Translation by Margaret Fuller)

Torquato Tasso

Preface by the Translator

IN PRESENTING TO THE PUBLIC this imperfect translation of a very celebrated production of the first German writer, I hope for indulgence from those who are acquainted with the original. There are difficulties attending the translation of German works into English which might baffle one much more skilful in the use of the latter than myself. A great variety of compound words enable the German writer to give a degree of precision and delicacy of shading to his expressions nearly impracticable with the terse, the dignified, but by no means flexible English idiom. The rapid growth of German literature, the concurrence of so many master spirits, all at once fashioning the language into a medium for the communication of their thoughts, has brought it to a perfection which must gradually be impaired, as inferior minds mould and adapt it to their less noble uses. It may become better suited to certain kinds of light writing, but must lose its condensed power of expression, as the English has done.

I may be allowed to quote Mr. Coleridge in apology for a some-what paraphrastical translation, not as presuming to compare mine with his Wallenstein, but to show that this accomplished writer deemed the rendering of the spirit, on the whole, more desirable than that of the letter. I would also shelter myself in the shadow of the same illustrious name with regard to the broken and lengthened lines too frequent in my translation. It is more difficult to polish a translation than an original work, since we are denied the liberty of retrenching or adding where the ear and taste cannot be satisfied. But there *is* no sufficient apology for imperfection. I can only hope by a candid acknowledgment of its existence to propitiate the critic, be-lieving that no setting can utterly mar the lustre of such a gem, or make this perfect work of art unwelcome to the meditative few, even to the tasteful many.

The beautiful finish of style is lost, and in lieu of the many-toned lyre on which the poet originally melodized his inspired conceptions, a hollow-sounding reed is substituted. But the contrasts between the characters, the beauty of composition worthy the genius of ancient statuary, must still be perceptible.

It is, I believe, a novelty to see the mind of a poet analyzed and portrayed by another, who, however, shared the inspiration only of his subject, saved from his weakness by that superb balance of charac-ter in which Goethe surpasses even Milton. This alone would give the piece before us a peculiar interest.

The central situation of Tasso, the manner in which his compan-ions draw him out, and are in turn drawn out by him, the mingled generosity and worldliness of the Realist Antonio, the mixture of taste, feeling, and unconscious feeling in Alphonso, the more delicate but not less decided painting of the two Leonoras, the gradual but irresistible force by which the catastrophe is drawn down upon us, concur to make this drama a model of Art, that art which Goethe worshipped ever after he had exhaled his mental boyhood in Werther.

The following remarks from an essay of A.W. Schlegel are probably new to the reader: "Goethe has painted Tasso from a close study of his works. He has even made use of extracts from his poems. Thus the greater part of what Tasso says about the golden age is taken from the beautiful chorus in the first act of Aminta. Many such things are lost upon those who are not familiar with the poems of Tasso, though they may not be insensible to the exquisite delicacy and care with which the portrait is finished throughout. In the historical circumstances, Goethe has preferred the authority of the Abbe Serassi to the more generally consulted Manso. Serassi denies that the princes ever encouraged Tasso to pass the bounds of deference. Generally it is dangerous to finish a real life by an invented catastrophe, as Schiller has done with regard to the Maid of Orleans; but such clouds of doubt rest on portions of Tasso's life, and what is know of it is so romantic, that more liberty may be taken."

DRAMATIS PERSONÆ

TORQUATO TASSO.
ALPHONSO, *the second Duke of* Ferrara.
ANTONIO MONTECALIVA, *Secretary of State.*
PRINCESS LEONORA, *Sister of the Duke.*
LEONORA SANVITALI, *Countess of* Scandiano.

The Scene *is at* Belriguardo, *a* Villa

TASSO

ACT I.

SCENE I.—A garden ornamented with busts of the epic poets. In front, on the right, is *Virgil*; on the left, *Ariosto*.

The PRINCESS, LEONORA SANVITALI, *with garlands in their hands.*

Prin.   You look at me and smile, my Leonora,
          Then turn away your face and smile again;
          Why do you not express to your companion
          Those pleasing, pensive thoughts.

Leon.   I mused, my princess,
          On the sweet rural peace we now enjoy;
          We live here like the careless shepherdesses,
          And like them pass the hours in weaving garlands.
          See what a variegated wreath is mine!
          How many flowers and buds! But thine is laurel.
          Thy lofty mind could joy in nothing less.

Prin.   And to an honored head I consecrate
          What I have twined amid such happy thoughts;
          To Virgil's.   [*She crowns the bust of* Virgil.

Leon.   And thou, Ludovico,
          Whose fancy like the spring, sportive and blooming,

{ *274* }

   Brought forth such wealth of buds and flowers, thou wilt not
   Disdain my motley offering.   [*She crowns* Ariosto's *bust.*

Prin. My brother has been kind indeed to send us
   Thus early to this dear retreat, where truly
   We live unto ourselves, and, undisturbed,
   Dream back the golden days of poesy.
   Youth's brightest hours I passed at Belriguardo,
   And May-time here gives them to me again.

Leon. Yes; all here smiles in tender youthful beauty;
   The warm airs woo us, and the plashing fountains;
   The heavy shadows of the evergreens
   Are not unwelcome. The young trees and shrubs
   Put forth new leaves with each day's warmer sun;
   And now from every bed flowers turn up to us
   Their loving, childish eyes. The gardener
   Released the citron and the orange trees
   To-day from their confinement. The wide heavens
   Are curtained o'er with one soft sleepy blue,
   Save that the now dissolving snows have edged
   The horizon with their vapors as a border.

Prin. Ah! why must a regret mar all this beauty?
   This lovely spring removes *thee* from my side.

Leon. Remind me not, dear princess, in this hour,
   That I so soon must leave thy gentle presence.

Prin. The city soon shall give thee other pleasures,
   And we shall be forgot.

Leon.   Duty and love
   Now call me to the husband who so long
   Has suffered my delay. I carry him our son,

Whom for a year he has not seen;
I joy that his improved mind and beauty
Will give such pleasure to a father's heart.
But for the rest, there is in splendid Florence
Nought that can vie with dear Ferrara's gems.
Florence is great but through the peoples's wealth;
Ferrara through her princess.

Prin.   Say rather through whose wise men
Whom chance brought hither and good luck detained.

Leon.   Chance scatters that which she alone collected:
Only the noble can attract the noble,
And hold them firmly bound as you have done.
You and your brother have assembled round you
Men worthy of yourselves and your great father,
Who kindled in this palace the twin lights
Of wisdom and of mental freedom, then
Our other realms were sleeping in the night
Of barbarous ignorance. To my childish ear,
Hippolytus and Hercules d'Esti
Were names of magic power. My parents loved
Florence and Rome; my heart turned to Ferrara,
Where Petrarch found a home, and Ariosto models.
Here the great men whom Italy reveres
Have all been entertained with honor due,
And honorably have repaid your kindness,
Sounding abroad the praises of your house.
Your grandchildren will glory in these days
Of splendid hospitality.

Prin.   Yes, if they feel like thee;
I envy thee such happy sensibility.

Act I, Scene 1

Leon.   Nay, thine is happier. How pure and tranquil
        Are thy enjoyments. My full heart impels me
        At once to speak what I so lively feel;
        Thou feel'st it deeper, better, and art silent.
        No meteoric lights can dazzle thee;
        Wit bribes thee not, and flattery wooes in vain,
        Still with fine taste, and as unnerring judgment,
        Thy soul appropriates the great and fair
        In feature new, familiar in the spirit.—

Prin.   It is not well to mask such flattery
        Beneath the guise of friendly confidence.

Leon.   A friend alone can justly praise and prize
        Such worth as thine. But since thou art so modest
        We will impute it to some happy circumstance
        Of education or companionship
        Thou hast it. And thy sister of Urbino
        Stands first amid the women of our day.

Prin.   'Tis true, Leonora, flattery could never
        So swell our hearts if we would call to mind
        How piece by piece we thankless have received
        Our all from others. All that I have learned
        Of ancient lore and speech is from my mother;
        And if in wisdom or in manners either
        Lucretia or myself can be compared
        With such a model, surely 'tis my sister.
        My rank, my name are gifts of a kind fate;
        I joy that I may hear when wise men speak,
        And understandingly receive those words
        Breathed to instruct and elevate their kind.
        Delighted listen I when eloquence

Pours forth the mingled treasures of the breast
Obedient to its glowing impulses. And whether
The poet tunes his lyre to eulogize
The deeds of princes, or philosophers
Refine upon the simplest, obscure action,
My ear is ready, and my mind can follow;
And this indeed is happiness!

Leon.   I too love
The poet's gentle yet inspiring influence,
Thy range is wider. I could live forever
Upon the isle of Poesy, nor weary
Of roaming through its laurel groves.

Prin.   Not laurel only—
The myrtle also decks that beauteous isle,
And in the fair companionship of Muses
May not a lady hope to meet some poet
Who rapturously may recognize in her
The treasure he was seeking far and wide?

Leon.   That arrow glanced aside. The jest doth touch me,
But goes not home. To all I would be just,
And admiration is the due of Tasso.
His inspired eye which roves from earth to heaven,
His ear which drinks the harmonies of Nature;
The past and present have enriched his mind,
And much that Nature scattered far apart
Combines there to a new and beauteous being.
The dead and mute find life and voice,
And daily glow with colors not their own,
And all false pomps fade to their native dulness.
He draws us to him in his magic circle,

    Then he seems near, and yet again so far,
    And oft appears to gaze on us when shapes
    From other worlds stand betwixt us and him.

Prin. Thou givest a faithful picture of the poet
    Enthroned above his shadowy world; but yet
    There *are* realities that *can* attract him.
    Tell me, those sonnets we so often find
    Upon these trees, breathing to us the perfume
    Of new Hesperian fruits, does thou not deem them
    Formed from the blossoms of true love?

Leon.   The songs
    Must charm the hearer; sweetly do they celebrate
    His lovely one; whether the poet raising her
    To heavenly height bows down before his angel,
    Or leads her through the fields of our poor planet,
    Wreathing her brow with earth-born flowers, or when
    As she departs he consecrates the turf
    Her delicate foot has trod, a very nightingale
    He fills each thicket with his soft complaining.

Prin. And when he warbles forth his beauty's name,
    Is it not Leonora?

Leon.   Thy name also!
    A happy ambiguity for him;
    And I am well content that he must thus
    Remember me in such sweet moments. This
    Is not a common love, whose only aim
    Is to possess its object and exclude
    All other worshippers from the chosen shrine.
    His love for thee need not forbid the poet
    From enjoying my lighter mode of being.

Neither of us he loves, if, as I think,
He clusters fancies born in other spheres
Around the chosen name of Leonora.
And even so with us, for we too love
Not Tasso, not the man, but the embodying
Of the soaring and impassioned in our nature.

Prin. Thou art learned in these matters, Leonora
Much thou hast said has only touched my ear,
And links not with my thoughts.

                                  How say'st thou?

Leon. The scholar of Plato cannot understand
A novice like myself. I meant but this—
In modern days Cupid no longer sports
A mischievous, spoiled child. A manly youth,
Husband to Psyche, counsellor to the gods!
No longer skips he with unseemly haste
From heart to heart. With mien and mind sedate
He chooses now his lodging, nor need fear
To repent his whims in sadness and disgust.

Prin. Here comes my brother. Let us not provoke,
By talking on this theme, more of the jests
Our quaint array already has called forth.

SCENE II

The former persons and ALPHONSO.

Alph. Is't possible that here I seek in vain
For Tasso? Where, fair ladies, is the poet?

Act I, Scene 2

Prin.   To-day we have not seen him.

Alph.   He retains then
His ancient love for solitude. But though
We cannot marvel that he would escape
The empty babble of a crowd of worldlings
To seek still converse with his secret spirit,
It is not well that he should feel impatient,
And thus transgress the boundary of a circle
Drawn at the spell of friendship.

Leon.   If I mistake not
Thou wilt soon lay aside all thought of blame.
To-day I saw him walking in the garden,
Carrying his book, and writing in his tablets.
From something that escaped him yester-eve
I think his work is finished, and to-day
He is probably giving the last touches,
And making such corrections as he deems
Needful to fit it for your princely eye.
When he has polished it to perfect symmetry,
He will present it for that approbation
So valuable in his eyes.

Alph.   Most welcome
Shall he be when he brings it, and left free
To his own will long after. Never yet
Have I so much desired the end of any thing.
I feel unceasing interest in its progress;
But he is always altering and improving,
And by his over-anxious care how often
He has deceived my hope!

Prin.   He strives,
Like a true poet, to give fit expression
To the rich breathings of his favorite Muse.
He understands what means the unity,
The well-ordered fabric of a real poem.
A string of sentiments and romantic stories
Following each other without end or aim,
Save to amuse the moment, nor aspiring
To leave a perfect image in the soul,
Cannot content a taste like that of Tasso.
Trouble him not, my brother. Works of beauty
Are not judged by the time that was consumed
In their production. And his private friends
Ought not to ask that he should sacrifice
The interest of so many future ages
To gratify them some poor moments.

Alph.   Dearest,
So let it be as it has ever been;
Thy mildness checks my too great eagerness,
And I give impulse to thy gentle wishes.
But I believe that I am right in wishing
To see the poem we have so admired
Known to our fatherland and to the world.
'Tis time that he should feel new influences:
The solitude he loves has cradled him
Too softly. Praise and blame he should encounter,
Bear both, and learn from both. For it is this
Which forms the manly character. The youth
Called into action both by friend and foe
Will learn to use his utmost strength. 'Tis then
That he may claim to be esteemed a *Man*.

Act I, Scene 2

Leon.   Thou wilt protect him in this novel scene,
       As thou hast ever done. 'Tis true that talent
       Is formed in solitude; but character,
       In the resorts of busy men, seeks shape
       And aliment. His natural mistrust
       Towards his fellow-men might but too probably
       Be mixed in time with hate and fear.

Alph.   He only
       Fears men who knows them not—and he who shuns
       Their converse soon misunderstands them. This
       Is Tasso's case, and thus, little by little,
       The freest mind becomes confused and fettered.
       He often doubts my favor, although never
       Has it been clouded towards him; and many
       Whom he distrusts, I know are not his foes.
       A letter lost, a servant who could leave him
       To mark some bad design—some black conspiracy
       Against his peace.

Prin.   Ah! let us never
       Forget, my brother, that each man is born
       With certain qualities that never leave him.
       And if a friend, when journeying in our company,
       Should lame his foot, is it not best and kindest
       To lead him by the hand, and walk more slowly?

Alph.   To call some true physician and attempt
       A cure were better still; since then we might
       Go gayly forward with the convalescent.
       Yet think not I would rudely touch his hurt,
       But fain would I give better confidence
       To his o'er-anxious heart, and often seek

Public occasions to bestow on him
Marks of the peculiar favor. All his troubles
I carefully inquire into; as lately
When he believed his chambers had been entered
With some wrong purpose. Nothing was discovered,
And then I calmly told him what I thought,
But with the utmost gentleness and patience.
Well! as for other matters, I this night
Must leave you, as affairs of consequence
Recall me to the city. Our Antonio
Returned to-day from Rome, and I must therefore
Hold council on the intelligence he brings,
And dictate my despatches. Ere we go
He would pay his respects to you, fair ladies,
And will be with us some few moments hence.

Prin. Is't not thy wish that we return with thee?

Alph. No; for I know your pleasure is to be
Here or at Consandoli, and I would not
Break in on your enjoyment of the season.

Prin. But why cannot you manage such affairs
As well here, without going to the city?

Leon. It is not well to carry off Antonio
Ere we have heard the news from Rome.

Alph.   We both
Shall visit you again as soon as may be:
Then shall he entertain you, and your smiles
Help me to recompense his faithful service;
And when all *that* is properly performed,
I shall admit the public to these gardens,

And animate the shades and walks with groups
Of young and pretty subjects.

Leon.   We know of old
Your highness loves such picturesque additions.

Alph. I could retort upon thee if I would.

Prin. This half hour Tasso has been walking towards us;
Yet still he dallies, seems irresolute,
And cannot quite decide to come or go.

Alph. Wrapt in his dreams as usual!

Leon.   Ah! he comes.

SCENE III

TASSO, *carrying a book covered with parchment.*

Tasso. I come, half fearfully, to bring my work,
And hardly dare to place it in thy hand.
I know too well it yet is incomplete,
While I present it as a finished book;
But I know not when I should cease to feel
Faults that on each survey start up to vex me;
And better thus than tax your patience further.
I will not preface such a gift by aught;
I can but say, such as it is, 'tis yours.

Alph. This day shall be esteemed a festival,
Which places in my hand a gift so wished for,
I almost feared never to call it mine,
Fulfilling hopes too oft and long deferred;

Tasso.   If you are satisfied, I must be so,
For I regard the work as yours in spirit.
The embodying, indeed, is mine; but all
Which gives my lay its worth and dignity
Takes rise from you. For if I were endowed
By Nature with the power to tell in song
The visitings of gentle Fancy, Fortune
Always refused to aid her sister's bounty;
The fire which flashed from the boy-poet's eye
Was often quenched with ineffectual tears,
Forced by his parents' undeserved distress;
And his lyre's sweetest tones could not alleviate
The sorrows of those dear ones: till thy grace
Sought out and drew me from this living grave
To liberty and light, wherein my soul
Her powers expanded, and gave forth a voice
Of love and courage. But for you this lay
Had never seen the light. Receive your work.

Alph.   Be *doubly* honored for thy modesty.

Tasso.   O, could I speak as I profoundly feel
My gratitude! My youth knew nought of arms;
Apart from action's busy scene I learned
From thee the varied forms of life. The wisdom
Of the commander, the heroic courage
Of youthful knighthood—if my lay could paint them,
'Tis from thy converse I have drawn their being.

Prin.   Enough! Rejoice in the delight thou givest.

Alph.   In the applause of all good minds.

Leon.   Of all the world!

Act I, Scene 3

Tasso.   This moment gives reward and joy enough.
        On you I thought whether I mused or wrote;
        To give you pleasure was my constant wish,
        My highest aim and hope. Who finds not
        A world in his friends' hearts, can never merit
        That the world hear his name. Why! in this circle
        My soul could live and find it wide enough;
        Experience, wisdom, taste have forged the links
        Which bind you to all after ages. What
        Can crowds do for the artist? Mingled voices
        Bewilder and confuse him. Only those
        Who feel like you shall understand and judge me.

Alph.   If in thy eyes we really represent
        The present and the future world, we should not
        Omit to give this thought some outward token:
        The crown which even heroes must rejoice
        To wreath around the temple of the bard,
        Without whom all their glory could not live,
        Some genius must have placed upon the head
        Of thy great ancestor for this occasion.
                      [Pointing to the bust of Virgil.
        Methinks he says, "If you would truly venerate
        The illustrious dead, do honor to the living,"
              *[*ALPHONSO *beckons his sister; she takes*
     the crown and approaches TASSO; *he draws back.*

Leon.   Wilt thou refuse the imperishable crown
        From such a hand.

Tasso.   O, pardon me; such honor is not for me.

Alph.   Soon shall the world pronounce it justly thine.

Prin.   (*Holding up the crown.*) Wilt thou deny me the rare pleasure,
        Tasso.

Without a word to tell thee what I think?

Tasso.   The precious burden from that dearest hand
      My head, though weak, shall not decline.

                [*Kneels down; she places it on his head.*

Leon.   Hail!
      Thy first crown becomes thee well.

Alph.   And soon
      Another shall be added at the Capitol.

Prin.   And plaudits there shall tell thee what the lips
      Of friendship can but whisper now.

Tasso.   O, take it
      From this unworthy head; my locks are singed,
      And thought burned from my brain as by the rays
      Of an o'erpowering sun. A feverish heat
      Inflames my veins. Pardon! it is too much.

Leon.   Rather shall it protect thy head when wandering
      In Fame's domain, which lies so near the sun,
      And yield a grateful shade.

Tasso.   I am not worthy
      Of such refreshment. Rather place it
      Amid the farthest clouds, that life-long toils
      May strive to such an aim.

Alph.   He who early wins,
      Best prizes this world's sweetest blessings. He
      Obtaining early, ill endures the loss

        Of that which long possessed seems part of life;
        And he who would possess must still be ready.

Tasso. And that requires a never-failing strength,
        Which now deserts me. In this prosperous moment
        My heart misses the courage which ne'er failed me
        In rudest shocks of past adversity.
        Yet once again, my princess, hear my prayer;
        Remove thy crown; it does, and must, oppress me.

Prin. If thou couldst humbly walk beneath the weight
        Of Nature's richest, rarest gifts, thou wilt not
        Sink under that of laurel garlands:
        Content thee in our will. Even if we wished,
        We could not take them from the brows they once
        Have consecrated.

Tasso.   Let me go then
        To that still grove where oft I mused in sorrow,
        To meditate my happiness. There no eye
        Can glance reproaches at my want of merit;
        And should some fountain give me back the image
        Of one who sits 'neath heaven's blue canopy
        Amid those lofty pillars, his brow crowned
        And his eye fixed in thought, I shall but fancy
        Elysium lies before mine eye. I ask,
        Who is the happy one? Some bard or hero
        From the bright by-gone day. Where are the others,
        His comrades and inspirers? O, to see them
        Bound in a circle by that strongest magnet
        Which links the answering soul of bards and heroes!
        Homer felt not himself; his true existence
        Was in the contemplation of two heroes;

And Alexander welcomes in Elysium
With like embrace Achilles and his poet.
O, might I share such greeting!

Leon.   Hush such fancies.
Dost thou disdain the present?

Tasso.   'Tis that present
Which elevates me to such rapturous thoughts.

Prin. I joy to hear thee talk in such bright spirits.
       [*Enter a page, who gives a letter to* ALPHONSO.

Alph. Antonio! In a happy hour he comes.
   Admit him.

SCENE IV.

The former persons and ANTONIO.

Alph.   Doubly welcome,
For thine own sake, and for the prosperous end
Of thine adventure.

Prin.   To us also welcome.

Anto. Can I express the pleasure of these moments?
To see you all at last, and find you satisfied
With all which I have done in your behalf,
O, 'tis full recompense for each vexation,
The wearing cares, and days of weariness.
I have fulfilled your wishes and am happy.

Leon. I bid thee cordial welcome, though thy coming
Is summons to my undesired departure.

Act I, Scene 4

Anto.　And this is bitter mixed in my full cup.

Tasso.　To me too, welcome.　May I also hope
　　　　Some benefit from thine experience?

Anto.　If thou should'st e'er incline to cast a look
　　　　From thy world into mine.

Alph.　　　　　　　　　　　Though from thy letters
　　　　I know the outlines of thy late transactions,
　　　　Yet many questions I would ask.　How finally
　　　　Was thy success obtained?　Full well I know
　　　　A faithful servant is hard tasked in Rome;
　　　　For there, the powers that be, take all, give nought.

Anto.　Not through my diplomatic skill, my lord,
　　　　Was all you wished obtained.　But many chances
　　　　Came to my aid, and Gregory, the worthiest,
　　　　The most discriminating head which ever
　　　　Wore the tiara, loves and honors thee,
　　　　Nor ever crossed my strivings in thy cause.

Alph.　His favorable thoughts must give me pleasure,
　　　　But not invite my confidence.　I know
　　　　As well as thou what sways the Vatican;
　　　　The wish for universal empire.　Talk not
　　　　Of favor, then, from princes or from men,
　　　　But say what helped thee most.

Anto.　The pope's high mind sees truly, great as great
　　　　And little things as little.　He is one
　　　　Who can command a world, yet love his neighbor.
　　　　He knows the strip of land he yields to thee
　　　　Is less worth than thy friendship.　He would have

Peace near him, that he may more undisturbed
Rule Christendom, and hurl his thunderbolts
With concentrated strength against the heathen.

Prin.   Who are his counsellors and favorites?

Anto.   Wise and experienced men possess his ear;
His instruments do honor to his choice.
Having long served the state, he knows her powers,
And how to sway those foreign courts, all which
He studied in succession as ambassador.
He is not blinded by his separate interests
To those of others, and his every action
Speaks a large purpose, and a plan matured
By many days of silent scrutiny.
There is no fairer sight than a wise prince
Swaying all interests to a just subservience
To that of the great whole; each man is proud
Of doing his commands, feeling that thus
He best performs his proper revolution,
Receiving light and heat as his sphere asks them.

Leon.   A fair thing to behold.

Alph.   Or rather help create. For Leonora
Loves not the dull part of a looker-on.
She fain would set those pretty hands to work
At this great game. Is it not so, my fair one?

Leon.   Thou canst not tease me now.

Alph.   I owe thee something
Since many days.

Leon.   I now am in thy debt,

        But too full of my questions to repay thee.
        (*To* ANTONIO.) What gave he to his nephew?

Anto.   Merely justice.
        The mighty one, who doth not help his own,
        Is blamed even by his people. He knows how
        To serve them, and the state through them.

Tasso.   Do Learning and Art joy also in his patronage?

Anto.   He venerates that learning which is useful,
        Or to instruct or regulate his people:
        And Art, when she adorns his Rome, or makes
        The whole world marvel at her palaces
        And stately temples. Near him nought is idle;
        What would be honored, still must work and serve.

Alph.   And dost thou think that we may be secure,
        No further obstacles cast in our way?

Anto.   A few more letters and thy signature
        Shall close the strife.

Alph.   Ever be blest the day
        Which gives such freedom to the present one;
        The future such security. And thou,
        Gaining such bloodless victory, dost deserve
        A civic crown. The fair ones should to-morrow
        Twine thee one of oak leaf. For as Tasso
        To-day enriched me with a glorious conquest,
        That of Jerusalem, so long contested,
        Thou seest we have meetly honored him.

Anto.   Thou solvest an enigma. Two crowned heads
        I saw with wonder as I entered.

Tasso.   Couldst thou
But see my sense of undeserved applause!

Anto.   I knew long since Alphonso's liberality
In his rewards.

Prin.   When thou hast seen
Our Tasso's work, thou wilt not deem us liberal.
We only claim to head the long procession
Of his admirers—to which future years
Shall add their thousands.

Anto.   Your applause is fame.
I dare not doubt where you approve. Who placed
This wreath on Ariosto's brow?

Leon.   'Twas I.
Thou hast judged well. The motley blooming garland
Better beseems him than the prouder laurel.
Nature paints in her own varying hues,
Not aiming at the sculptor's cold ideal;
Yet, wandering through his tale's fantastic page,
Frequent we bow the knee at wayside shrines;
There the heart's natural deities smile on us,
Fixed by the enchanter's wand in all life's bloom.
Contentedness, experience, and wit,
Imagination, pure taste, and sound judgement,
Combine to illume the heaven of his mind,
A new, and O, how radiant constellation!
His sages rest beneath the blossoming bough
Which sheds its snowy treasures o'er their slumbers;
Or, crowned with roses, touch the thrilling lute,
And wisdom speaks in love's melodious tones;
The brooks soft murmur lures your wandering eyes

To the strange glittering forms that dwell beneath
Its amber waves. The air, the grove, the meadow,
Teem with creation of his lavish fancy:
There Prudence dances in a robe of green,
And Wisdom thunders from a golden cloud.
But he, who framed, is Monarch of this realm,
And all which seems incongruous in the parts
Finds place and aim in the romantic whole.
He who could wear the garland in his presence,
Deserves it for his boldness. Pardon me
If I talk largely or extravagantly.
These crowns, these poets, and these rural robes
Lead me out of myself.

Prin.   Who knows so well
To praise the one must learn to prize the other.
Thou shalt read Tasso's lays, and tell to us
All we have *felt*, and thou canst understand.

Alph.   Come with me now, Antonio. I must ask
Some questions more, and after will resign you
Entirely to these ladies. Now, farewell.

ACT II

SCENE I.—*A Hall.*

The PRINCESS, TASSO.

Tasso. As with uncertain steps I follow thee,
Wild and disordered thoughts oppress my mind,
And ask some hours of solitude to still
Their feverish tumult. Yet to gaze on thee
Is like the dawning of another day,
And must unloose my bonds. Yes; I must tell thee.
Our unexpected visitor has waked me
With most ungentle touch from my sweet dream.
His words, his presence, have with sudden force
Roused up new feelings to confuse my soul.

Prin. It is impossible that an old friend,
After an absence passed in scenes unlike
Those which we knew together, should appear,
In the first moment of reunion, near
And dear as when we parted. Yet we should not,
Impatient, deem that we have lost him. Soon
The strings respond again to their concordance,
And harmony makes glad the waiting heart.
He is unchanged within. The jars arise
But from another atmosphere. Antonio,
When he has learned to know thee and thy works,
Will hold forth eloquently in thy praise,
As late in Ariosto's.

Tasso.   Ah, believe me,
Those praises were delightful to my ear;

>   My heart soft whispered as he spoke; and thou
> Mayst thus enkindle in some soul of honor
> These incense-breathing fires. Though lowlier gifted,
> Sincere has been thy striving, great thy love.
> What pained me was the picture of *his* world,
> With all these glowing, grand, and restless shapes,
> Which such a man can charm into his circle,
> Submissive to the spells his wisdom frames;
> For as I gazed, *my* world sank in the distance
> Behind steep rocks, on which I seemed to fade
> To echo—to poor shadow of a sound—
> Bodiless—powerless.

Prin.   And but now, how dear
> Thou felt'st the ties which bind the bard and hero;
> Born to adorn their day with noble rivalry,
> By envy unprofaned. The heroic deed
> Which fires the bard is beautiful; nor less so
> The generous ardor which embalms the deed
> In lays whose fragrance breathes o'er far-off ages.
> *Thou* must live tranquil, or thy song is marred.

Tasso.   Here first I saw how valor is rewarded.
> I came here at a time when feast on feast,
> Given to celebrate Ferrara's glory,
> Dazzled my boyish eye, as in the lists
> Knighthood displayed its prowess. The first men,
> The fairest women of our day, looked on—
> Flowers of our fatherland, bound in one garland.
> When the lists opened, when the trumpet sounded,
> Helm and shield glittered, courses pawed the ground,
> Pages ran to and fro, the lances shivered,
> And rising clouds of dust hid for a moment

The victor's triumph and the vanquished's shame.
O, what a spectacle of worldly splendor!
I felt my littleness, and shrank abashed.

Prin.   How differently did I pass those moments
Which sowed ambition in thy heart! The lore
Of sufferance I was painfully receiving.
That feast which hundreds since have vaunted to me
I could not see. In a far, dim apartment,
Where not an echo of this gayety
Could penetrate, I lay. Before my eyes
Death waved his broad, black pinions. When the light
Of motley raging life returned upon them,
It showed as through a dusky veil obscured.
In those first days of unhoped convalescence,
I left my chamber leaning on my women.
I met Lucretia full of joy and health,
And guiding thee, their harbinger, to me.
Thou wert the first who welcomed me to this
New lease of life; I hailed it as an omen,
And hoped much *for* and from thee; nor have I
Been by my hope deceived.

Tasso.   And I,
Who had been deafened by the tumult, dazzled
By the excess of light, and roused by many
Passions unknown before, as with thy sister
I met thee in that long still gallery,
Was like one much harassed by magic spells
Beneath the influence of celestial spirits.
And since, when wild desires distracting pant
After their thousand objects, has the memory
Of that hour bridled them, and turned aside

        My thoughts from their unworthy course. But some
        Wildly and vainly search on ocean's sands
        To find the pearl which lies fast locked, the while,
        In its still, secret shell.

Prin.   Those were fair days,
        And had not Duke d'Urbino wed my sister,
        Our happiness were still unclouded. But
        We want her life and courage, her gay spirit
        And various wit.

Tasso.   I know that thou
        Canst ne'er forget her loss. O, I have felt it
        Often and keenly—often have complained
        In solitude that I could not supply
        What thou hast lost in her; could nothing be
        Where I desired so much. O that I might be something,
        And not in words, but deeds, express to thee
        How my heart worships thee. In vain, alas!
        I cannot gladden thee, and often vex thee;
        In my bewilderment have injured those
        Thou wouldst protect, have marred and frustrated
        Thy cherished schemes, and still go farthest from thee
        When I most sigh to approach thee.

Prin.   I have never
        Doubted thy wishes towards me, and grieve
        Only that thou shouldst hurt thyself. My sister
        Can live with every one in his own way.
        Might'st thou but find thyself in such a friend.

Tasso.   In whom, except thyself, can I confide?

Prin.   My brother.

Tasso.   He is my sovereign.
Not the wild dreams of freedom bar the way.
I know, I feel, man was not born to freedom;
And to a worthy heart 'tis happiness
To serve a worthy prince. But I cannot
Serve him and trust him as an equal friend.
But must in silence learn his will and do it,
E'en should mine own rebel.

Prin.   Antonio
Would be a prudent friend.

Tasso.   And once I hoped
To have him for a friend, but now despair.
I know his converse and his counsel both
Are what I need. But then the assembled gods
Showered in his cradle rich and varied gifts,
The Graces held back theirs. And whom they slight
(However favored by all other powers)
Can never build their palaces in hearts.

Prin. O, but he is a man worthy of faith:
Ask not so much—he will redeem all pledges
His words and manner give. Should he once promise
To be thy friend, he would do all for thee.
O, I will have it so. It will be easy,
Unless thou art perverse. But Leonora,
Whom thou so long hast known, and who is surely
Refined and elegant to the degree
Of thy fastidious taste's exaction, why
Hast thou not answered her proffered friendship?

Tasso. I had declined it wholly but for thee.
I know not why, I cannot frankly meet her,

<blockquote>
And oft, when she would benefit a friend,
Design is felt, and her intent repulsed.
</blockquote>

Prin.   This path, Tasso
<blockquote>
Leads through dark valleys and still lonely woods;
Hope no companion if thou wilt pursue it.
There canst thou only strive, that golden time
Which thy *eye* vainly sees within thy *mind*
To form and animate. Even that I fear
Thou vainly wilt essay.
</blockquote>

Tasso.   Ah, my princess,
<blockquote>
Do all hearts vainly sigh! That golden time,
Is it quite gone? that age of blissful freedom,
When on the bosom of the mother earth
Their children dreamed in fond security;
The ancient trees sheltered from noonday heat
The happy shepherds with their shepherdesses;
The streams could boast their nymphs. Fawns were familiar;
Snakes had no venom, and the fearless birds
And unmolested rangers of the forests,
Every gay creature in its frolic play
Taught man the truth—All which can *bless* is lawful.
</blockquote>

Prin.   My friend, the golden age indeed is past;
<blockquote>
Only the good have power to bring it back.
And (shall I frankly tell thee what I think?)
The poets feign in all their pretty tales
Of that same age. Most like 'twas then as now,
United noble hearts *make* golden days,
Interpret to each other the world's beauty.
Change in thy maxim but one single word,
All is explained. All which is *meet* is lawful.
</blockquote>

Tasso.   Might then a synod of the wise and good
decide on what is meet; for now each one
Says that is meet which to himself is pleasing,
And to the crafty and the powerful
All is permitted, whether just or not!

Prin.   A synod of good *women* should decide;
It is their province. Like a wall, decorum
Surrounds and guards the frailer sex. Propriety,
Morality, are their defence and fortress,
Their tower of strength; and lawlessness their foe.
And as man loves bold trials of his strength,
So woman, graceful bonds, worn with composure.

Tasso.   Thou think'st us rude, impetuous, and unfeeling?

Prin.   Not so! Your striving is for distant good,
And must be eager to effect its end;
But ours for single, limited possessions,
Which we would firmly grasp, and constant hold.
We have slight hold upon your hearts; that beauty
Which wins them is so frail; and when 'tis gone
Those qualities to which it lent a charm
Are worthless in your eyes. But were there men
Could know a woman's heart, could feel what treasure
Of truth and tenderness is hoarded there,
Could keep the memory of by-gone bliss,
And by its aid could penetrate the veil
That age or sickness o'er her casts, and did not
The gaining of one gem, instead of quieting,
Excite desire for the others,—then to us
A beauteous day would dawn, and we should know
Our golden age.

Act II, Scene 1

Tasso.   Thy words call up
Sharp pains that long have slept within my breast.

Prin.   What mean'st thou, Tasso? Frankly tell it me.

Tasso.   I hear that noble princes ask thy hand:
I always knew it must be so, yet have not
These trembling apprehensions taught my heart
To encounter such misfortune. Though 'tis natural
That thou shouldst leave us, how we shall endure it
I know not.

Prin.   Free thy mind
From all such fears; I dare to say, forever.
I do not wish to go, nor shall, unless
My friends disturb my home by vain dissensions.

Tasso.   O, teach me but what I shall do for thee;
My life is thine, my heart beats but to praise,
To adore thy excellence; my all of bliss
To realize the beautiful in thee.
The gods are separate and elevate
Far above man as destiny o'er prudence,
And plans formed by the foresight of us mortals,
Waves which o'erwhelm us with destroying press,
To their wide ken seem but as the brook's ripple.
The wild tornadoes of our atmosphere
Reach not those azure heights where they are throned.
They hear our wailings with as light regard
As we do children's for their shattered toys.
But thou, serene as they, art not removed
From sympathy, but oft, sun-like, dost pour
Down from thy heights floods of consoling light
Upon these eyelids wet with dew of earth.

Prin.   All women ought to love the bard, whose lay
          Like theirs can praise them. Soft and yet heroic,
          Lovely and noble, hast thou painted them;
          And e'en Armida's faults are half redeemed
          By tenderness and beauty.

Tasso.   From one model
          I pictured all; if any shall be deemed
          Worthy of immortality, to that model
          They owe it. My Clorinda and Hermione
          Her unheeded but undying faith. Olindo,
          His sorrow and Sophronia's magnanimity,
          Are not the children of my fancy; now
          They exist, and if profound reality
          Give interest to a picture, shall endure
          The story of a nobly-placed devotion
          Breathed into song.

Prin.   Thy poem's highest praise
          Is that it leads us on, and on. We listen,
          We think we understand, nor can we blame
          That which we understand, and thus become thy captives.

Tasso.   Thy words breathe heaven, princess; but I need
          The eagle's eye to bear the new-born light.

Prin.   No more at present, Tasso. If some things
          May suddenly be seized, yet love and virtue
          (Nearly, I think, related to each other)
          Ask in their quest patience and self-denial.
          Forget not this. And now adieu, my friend.

Scene II

Tasso, *alone.*

Tasso.   Is it permitted thee to ope thine eyes
And look around—above thee? Did these pillars
Hear what she spake? They were the witnesses
How a descending goddess lifted me
Into a new, incomparable day.
What power, what wealth, lie in this new-traced circle!
My happiness outruns my wildest dream!
Let those born blind think what they will of colors,
To the cleared eye wakens a novel sense.
What courage, what presentiment! Drunk with joy.
I scarce can tread the indicated path,
And how shall I deserve the choicest gifts
Of earth and heaven? Patience, self-denial,
Must give me confidence—they shall.
O, how did I deserve that she should choose me!
What shall I do to justify her choice?
Yet that choice speaks my worth. Yes; I am worthy,
Since she could think me so. My soul is consecrate,
My princess, to thy words, thy looks. Whate'er
Thou wilt, ask of thy slave. In distant lands
I'll seek renown with peril of my life,
Or chant in every grove thy charms and virtues.
Wholly possess the creature thou hast formed;
Each treasure of my soul is thine. I ne'er can
Express my vast devotion with the pen
In written words. Ah, could I but assist
The poet's by the painter's art! Did honey
Fall from my lips! Now never more shall I

Be lonely, sad, or weak. Thou wilt be with me.
Had I a squadron of the noblest men
To help me do thy bidding, some great deed
Should justify the boldness of a tongue
Which dared to ask her grace! I meant it not—
I meant not to speak now. But it is well;
I take as a free gift what I could never
Have claimed. This glorious future! This new youth!
Rise, heart! O, tree of love! may genial showers
Call out a thousand branches towards heaven!
Unfold thy blossoms, swell thy golden fruit
Until the loved one's hand be stretched to cull it.

Scene III

Tasso, Antonio

Tasso. Be welcome to me as if now first seen.
Thy coming is most happy. Welcome, welcome!
For knowing now thy worth, I long to proffer
A heart and hand which thou must not disdain.

Anto. I thank thee for thy gifts, but must beware
Lest I abuse thy generosity, accepting
Where I cannot repay. Pardon my providence;
'Tis best for both I be not over hasty.

Tasso. No one can blame the prudence which we need
At every step; yet in some precious moments
The heart suffices to direct our way.

Anto. Let each for himself decide when these occur,
Since each must bear the weight of his own error.

Act II, Scene 3

Tasso. Well, be it so. I now have asked thy friendship,
Swayed by a wish the princess has expressed,
And she could not expect that I should urge it.
Time and acquaintance may perchance give value
To what thou now almost disdain'st.

Anto.   Moderation
Is still reproached as coldness by those men
Who give impetuous heat the name of tenderness—

Tasso. Thou blamest what I blame and shun. Though young
I know that constancy and vehemence
Seldom combine.

Anto.   Act wisely as thou speakest.

Tasso. Thou hast a right to advise and warn me, since
Experience is thy friend and guide. Yet trust me,
The heart so learns all that she teaches;
In secret, practises what thou dost think
To teach as new.

Anto.   Pleasant enough it were
To muse about one's self, if but as useful.
No man can know himself from contemplation,
Measure his faculties upon a scale
Made by himself. No; he must read his own
In the hearts of other men, and life alone
Shows forth the living man.

Tasso.   With applause
And reverence I listen.

Anto.   And yet thou thinkest
Something quite different as I am speaking.

Tasso.   Thus shall we ne'er approach to one another.
It is unkind, it is discourteous,
In thee, thus obstinately to misinterpret
My words and thoughts. Before the princess asked,
I longed to know thee. I was told thou wert
Creative still of good to others; ever
Assisting them, and heedless of thyself.
With firm heart sail'st thou o'er life's changeful sea.
I seek thee, ask but for a little part
Of thy large treasure. I feel confidence
Thou'lt not repent such bounty towards me;
But when thou know'st my heart, will be my friend,
Such as I need. I fear not to avow
My inexperience and unripe judgment.
My future were a fair one did I know
But how to meet and use it. Would'st thou teach me?

Anto.   Thou ask'st that I this moment give a pledge
What time and thought should justify.

Tasso.   Yet love
Will in a moment yield what toil would never
Claim as a reward. I *claim*, I do not *ask* it.
I claim it by two words of strongest might—
Virtue and Leonora send me to thee;
She wishes that we should be friends. O, let us
Haste, hand in hand, unto her heavenly presence;
United offer fealty. Noble Antonio,
Grant me that sweetest pleasure to the good
Frankly to pour the heart out to a better.

Anto.   Full sailed as usual! Used to conquer, every where
To find ways broad, doors open. Be it so!

Act II, Scene 3

     I yield to thee thy luck—but truth compels me
     To say that natures so unequal poised
     Never could bend unto one point.

Tasso.   Unequal
     I know we are in years and in tried worth:
     In courage and good will, I yield to no one.

Anto.   From will to deed the road is not so easy
     As it may seem to thee. When the goal's reached
     The victor claims a crown, which is not always
     Given to the worthy. But some crowns there are
     Much easier gained—a careless hand may pluck
     Such from the trees during an idle stroll.

Tasso.   Some gifts, indeed, immediate from the gods,
     Nor labor nor experience could obtain!

Anto.   Blind Fortune is the deity of such.

Tasso.   Justice protects her eyes by bands against
     Influences which might distort the truth.

Anto.   The fortunate are right to praise their deity,
     Give her discrimination, Argus eyes,
     Name her Minerva, proudly wear her trappings
     As armor from the fight.

Tasso.   Thou needs't not
     More plainly speak. It is enough. I look
     Into thy deepest heart, and know thee now:
     O, did the princess know thee too! Thy tongue,
     Thy eyes, will aim their poisonous darts in vain
     Against my brows defended by this garland.
     The envious have no claim to such; yet bring me

The man who has reached that whereto I strive,
A hero such as history alone
Has given to my knowledge, or a poet
Who may compare with Homer and with Virgil,
(And such a one, deserving far more highly,
Would be far more abashed to win this crown
Than thou hast seen me,) I will humbly kneel,
Happy to place it at his feet.

Anto.   Till then
Remain worthy possessor of thy garland.

Tasso. I fear not scrutiny, but will not bear
Such uncalled-for contumely. The prince decreed me
The crown. The princess' hand has woven it—
Who has a title to gainsay my right
To wear it!

Anto. This fury, this high tone,
Beseems neither this palace, nor is it meet
From thee to me.

Tasso.   Then why from thee to me?
Or is truth banished from the palace; freedom
Cast into chains, oppression to be borne
By noble hearts! Here should the swelling spirit
Find room, if any where, nor fear the greatness
Of earthly powers. With me it shall be so!
Only the high blood of our ancestors
Gives claim to approach the prince; why not our own?
Why must the large soul put on chains like these?
They are for little minds; fit for the envious
To mark their shame! Yet such should not be here,
Nor spiders' webs deform the marble walls.

Act II, Scene 3

Anto.   Thou justify'st my scorn. Rash boy! dar'st thou
       Claim confidence and friendship from a *man*?
       Unmannerly as thou art.

Tasso.   Better unmannerly
       Than like to thee, of cold, ignoble temper.

Anto.   Thou art yet young, and timely chastisement
       May moderate this folly.

Tasso.   Not young enough to bow down before idols;
       And old enough with scorn to face the scorner.

Anto.   No doubt thou art a mighty conqueror:
       When singing to thy lute thou art so doughty.

Tasso.   My hand has not been much acquainted with my sword,
       Yet I trust it.

Anto.   In fortune trust,
       Who still has favored thy presumption.

Tasso.   Now
       Is come the time for combat. I had not
       Wished it should be with thee; but thou wilt have it.
       Heap coals on coals, and heat my inmost heart,
       Till the desire for vengeance boils up foaming.
       Draw! if report speaks truly of thy manhood.

Anto.   Thou think'st as little *who* as *where* thou art.

Tasso.   No sanctuary can compel me to suffer
       Such insults in its bounds. *Thou* dost infringe it,
       Not *I*, who hither came to offer thee
       Love, veneration, confidence, my all.
       'Tis thou, thy words, and not my swelling heart

So greatly outraged, that profane this place.

Anto.   What lofty rage pent in one narrow breast!

Tasso.   Well, here is space to give my bosom air.

Anto.   Needs not the sword; with *words, that* may be done.

Tasso.   If thou, indeed, art noble, show it now!

Anto.   Noble I am, and yet know *where* I am.

Tasso.   Come down into the court, then.

Anto.   At *thy* bidding?

Tasso.   Thou art a coward.

Anto.   Those are cowards
Who storm and threaten where they feel secure.

Tasso.   No place compels to suffer this. (*Draws.*) Follow me
Or draw on peril of contempt as well
As hatred.

SCENE IV.

The former persons and ALPHONSO.

Alph.   What unseemly strife is here?

Anto.   It is not strife! Composedly I seek
To calm this madman!

Tasso.   'Tis thy look alone
Can calm me, prince.

{ *312* }

Act II, Scene 4

Alph.   Speak truly, both;
   What leads you thus to violate propriety?

Tasso. This man so noted for his courtesy
   And wisdom, hath to me so borne himself,
   So rude and so ungenerous, 'twere shame
   In the most coarsely nurtured menial.
   I accosted him in kindness; he repulsed me.
   I persevered; more bitterly he taunted me,
   Until the heart's sweet flow was turned to gall.
   If I have angered thee, it is his fault,
   For he designedly did chafe my passion.

Anto. What a poetic flight! Is it permitted
   By a few calm words to put down all his rhetoric?

Tasso. O, speak but truth! Tell each malicious word,
   Each sneer. Do but full justice to thyself.

Anto. If thou hast more to say, now say it, else
   Give me my turn, and interrupt me not
   Whether 'twas I, my prince, or this hot head
   Began the quarrel, which of us had right
   I think is not the question.

Tasso.   Not the question!
   Which of us did begin, and which was right?

Anto. Not wholly as it seems to thy wild mind.

Alph. Antonio!

Anto.   Then please your highness,
   Let him be silent while I speak, and then
   Talk as he will. Thou wilt decide. I neither

Accuse him nor defend myself; not yet
Can think it best to offer satisfaction
As he demands. He is not now my equal,
But subject to a heavy penalty
From which thy grace alone can set him free.
He threatened me, and urged me to the combat;
Even at thy coming scarcely sheathed his sword;
And I, but for thy timely interruption,
Must also have forgotten duty.

Alph. (To TASSO.)   How?

Tasso.   My heart, I do assure your highness, speaks me
(As I think you will) free from blame. 'Tis true
I challenged, threatened, him, and was the first
To draw the sword. But he had injured me
With his envenomed tongue beyond endurance,
Filling each vein with poison, till I fevered
Into delirium; he, the while, sedate,
Cold blooded, calculating, sneering at me.
(Thou know'st him not.) I offered him my friendship;
He trampled on the gift. Had not I then
Been roused to anger, sure I were unworthy
Thy favor. Pardon if I have forgotten
Those small proprieties of time and place.
Be angry when thou seest me suffer insults.
Methinks the grace your highness shows me should
Have guarded me in converse with thy servant.

Anto.   How the youth sails along beneath the burden
Of his offences! or, like dust from raiment,
Would careless shake them off! 'Twere marvellous,
Did not all poets love the impossible.

But whether thou or thine, my prince will judge
The offence thus insignificant, I doubt.
Majesty, like religion, should protect
All busied in its service. At the foot
Of thrones and altars passion should be tamed.
Swords sleep i' the scabbard, lips forbear to threaten;
There's space enough elsewhere for noise and strife.
Thy sire, who built these walls, cared for their peace,
And the security of his descendants,
Enacting rigorous laws against transgressors.
Then, no respect to persons, no indulgence,
Held back the arm of justice in such cases.
In consequence, the walls have long been undisturbed
By scenes like this to-day. Shall it be pardoned,
And liberty be given to wild brawlers
To anger and assail the temperate
While in the discharge of duty?

Alph.   I impartially
Have heard you both; and you have both done wrong,
Since 'tis so hard to decide. But if Antonio
Have wronged thee, Tasso, he shall meet thee,
Though I would fain settle thy differences.
Meanwhile thou must be prisoner in thy chamber—
The gentlest punishment for such offence.

Tasso. Is this thy judgment, prince?

Anto.   Say, rather, *father.*

Tasso. (*To* ANTONIO.) I have nought more to say to thee.
(*To* ALPHONSO.) O prince!
Thou send'st me to imprisonment; so be it.
I bow my head submissive to thy order;

My heart is silenced. I can scarce perceive
To where or how I am. Was it a crime?
It was—else why should I be punished?—yet
I cannot feel it such.

Alph.   Talk not of crime; it was a youthful folly.

Tasso.   Well, call it so! I cannot understand.
I, childlike, think I see and object clearly,
Which the next moment turns a new side to me,
And shows me how imperfect was my knowledge.
But I can hear thy sentence and obey it.
Too many words have already been wasted:
Henceforth, obedience shall be blind and silent.
Weakling! thou thought'st thyself on level earth,
And art thrown headlong from the halls of the gods.
Now I will do the thing that's forced upon me,
With a good grace, as doth become a man.
Receive the sword thou gav'st me when I followed
The cardinal to France; if not with honor,
Without disgrace. Thy gift I have worn ever;
Take from my saddened heart what filled it formerly
With hope.

Alph.   Thou quite mistak'st my feelings toward thee.

Tasso.   I can obey better than understand.
A splendid gift fate calls me to renounce;
This crown must not adorn a prisoner's brows;
Receive again what I had idly fancied
I might forever wear. Too early given,
My happiness is early taken from me,
Lest I grow arrogant. Nor do the gods
A second time bestow such gifts. O, men

Are deeply tried. Nor could we live beneath it,
Had not Nature given strange elasticity,
Rebounding from severest pressure. Poverty
Compels to part with our most precious jewels,
And from our opened hands oft gems escape
Which toil and searching never will bring back.
A kiss and tear consign thee to decay.
This weakness be permitted. Who weeps not
When the immortal pales before decay!
I twine the garland round the sword, although
Not won by trial of its temper. Rest,
As sometimes on the coffin of the valiant,
Upon the grave of all my bliss and hopes;
I lay them at thy feet; for what are weapons
Against thy anger? And when thou disdain'st,
What coronal gives honor? Now I go
To the imprisonment thou hast commanded.

> [*Exit. The prince signs to a page to*
take away the sword and garland.

SCENE V.

ALPHONSO. ANTONIO.

Anto.   What mad enthusiasm! How he raves
About his character and destiny!
The youth fancies himself an elected being,
To whom all is permitted. Punish him;
The man shall thank you.

Alph.   Too far, I fear,
His punishment is carried.

Anto.   If thou repentest,
Give him his sword. Let that decide between us.

Alph.   Perhaps I may decide on that. Tell truly
How thou didst irritate him so.

Anto.   I cannot
Explain to thee. Though as a *man* I might
Have pained him, as a nobleman I did not
Offend his honor. Nor by words did he
Insult me in his passion.

Alph.   What you say
Confirms me in my first impression. When
Such difference has risen, 'tis just to blame
The wisest most. Thou should'st have born with him,
Enlightened him. Nor is it now too late.
I wish for peace among my friends. 'Tis easy,
If thou wilt lend thy aid. Let Sanvitali
Soothe him with soft words; then go thou unto him,
And free him in my name, and offer him thy friendship;
Speak to him as thou shouldst, and show paternal kindness.
Easily couldst thou win his worthy heart.
When we are gone, the ladies will complete
The good work that thou must begin. I see
Thou art the old Antonio. No sooner
One intricate affair is brought to end,
Than thou begin'st another. Might but this
Terminate happily as thy embassy.

Anto.   I am ashamed, and see, in thy clear judgment
My error mirrored, and obedience follows
The noble master who prefers convincing,
Where he has power to command our wills.

ACT III

Scene I

The Princess (*Alone.*)

Prin.   Where tarries Leonora? Every moment
Perturbs me more. I cannot learn distinctly
What happened—which of them was faulty.
Does she delay? I must not meet my brother
Or Antonio, till I have composed myself,
And will not be till I know the truth.

Scene II.

Enter Leonora.

Prin.   How was it Leonora? What has happened?
How fares our friend?

Leon.   I learned no more
Than we have heard. Tasso had drawn, thy brother
Came in and separated them; 'tis said
Tasso began the strife, for he was sent
To his apartment as a prisoner.
Antonio is free, and with thy brother.

Prin.   I know Antonio must have injured him,
Or, cold and distant, jarred his excited mind.

Leon.   I doubt it not. A cloud was on his brow
Just as they met.

Prin.   Why do we
Neglect the soft voice of the heart? A God
Speaks in the heart, but we forget to listen,
Though nought so clearly can disclose to us
What we should seek, what shun. Antonio
Appeared this morning even more reserved
And blunt than usual; and my heart gave warning
As Tasso near him stood. See but the outward guise
Of both! The face, the voice, the look, the tone,
How different, and how discordant framed!
Ah, hope deceived me; they could ne'er be friends.
Both are intelligent, noble, well-nurtured,
My friends. I hoped to bind them close to one another;
I beckoned Tasso on. How eagerly,
How warmly, sought to fulfil my wish!
Had I but spoken to Antonio first!
I felt reluctant, just at his return,
In these first hours to introduce the subject.
I trusted in his courtesy, nor feared,
In a wise man, a boy's impetuosity.
Well, it is over; and these thoughts are vain.
Advise me what I now can do.

Leon.   How hard
It is to advise well, thou must surely feel,
After what thou hast said. No misunderstanding
Is this between like-minded men. *Such* difference
Words might accommodate, or arms if needful.
These must be enemies, I long have felt;
Because Dame Nature did not will the two
Should, meeting, form a whole. Yet might it be,
Could they be wise, and balance one another.

        The whole thus made might lead a world in chains.
        This thought is bootless, though we may compose
        The quarrel of to-day. This was but earnest
        Of what must be. 'Twere best if Tasso journeyed
        For some short space from hence either to Rome
        Or Florence, where I soon shall go, and might
        Exert a friendly influence on his spirits.
        Thou here might'st mollify Antonio,
        And time, perhaps, would do the rest.

Prin.   Thy plan
        Takes from me what it gives to thee. Is that
        Quite just, my friend.

Leon.   It takes from thee
        What thou couldst not enjoy in present circumstances
        If thou retain'st it.

Prin.   So coolly shall I
        Banish a friend?

Leon.   Thou wilt receive him back
        More happy.

Prin.   I know my brother never
        Will give consent.

Leon.   If we persuade him
        He will.

Prin.   Condemn my friend!

Leon. To save him.

Prin.   No; I cannot say yes.

Leon.   Not to avert such evil?

Prin.   Thou art not sure that what gives me such pain
Will do him good.

Leon.   That we shall see.

Prin.   Urge me no more!

Leon.   Who firmly can resolve
Conquers each obstacle.

Prin.   Well, he shall go,
But soon return, and we must have a care
That the duke give order for his maintenance
Abroad as here. Do thou persuade Antonio
To forget his wrath and influence my brother.

Leon.   A word from thee, princess, would more avail
Than all that I could say.

Prin.   Thou knowest, Leonora,
I am not like my sister of Urbino,
And cannot beg for myself or those I love.
I ask but peace, and thankfully receive
My generous brother's gifts, but never seek them.
One of my friends has often scolded me.
"Call'st thou this disinterestedness, she says,
To neglect thy friends' need as thine own?" In silence
I suffer the reproach, nor can resolve
To take another course. But now, most luckily,
A part of what I inherit from my mother
Is due, and I am free to aid my friend.

Leon.   And I will be thy steward; for we know
Our Tasso is no manager.

Act III, Scene 2

Prin.   Take him, then,
If I must part from him. Before all others
I would to thee resign him, and I see
That it is best to do so. So I must
Practise again that lore of resignation
I have been conning from my earliest years.
It is not hard for me to lose, for never
Feel I security in the possession
Of any precious thing.

Leon.   I hope to see thee happy,
As thou so greatly dost deserve to be.

Prin.   Happy! My Leonora, who *is* happy?
My brother I might deem so; his strong heart
With fortitude bears each decree of fate.
But he has ne'er received what he deserved.
My sister of Urbino—is she happy?
The beautiful, the noble, the high-minded—
Had she but children, she indeed were happy.
But as it is, her youthful husband's business
Can ne'er make her forget his disappointment;
No joy dwells in their house. Our mother's wisdom,
Her knowledge, her bright wit and generosity—
Could they preserve her from bewilderment?
They took her children from her, and she died
Unreconciled with God, and far from us.

Leon.   Think not of all which to each soul is wanting;
But think what they possess—how rich, my princess,
Art thou.

Prin.   One word, Leonora,
Tells all my riches—patience is my wealth,

Accumulating since my earliest youth.
When all my friends, my brother and my sister,
Joined in the dance and merry roundelay,
Sickness and sadness were my boon companions,
Who, in my lonely chamber, sat with me;
Yet I had my songs, too, lending their sweetness
Even to that forlorn estate; and music
For a time charmed away the thought of pain.
But soon did my physician send from me
That gentle soother to my sufferings.

Leon.   But many hearts clave to thee even then,
And now thou'rt well, and feelest life more fully
Than if thou always hadst been so.

Prin.   I am well;
That is, I am not sick, and many friends
Tenderly minister to me—and *one* I had—

Leon.   Thou hast him yet.

Prin.   But soon must lose him. What significance
Lay in the moment of our meeting first!
But lately freed from pain and sickness, coyly
I looked back upon life—the light of day
And of loved faces gladdened me again—
I sipped hope's sweetest balsam. Friendly forms
From the fair future leaned and beckoned me.
Came to me from the distance, by my sister
Conducted, came this youth to me. The soul
Was open to receive him, and must ever
Retain him in her hall of imagery.

Leon.   Repent not of that hour. To know the good
Is happiness which fate can ne'er tear from us.

Act III, Scene 2

Prin.   The lovely, the superlatively good
        Is like the fire, which, blazing on thy hearth,
        Or from thy torch gives pleasure to thy dwelling,
        Never to be dispensed with when once known.
        But let it leave the spot which was reserved
        For its abiding place, rove through thy chambers,
        How dangerous, how fatal! O my friend,
        I talk too much, and ought to hide from thee
        How weak, how sick I am!

Leon.   Through confidence
        Is sickness of the mind solaced.

Prin.   Could it
        Be cured through confidence, I soon were well,
        For mine in thee is perfect. Let him go.
        But ah! the lonely days that I must pass—
        The sun no longer chasing from my eyelids
        The dream which painted him. No hope of meeting
        Shall fill the awaking soul with joy and eagerness.
        I shall look for him in each shady alley,
        And look in vain. How sweet the anticipation
        Of passing with him the calm evening hours,
        With every conversation still increasing
        The desire to know each other more completely,
        And each new day bringing new harmony
        To our accordant souls! Now all is dark.
        The splendor of the sun, the life of day,
        The thousand-sided world, its changing images
        And glittering presence mantled o'er by night.
        Once every day was as a separate life,
        Care and fear distant far. We rudderless
        Sailed, joyous-carolling, on the sea of Time;

But now, a cloudy future fills my breast
Like a tormenting present.

Leon.   The future
Shall bring thy friend, and with him fairer days
Than those thou mournest now, as fled forever.

Prin.   I should prefer keeping what I possess;
Change may be entertaining, seldom useful.
With youthful longing did I never seek
To draw new lots from the urn of the great world.
Seeking new objects for a craving heart,
I venerated him, and therefore loved him.
I loved him, too, because near him my life
Assumed a beauty never known before.
At first I thought, I will remove from him;
But my resolve gave way. I drew still nearer,
So sweetly lured, now so severely punished.
And some bad spirit fills my cup of joy
With bitter beverage from a kindred vine
To that whose juice I late delighted quaffed.

Leon.   The world's strong influence and Time the comforter
Will do for thee what friendly words cannot.

Prin.   The world! ah, what fair things move on its surface,
And oft seem but a step removed from us,
And lead us step by step on to the grave
Of all our longings, all our hopes! How seldom
Men find what Nature seems to have formed for them—
Or hold such when obtained! They leave us or we lose them.
We find a treasure, and we know it not;
Or, if we know it, it is taken from us.

SCENE III

LEONORA, *alone.*

Leon.   The generous heart! how gloomy is her lot!
        Unmerited by such noble being.
        Ah! is it by her loss I seek to win?
        And shall I selfishly monopolize
        The heart, the talents, which I share with her,
        Though not in equal measure? Is this honorable?
        Am I not rich enough? Have I not all?
        Husband and son, beauty, and wealth, and rank—
        All these I have, and I must have him too.
        I love him then! I blush not at the avowal.
        How sweet to gaze into his beauteous mind!
        A happiness immortalized by him,
        Charms hallowed in his lay, indeed have claim to envy!
        Not only to possess what others sigh for,
        But every one shall know my *luck*; my name
        Be echoed through my fatherland, and this
        Is consummation of all other happiness.
        Let Laura boast her Petrarch! I would not
        Exchange with her. The afterworld be judge.
        How splendid, in the flush of present life
        To approach with him the no less brilliant future!
        Time, age, and rumor have no power o'er him,
        And all he touches shares his attributes.
        I still shall be adored, living and lovely,
        When by the circling hours my real charms
        Have, one by one, been stolen away. O, yes,
        He must be mine! I take so little from her.
        Her inclination for this worthy man

Is like her other feelings, whose pale moonlight
Falls coldly on the wanderer's path, nor sheds
One ray of mirth or joy. She will be happy
If he is distant, and content as when
He daily wandered at her side; nor will I
Leave her, or take him quite away from her.
I will return sometimes. It shall be so.
Here comes my rougher friend. 'Tis I must soften him.

SCENE IV.

LEONORA. ANTONIO.

Leon. Thou bring'st us war instead of peace. 'Twould seem
Thou camest from a camp, a field of battle,
Where strength has empire, and commands the sword,
Rather than Rome, where solemn *benedicites*
Soften each fiat of tremendous power.

Anto. I am to blame, fair friend; yet pardon me.
'Tis dangerous always to be so prudent,
Always upon one's guard, and vigilant;
The evil genius, lurking near, demands
A sacrifice from time to time: unhappily,
This time I make it at my friend's expense.

Leon. Thou hast so long held intercourse with strangers,
Bringing thyself in close contact with minds
Of different poise and fabric, now thy friends
Much feel the inconvenience of such habits.

Anto. There is the danger, my sweet friend; with strangers
We are reserved, observing; seeking still

To make their favor subserve to *our* aims.
With friends we're free, confiding in their love;
Indulge each freak of fancy, and thus injure
Most frequently the beings we most love.

Leon. I joy to find thee in tranquil mood,
Which brings back these reflections.

Anto.   Yes, I am vexed
That I have acted so intemperately.
But it is trying to a man who comes
Heated and weary from his toil, and seeks
The refreshing shade, to nerve himself anew,
To find an idler stretched at length beneath
The sheltering tree he looked to. Is't surprising
If in his bosom dwells some transient anger?

Leon. Didst thou feel rightly, thou wouldst gladly share
The shade with one who your repose might gladden
By eloquent discourse or melody.
The tree is broad, my friend. There's room enough.

Anto. This simile doth but o'ercloud our meaning
And ward off the conclusion, Leonora.
Many of this world's goods I am content
To share with others; but there is a treasure
I could not share but with the well-deserving.
There is another which not willingly
I would share with the *best* deserving. Wouldst thou
The names of these two treasures? Hear! The laurel
And woman's favor.

Leon.   Did the crown
On the youth's brow offend so grave a man?

For his long labor, his sweet poesy,
Could a more meet reward have been devised?
A merit that is supernatural, based
On aerial tones, and the fair pictures, offspring
Of an excited fancy; by a symbol
He should be recompensed; and if he hardly
Touches the earth in resting from his flight,
The unfruitful laurel hardly touched his head,
Fit emblem of the unfruitful admiration
Which is his portion; and around the heads
Of martyrs thou art pleased to see the halo,
And laurel crowns are not for happy hearts.

Anto. Thy sweet mouth, haply, all this variety
May teach me to contemn.

Leon.   At its just rate
To prize each good thing needed not to teach thee.
But even the wisest sometimes need fresh lectures
Upon the value of their own possessions,
Which cease to shine, familiar to the eye.
What seek'st thou for a phantom with thy jealousy
Of favor and of honor? Could the prince
Or could thy friends spare or supply thy services?
As real and as living as those services
Should be their guerdon. Could a laurel garland
Add honor to the prince's confidence,
The people's confidence, so lightly borne,
So fully justified?

Anto.   The smile of beauty
Would gild my honors fairly; what of that?

Leon. Thou couldst dispense with that better than Tasso.

        Wise, self-collected, need'st thou tender care?
        What can a woman do for thee? Round thee
        Reign order and security. For thyself
        Thou carest as for others. Hast already
        All we would give thee. But the bard requires
        Those small attentions women love to render.
        The thousand things he wants, a woman finds
        Such pleasure in providing. Though he fain
        Would have the finest linen, richest silks,
        Nay, even embroidery, and ill endures
        Aught coarse or servile near him, yet he knows not
        The ways and means to gratify his tastes.
        When he has reached a thing, he cannot keep it;
        Is always lacking either gold or care.
        He is so heedless that he never takes
        A journey without losing the third part
        Of his attire and ornaments. At home
        His servants steal from him. And thus it happens
        One must be thinking for him all the while.

Anto.   And thus his very faults make him beloved.
        Fortunate he, whose foibles are deemed
        So charming, who in manhood is permitted
        To play the boy, and be for weakness praised.
        Pardon some little bitterness, my fair one.
        Thou dost him less than justice, it thou tell'st not
        How provident he is in one respect:
        'Tis said he is provided with two loves,
        And, playing off the one against the other,
        Holds them both fast by petty artifice.
        Should this be true?

Leon.   What surer proof could be

That simply friendship governs us? But why
Should we not love the ardent soul which lives
And breathes its beauteous world of dreams for us,
For us alone?

Anto.   Well, spoil him as thou wilt;
His selfishness reward with love; neglect
The friends who dedicate their true souls to you;
Pay homage to the proud one; break forever
The circle drawn by tender confidence.

Leon. Nay, we are not so blindly partial, neither.
We know the failings of our friend, and oft
Rebuke and try to form him to a state
Where he more fully may enjoy himself,
And pleasure others.

Anto.   Yet praise his faults.
I've known him long; for easy 'tis to scan
A soul too haughty to hide aught. Sometimes
He sinks into himself as if his bosom
Contained a world more lovely than the outward,
Which he repulses or forgets. Then, suddenly,
Let joy or grief, anger, or only whim
Cast the least spark, the hidden mine blows up.
He will seize every thing, hold every thing;
Will have his thoughts fulfilled; claims on the moment
What years of preparation might produce;
And often, too, does what years of repentance
Cannot repair. He asks the impossible
From himself as others. The results of all things
He all at once would seize and comprehend.
Scarce one among a million can do this,
And he is not that one.

Act III, Scene 4

Leon.   Himself he hurts;
Not others.

Anto.   Ah yes, others!
Canst thou deny that in the moods of passion,
Which come so unexpectedly upon him,
He dares to scorn, reviles the prince himself,
And even the princess? Granted that his anger
Is transient; these bad moments come too often.
Nor has he mastery o'er his heart or lips.

Leon.   I think it would be well for him and us
Were he removed for some short space from court.

Anto.   Perhaps so, perhaps not. This is no time.
I would not seem to wish his banishment:
I'll trouble him no more; and if he will
Be reconciled with me, and hear my counsel,
I'll compass more tranquility for us all.

Leon.   Talk'st thou of counselling? I deem but now
Thou didst portray him as impracticable.

Anto.   Yet still I hope. In any case 'tis better
To hope than to despair. Of possibilities
Who gives account? Besides, as the prince loves him,
He must remain. And if in vain we strive
To mould him to our wishes, we have long
Been trained to tolerate such companions.

Leon.   So calm,
So passionless, I had not hoped to find you:
A mighty change, methinks.

Anto.   My riper years

Have the advantage; if I go astray,
Experience shows how to repair my error.
But now thou wishedst that we might be reconciled,
I pray thee to continue thy good offices.
Strive to bring Tasso to a calmer mood,
And call me when he is prepared to meet me;
Go to him now, for we set forth to-night.
Farewell.

Leon.   (*Alone.*) We differ then, good friend;
My interest and thine cannot be linked.
I'll use the hour, and win him to my side.

ACT IV

Tasso.

Tasso. (*Alone.*) Am I awakened from a dream? And has
Its sweet illusion fled forever? Is it
That heavy slumber seized me in the noon,
The overpowering blaze, of happiness,
Which fetters still my eyelids? Those gay hours
That, crowned with roses, played about my head,
Where are they fled? and those in which my soul,
With eagle longing, winged its upward flight
To realms of bluest ether? They are fled;
And yet I live, if life it may be called.
And is it my own fault that I am here?
Or do I suffer being innocent?
Nay, was't not a good act incurred this punishment?
I was too hasty to bespeak his favor.
Deceived by that false faith of heart which deems
That all of human face and form are men,
I rushed to his embrace with open arms,
And met hard bolts and padlocks, not a breast.
I should have fortified myself with calm reserve
Against a man I always had suspected:
But be that as it will—one certainty
Remains with me—she stood near me. Her look,
Her tones, and the dear memory of her words,
There are forever mine; nor time, nor fate,
Nor wildest change can ever steal them from me.
And though my love were boldness, though too lightly

I gave a flame admittance to my bosom
Which may consume my life and mar my fortunes,
Yet I can ne'er repent, or wish it otherwise.
When my heart's idol gave the beck, I followed,
Not heeding though the path led to destruction.
So be it. I at least showed myself worthy
Of her most precious confidence, which came
Like incense to my soul, and breathes there still.
Even in this hour when, harshly grating, open
The black-draped portals of long-mourning time.
'Tis done—the sun of favor set forever!
The prince has turned away his face from me,
And I must walk a gloomy, narrow path;
And they, the hideous and ambiguous brood,
The worthy offspring of old night, fly round me,
And raise their hateful note to screech my ruin.
Where shall I turn to shun these loathed attendants?
How 'scape the precipice that yawns for me?

SCENE II

LEONORA. TASSO.

Leon.   Ah, what has happened? Whither, dearest friend,
Have jealousy and anger hurried thee?
How has it happened? We are all amazed.
Thy sweetness and thy kindly tone of feeling;
Thy swift perception, and clear understanding,
Which gave to each his due; thy equanimity,
Teaching to bear what is so hard to vanity;
And thy wise mastery o'er tongue and lips,—
Where were they all, my friend, this luckless day?

Act IV, Scene 2

Tasso. They all are gone; thou find'st thy friend a beggar.

Yes, thou art right; I am no more myself—

Yet know I am not less than what I was.

This seems a riddle, but I can explain it.

The still moon that enchanted thee at night,

To soul, to sense, alluring and yet soothing,

By day is but a cloud, pale, insignificant,

Before the sun's broad glare. And thus with me;

I've lost my lustre since the glare of day.

Leon. I do not understand thy meaning—speak

More frankly. Say, has that harsh man so sickened thee

That thou forgettest thy friends? Wilt thou not trust me?

Tasso. I'm not injured. I must be the injurer,

Since I am punished. Knots that words have tied

The sword might loose; but I—I am a prisoner!

Know'st thou thy visit is paid to a prison?

The prince chastises me as pedagogues

Their pupils, and with *him* I may not reckon.

Leon. Thou seem'st more deeply moved than the case calls for.

Tasso. Think not I am so weak, so childish weak,

To be so moved by such an incident;

But for the state of things which it betokens.

Yet let my enviers, my foes, beware;

The field is free and open.

Leon.   But mistakenly

Such deem'st thou many, as I surely know;

Nor is Antonio so minded towards thee

As thou believest.

Tasso.   And if it be so,
I can't endure his character, and always
Shrink from encountering his stiff worldliness,
And that he always seeks to play the master,
Nor waits to know the riches of his hearers,
But tells you what you better knew before.
He hears not what you say, or misinterprets it;
And so to be mistaken by such arrogance,
Smiling and fancying he knows you wholly,—
Has read you at a glance!—I am not old enough,
Patient or wise enough, to smile it back
With answering thoughts. And since, perforce, we must
Have broken asunder, better now than later.
Thy prince, the lord who fosters and sustains me,
He is my master, and I know no other.
Free will I be in thought and poesy;
In acting, the world limits us sufficiently.

Leon. Antonio oft speaks of thee with esteem.

Tasso. O, no! he speaks with kindness, thou shouldst say,
Or some such word. He knows how to insert
Such smooth qualifications that his praise
Doth turn to blame; nor would aught vex me more
Than praise misused by such a mouth.

Leon.   Yet hadst thou
But heard as I how fitly he could talk
Of thy exalted talents, thou wouldst not
Have called it praise misused.

Tasso.   A selfish mind
Cannot escape the pangs of envy. Such

       Can pardon others' wealth and rank; for these
       They think they may obtain themselves, if chance
       Favor them in their turn; but gifts which Nature
       Alone can give, which neither toil nor patience,
       Valor nor wealth, nor prudence can attain,
       They cannot pardon others their possession.
       Shall he love them in me?—he who vainly
       Has paid his stiff and formal court to the Muses,
       And as he the thoughts, culled from many poets,
       Together binds—tasteless amalgamation!—
       Fancies that he is one; can he forgive me
       My natural gift? No! Far more willingly
       Would he resign me to the prince's favor,
       Which yet he gladly would monopolize,
       Than that prerogative with which the Nine
       Endowed the poor and orphan youth.

Leon.   Sawest thou
       But with mine eyes! Indeed thou art deceived.

Tasso. Well, then, I would remain so. I regard him
       As my worst foe, and most unwillingly
       Should I think milder of him. It is folly
       To aim at perfect impartiality.
       Freedom from prejudices, if entire,
       Destroys originality of mind.
       Are other men so just in judging us?
       No, no. Man must have in his narrow being
       The double impulses of love and hatred.
       Are there not day and night? sleeping and waking?
       And I must hate this man—must have the pleasure
       Still worse and worse to think of him.

Leon.   Unless
You check these feelings, how, my friend, is't possible
You should continue at this court? You know
He cannot be dispensed with here.

Tasso.   Fair one, I know
I might have been long since.

Leon.   Never!
Thou knowest how dear is thy society
Both to the prince and princess. And Leonora
Comes hither for thy sake almost as much
As theirs so near in blood. And they all love
And trust thee fully.

Tasso.   Trust me?
O Leonora! what a word is that!
Speaks the prince ever of his state affairs,
Of aught of consequence, to me? Or if
He speaks of such before me to his sister,
Or other friends, he never turns to me.
'Tis always, "When Antonio comes we'll do it;"
"Write to Antonio;" "Ask Antonio."

Leon.   Wilt thou complain where there's such cause for gratitude?
Is it no compliment to leave thee free,
Requiring nought but thy society?

Tasso.   He leaves me free because he thinks me useless.

Leon.   Thou art not useless even when thou art
To all appearance quite inactive. But
Why is it that you cherish this chagrin,
Like a belovéd child, close to the heart?

       Thou art not happy here where chance has planted thee;
       I long have thought it. If I dared advise thee,
       I'd say, Leave for a while this place.

Tasso.   Spare not
       Thy patient, sweet physician; give the draught,
       Though it be bitter. But can he recover?
       O, no! I see he is beyond all remedy.
       If I could pardon your Antonio
       He would not me; and he it is is needed,
       Not I. And he is prudent; I alas,
       Too much the opposite. So he can harm me;
       I know not to resist, nor do my friends
       Attempt it. They are wise, and I will go.
       The thought that you so lightly could resign me
       Will lend me strength and courage: so, farewell!

Leon.   At distance placed, things show in fair proportion,
       Which look confused seen nearer. Someday thou
       Wilt learn to prize the love which here flowed on thee,
       And which no other scene shall e'er supply.

Tasso.   That will I try. I will know the world's way;
       How easily it leaves one lonely, helpless,
       And like the sun, and moon, and other idols,
       Runs on its course, nor casts a look behind.

Leon.   If thou wouldst listen to my counsels, Tasso,
       Thou never need'st repeat the sad experience;
       If thou wilt go to Florence, I myself
       Will tenderly care for thy comfort. I
       Set forth to-morrow, there to join my husband.
       He would rejoice to see thee my companion.

Thou knowest what a prince that city boasts;
What noble men, what lovely women. Couldst thou
Be happy there? Reflect, and then decide.

Tasso. Thy plan has charms; it is conformable
To certain secret wishes of my soul.
But 'tis so new, I cannot answer yet.

Leon. Well, I will leave thee with the fairest hopes
For thee and me, and for this house: I do not
Believe thou canst contrive a better plan.

Tasso. Yet stay one moment, fairest friend, and say,
How is the princess minded towards me?
Speak freely. Is she angry? Doth she blame me?

Leon. Knowing thee well, she easily acquits thee.

Tasso. Doth she esteem me less? Flatter me not.

Leon. A woman's heart is not so lightly altered.

Tasso. Can she be willing, then, to let me go?

Leon. She wishes thee to go for thine own sake.

Tasso. Shall I not lose the prince's grace forever?

Leon. Thou mayst trust in his magnanimity.

Tasso. We leave the princess quite alone. Thou goest,
And I, though little to her, yet was something.

Leon. We have companionship with distant friends,
If we can know them happy; nor shalt thou
Depart from hence dissatisfied. The prince
Commands Antonio to seek thee. He

Now blames himself for his past bitterness.
I pray thee, meet him calmly when he comes.

Tasso.   There is no mood in which I may not meet him.

Leon.   And would to Heaven, my dear friend, thy eyes
Might e'er be opened to the truth,
That in thy fatherland there's not a being
Would hate, or persecute, or injure thee.
Thou errest greatly in these thoughts: thy fancy,
Which framed such beauteous fabrics to delight
The hearts of others, here, alas! has woven
Sad-colored ones to thine own hurt. I'll do
All that I can to disentangle them,
And make thee free and gladsome. Now, farewell!
I hope a favorable answer from thee.

SCENE III

TASSO, *alone.*

Tasso.   So! when I'm calm and sane, I shall perceive
Nobody persecutes me—I have no enemy.
These are chimeras of my troubled brain!
I shall acknowledge I do great injustice
To real friends, in treating them as foes,
This hour, which, clear as noonday sun, displays
My injuries. Their malice should have taught me
To praise their kindness. I should thank the prince
For his large bounty, at the very moment
He weakly suffers his eyes to be blinded,

And his hand guided by my enemy.
Now he has been deceived he cannot see.
Who the deceivers are I cannot show.
He could so easily admit their influence,
They are so crafty. Shall I, then, keep still,
Or wholly yield? Who is't advises this?
Who with such seeming tenderness would lead me?
Leonora Sanvitali—the soft siren.
I know her now! Why did I listen to her?
Do I not know her wily heart, still turning
To all that brings her favor and advantage?
How willingly I have deceived myself
About her also! Yes! 'twas really vanity
Cheated me so. I knew her, and yet trusted her.
She may be false to others. I would think
To me her heart is warm, and will be faithful.
I understand her now, although too late.
Her heart was warm towards the favored one—
Was faithful to my luck. Now I am fallen,
She turns from me to join the fortunate.
Now comes she as the agent of my foe,
Steals in and hisses out her sugared words.
The smooth-tongued snake! How gracefully she did it!
How sweetly counterfeited love! Yet could not
The hollow flattery deceive me long.
Falsehood was written on her brow; and soon
I feel it when one seeks unfair advantage
Over my heart. I shall depart immediately—
Shall go to Florence. And wherefore Florence?
I understand it all. There reign the Medici.
They're not, indeed, at open variance
With the house of Este; yet do jealousy

And envy, with cold hands, hold them asunder.
Should I be honored by that noble prince
With marks of favor, such as I may surely
Expect from him, the courtiers of Alphonso
Could easily deprive me of his favor.
Yes, I will go, but not as you advise;
I will away, and farther than you think.
Why am I here? What now detains me here?
Each word I understand so perfectly
Which I allured from Leonora's lips.
I took in every syllable and now know
Precisely what the princess thinks. "Despair not;
She wishes thee to go for thine own sake."
O, felt she rather and o'ermastering passion,
Rending its way unthinking of my safety!
More welcome the cold hand of death than hers
Which can so willingly let go my hold;
As cold and stiff indeed. Yes, yes, I go.
Now guard thyself, and let no new illusion
Of friendship or of happiness deceive thee.
No man can cheat thee if thy false heart aid not.

SCENE IV

TASSO. ANTONIO

Anto.   I have come hither, Tasso, to talk with thee,
If thou canst quietly give ear to me.

Tasso.   Since I'm debarred from acting, as thou knowest,
Waiting and hearing must become me well.

Anto.   I find thee then composed, as was my wish,
        And shall speak frankly. First of all, I break,
        In the prince's name, the weak band that confines thee.

Tasso. Caprice, which took my freedom, now restores it.
        I must accept it so, and ask no question.

Anto.   Then, for myself I have, it seems, impelled
        By passion, wounded thee unconsciously,
        Not feeling at the time the venom of my words;
        But no insulting phrase escaped my lips.
        Thou art not injured as a nobleman,
        And as a man wilt not refuse the pardon
        I come to crave.

Tasso.   Which is most cruel,
        To wound me in my feelings or mine honor,
        I'll not inquire. The one scratches the skin,
        The other pierces to the marrow. Easily
        The dart is turned on him who shot it.
        The opinion of the world is satisfied
        By a well-guided sword. A sickened heart
        What remedy shall heal?

Anto.   Yet let me urge thee—
        I but express the prince's wish, who sent me.

Tasso. I know my duty, and must yield. I pardon thee
        As far as in me lies. Some say the sword,
        By friendly touch, can heal the wounds it made.
        This power man's tongue possesses, nor through stubbornness
        Would I retard my cure.

Anto.   I thank thee, and would gladly prove the extent

    Of my good will to thee. Say, is there aught
    Which I can do in furtherance of thy wishes?

Tasso.   Thou bring'st me freedom! Wilt thou aid to use it?

Anto.   Express thy meaning more distinctly.

Tasso.   Thou knowest
    I've brought my poem to an end; yet much it wants
    To its completion. When, to-day,
    I showed it to the prince, I meant to have proffered
    A request that I might have permission now to visit
    My friends in Rome. In letters they have sent me
    Various criticisms on my work.
    Some I adopted; with regard to others,
    Remain more doubtful, and would fain discuss them
    With my accomplished censors satisfactorily,
    Which I, in writing, cannot do. To-day
    I found no fitting time to ask the prince,
    And am no longer confident enough.
    But wouldst thou undertake to do it for me?

Anto.   But is it, then, desirable to go
    Just at the moment when thy poem's close,
    So long expected, highly recommends thee
    To the favor of the prince and princess. For
    The days of favor are the days of harvest.
    One must be busy, and not leave the field;
    If thou goest now, thou probably mayst lose
    The fruit of all thy labor past. The princess
    A mighty goddess is, nor must she be slighted.
    Respect her influence, and remain with us.

Tasso.   I do not fear to go. The prince is noble;

Has always treated me with generosity.
From his heart alone would I receive a favor,
Nor would propitiate him by artifice,
Or watching of his moods. So shall he never
Learn to repent what he has done for me.

Anto. Yet do not now ask his consent to go;
He will refuse, or grant it most unwillingly.

Tasso. He'll give it willingly, if rightly asked.
Thou mightst obtain it if thou wouldst.

Anto.   Thy reasons
He will not think sufficient.

Tasso.   My poem
Doth render one in every stanza. High
Is placed my aim, though perhaps unattainable
To powers like mine. In diligence and toil
I've not been wanting. In the quiet walks
Of the fair day, the stillness of the night,
Still I was weaving, coloring, my lay.
In all humility I strove to emulate
The great masters of the former world. I hoped
The noble deeds of a more modern time
To revive from the long sleep that had o'erpowered them,
And with my heroic warriors to share
The glory of their holy war. And if
The lay be destined to awake the best,
It must also be worthy of the best.
'Twas Alphonso inspired what I have written;
Now let him give me space for its perfection.

Anto. Are there in Rome, then, more accomplished critics

        Than in the prince and others of Ferrara?
        Finish thy poem here, then go to Rome
        To enjoy the fruits of thy success.

Tasso.   As was Alphonso
        The first to inspire me, he shall be the last
        To instruct me. Thy opinion, too, and those
        Of the wise men who grace this court, I honor.
        You shall be umpires when my Roman friends
        Fail to produce conviction. These I wish
        Also to hear. Gonzaga has assembled
        A noble council for my trial: Bargo,
        Antonio, and Speron Speroni,
        Angelio, Flaminio de Nobili,—
        Names doubtless known to thee. My mind would willingly
        Submit to their decision.

Anto.   Thou art so occupied
        With thine own feelings thou forgett'st the prince.
        I tell thee he will not give leave, or, if
        He does, it will be angry. And shall I
        Become the means to draw his wrath upon thee?

Tasso.   So thou refusest the first time, I ask
        A proof of thy late proffered friendship.

Anto.   Can I
        Give stronger proof of friendship than the present—
        Denying what I know would do thee harm?
        'Tis a false love which cares to gratify
        The wishes of the loved, not taking heed
        Whether it be for lasting good or ill.
        Thou fanciest at this moment what thou wishest
        Must be the best thing possible. 'Tis thus

      We erring mortals strive through a chimera
      To remedy our want of power and truth.
      My duty bids me seek to moderate
      The heat which now is leading thee astray.

Tasso.   This tyranny of friendship I esteem
      The most insufferable of all despotisms.
      Because thy opinion differs here from mine,
      Of course thou must be right. Although I doubt not
      Thou wishest my best good, yet do not ask
      That I shall seek it only in thy way.

Anto.   And dost thou then demand that in cold blood
      I do this which I know will work thee ill?

Tasso.   Dismiss that care. Thou shalt not thus escape.
      Thou hast declared me free. The door lies open.
      I go myself to the prince if thou wilt not.
      The prince sets forth immediately; here is
      No space for delay. Choose! Be assured,
      If thou goest not, I shall, whate'er the result.

Anto.   Act not so rashly! I will only ask
      That thou wilt wait until the prince return.
      Speak not so suddenly, lest thou repent it.

Tasso.   This very hour I'll speak with him. My feet
      Burn on this marble flooring; and my spirit
      Will not be pacified until the highways
      Cast up their dust around me, hastening hence.
      I pray thee go! Thou seest I am unfit;
      I cannot promise to command myself.
      Alphonso is no tyrant; and, in happier days,
      I willingly obeyed him; now, I cannot.

    Leave me in freedom to recall my senses,
    All scattered now, and I shall soon return
    To duty and my friends.

Anto.   Thou art then skilled
    In sophistry. I scarce know how to act.

Tasso. If thou wouldst win my confidence, wouldst have me
    Trust in thy late fair-spoken words, grant now
    The boon I ask. At thy request, Alphonso
    Will, without anger, let me go; and I
    Will warmly thank thy friendly intercession.
    But if thou still dost hate me, and wouldst have me
    A hapless exile from this court forever,—
    Helpless cast forth to the wide world,—thou canst not
    Take surer means to wreak thy vengeance on me,
    Than by refusing thy assistance here.

Anto. Since thus obliged to harm thee one way, Tasso,
    I take the one thou dost prefer. The issue
    Will show thee which was wrong, and which was prudent.
    I say to thee, beforehand, that thou hardly
    Wilt leave this house behind, before thy heart
    Will sigh to turn again, although thy obstinacy
    May urge thee forward. Pain, confusion, sadness,
    Wait thee in Rome, where thou wilt miss thy aim.
    I do not say this to deter thee, only
    I prophesy to thee that I may promise
    T'assist thee in the troubles I foretell.

SCENE V

TASSO, *alone.*

Tasso. Yes, go, and please thyself upon the way
With thoughts how well and wisely thou hast talked.
For once I have been able to dissemble. Thou
Art a great master, and I am not slow
In learning what I will. Thus life constrains us
To seem the thing our flush of youthful courage
Almost disdained to look upon. Now clearly
I penetrate the screen of courtly policy.
Antonio wishes me away, but will not
Be seen to wish it; thus he plays the moderator.
The prudent, who would strengthen my weak judgment
Elects himself my guardian, and would lower me
To childhood, since he could not quite to servitude;
Thus clouding o'er the piercing ken of the prince
And princess. He thinks Nature, while endowing me
With many splendid gifts, saw fit to balance
Her grace by a large portion of like follies,
Unbounded pride, a gloomy turn of thought,
And an exaggerated sensibility.
"But since his character is formed, we must
Bear with him, and hope the best;
So shall each good trait yield unlooked-for-pleasure.
And 'tis the only way; for as he is
Be sure he'll live and die."—And then, Alphonso,
Where is the firm, clear mind, so steady towards
His foes; so faithful, tender to his friends?
It is my fate that e'en those who to others
Show themselves kind and true, will turn from me,

Will coldly leave me on most light occasion.
Was not the coming of this man sufficient
To alter all my fortunes in an hour;
Razing the palace of my happiness,
Nor leaving one stone upon the other? Ah,
That it must be so! must be so to-day!
But now I was the centre of a circle;
All things pressed towards me; now all recede.
But now each being in my circle's range
Strove to draw near me, nay, to mingle with me.
Now equally they strive to repulse or shun me.
And wherefore? Does this man carry such weight,
Poised in the scale, 'gainst all my worth and love?
All fly me now. Thou too, belovéd, thou,
O princess of my soul, couldst thou forsake me!
Yes, yes, 'tis so; or else she would have cheered
These black hours by some token of remembrance.
Yet how have I deserved it? 'Twas so natural
To this poor heart to love her. Her first tones
Thrilled through that heart, and chained me here forever.
My eyes are dimmed whene'er I look upon her;
My knees bend under me; I scarce can stand
Before the light of that divinest face.
How has this heart bowed down in worship to her.
And now,—hold firm, fond heart,—she too has left me.
Excuse her, but dissemble not the truth.
Yes, it is so! and yet there is a breath
Of faith within me fain would waft away
These cold and leaden tidings. Yes, 'tis so,
And fate, e'en now, is busy inscribing it
On the brazen rim of the o'er-full grief tablet.
Now are my enemies indeed triumphant,

And I am driven from my chiefest stronghold—
Must yield myself a captive to the squadrons.
Her hand will not be stretched to raise the falling,
Her radiant glance cast to recall the flying.
Despair now has me in his talons: still
Weeping I shall repeat, *"Thou too—thou too!"*

ACT V

ALPHONSO. ANTONIO.

Anto.   At thy command, I went again to Tasso,
And left him but a moment since. I urged him,
Persuaded him; but he is obstinate.
Nothing will serve him but the asked permission
To visit Rome for some short space.

Alph.   I grieve,
And 'tis as well to confess as to increase it
By effort at concealment. If he goes,
The wily Medici, or else Gonzaga,
Will be sure to entice and keep him from me.
For this 'tis which enriches Italy,
Beyond all other lands, with the productions
Of genius in its varied workings, that
Her princes strive who shall possess and favor
The gifted men whose minds inform such works.
A general without army is that prince
Who attracts not men of genius to his banner;
And who the voice of Poesy loves not
Is a barbarian, be he who he may.
'Twas I discovered and developed genius
In Tasso. 'Tis my pride that he's my servant;
And I have done so much for him that now
To lose him is most grievous.

Anto.   And the fault

Is mine, that I so needless angered him.
I have to thank thy grace which pardons me;
I shall be comfortless if thou believe not
That I have done my best to reconcile him.
O, give me the assurance that thou dost so,
That I may calm, may trust myself once more.

Alph.   Fear not, Antonio; I cannot blame thee.
I know as well his disposition as
All I have done for him, and pardoned in him,
Nor e'er constrained him, asking aught again.
Much can man conquer; his own will can only
Adversity, or Time the underminer.

Anto.   When many toil for one, 'tis surely just
That *one* should strive to return their favors, using
What means he has for benefiting them.
He has such a rich, adornéd mind,
Such hoards of knowledge, is he not more bound
Than common men to live lord of himself?
And does the poet e'er remember this?

Alph.   Repose is not desirable to man,
Thus foes are given him to stir his valor,
And friends, as well, to exercise his patience.

Anto.   That simplest duty of a reasoning being,
To choose what meat and drink are proper for him,—
Since Nature does not limit man, as she
Has done the other animals, by instinct,—
Does he fulfil it? No; but like a child
Swallows each viand which allures the palate.
Who ever saw him temper wine with water?
Spices, sweet things, strong drink, he likes them all—

So takes them all, not heeding consequences;
And then complains of an o'erclouded brain,
His heated blood, and his excited feelings,
And scolds about his nature and his destiny.
Oft have I heard him rail at his physician
In bitterness and folly. 'Twas ridiculous
If aught can be which plagues our fellow-creatures.
"I have this ail," says he, frightened and fretful;
"I would be cured." "Then," says the doctor, "shun
This thing or that." "I cannot; 'tis impossible."
"Then take this drink." "O, but it tastes too horribly;
My blood rises against it." "Well, drink nought but water."
"I could not more detest water alone
In hydrophobia." "Then I cannot help you;
You must grow worse and worse each day you live thus."
"You are a fine physician, truly! Are there no remedies
Which are not worse to endure, than is
Thy present ill?" Your highness smiles;
But you have often heard all this, and more.

Alph.   Yes, I have heard and have excused it all.

Anto.   'Tis certain, so irregular a life
Poisons our slumbers with wild, painful dreams,
And finally can make us dream at noonday.
Such dreams are his! Thinking himself surrounded
With foes and rivals, all who see his talents
Forsooth, must envy, hate, and persecute him.
With what fond fancies doth he weary thee!—
Locks broken, intercepted letters, daggers, poison;
And when thou mad'st inquiry, what has been
The invariable result? 'Twas all his fancy!

The protection of no prince gives him security,
The bosom of no friend gives him repose!
Can such a man add to thy happiness?

Alph. He does not add directly to my happiness.
That I cannot expect from all my friends,
But use each one according to his nature;
And thus each serves me well. This lesson learned I
From the wise Medici, and from the pope,
Who, with such gentleness and patience, bore
The freaks and follies of those men of genius
Who needed them so much, and knew it not.

Anto. Yet sure, my prince, all are best taught to prize
Life's blessings by the toil of winning them!
Had he been forced to struggle for all this
Which Fortune, open-handed, pours upon him,
His character had gained more strength through experience,
And he from step to step become more satisfied.
Is it not luck enough for a poor gentleman
To be the elect companion of his sovereign,
And freed from pains and cares of penury?
And when he is advance still further, raised
O'er his sometime superiors, and loaded
With marks of favor and of confidence,
Should he not feel delight and gratitude?
And Tasso has obtained, beside all this, the noblest
Reward of youthful effort; since his country
Already knows and looks on him with hope.
Believe me, his capricious discontents
Rest but on the broad bolster of his luck.
He comes—dismiss him kindly—let him seek
In Rome or Naples what he misses here,

And what here only he can find again.

Alph.   Will he go with us to Ferrara first?

Anto.   No! he prefers staying at Belriguardo,
And sending to the city for such things
As he may need for the intended journey.

Alph.   Well, let it be so, then. My sister goes
With us to accompany her friend, and I
Shall ride before and be there to receive them.
Thou follow us when thou hast cared for him.
Make thou arrangements, and direct my warder
That he may stay here till his stores arrive,
And I prepare some letters I will give him
To friends of mine in Rome. He comes. Farewell!

SCENE II

ALPHONSO. TASSO.

Tasso.   (*With an air of reserve.*) The grace which thou so oft hast
shown to me
To-day displays in broadest light. The trespass
So heedlessly committed thou hast pardoned;
Hast reconciled me with mine adversary;
And now dost graciously give me permission
To leave thy side in happy confidence
That thou wilt not forget, nor cease to favor me.
I go in hopes that change of scene will cure
The malady that now distresses me,
And move my spirit with new life, so that,

Returning, I may merit those kind looks
Which cheered me when I came to thee at first.

Alph.   I wish thee luck and pleasure in thy journey,
And trust thou wilt return quite well and happy,
And wilt requite me richly for each hour
Thou has stole from us. I shall give thee letters
To my ambassador and friends at Rome.
I hope thou wilt treat them with confidence,
As being mine; for I must still regard thee
As mine, though thou dost leave me voluntarily.

Tasso.   Thy goodness overpowers me. I can scarcely
Find words to thank thee. Hear a prayer instead,
To which this goodness now emboldens me.
My poem, I have striven to perfect it;
And yet it falls far, far beneath the standard
E'en of my present tastes.   Now, then I visit
The Eternal City, where the very air
Is instinct with the spirit of past greatness,
I am again a pupil, and may hope
To make my poem a more worthy gift;
But now I shame to know it in thy keeping.

Alph.   Wilt thou reclaim thy gifts in the same day
They were bestowed? Besides, I do believe
thou art in error: let me mediate
Between thee and thy poem: have a care
Lest thou refine away that glow of nature
Which animates thy verse; no sickly hues,
Mixed by fastidious taste, could recompense us.
List not too much to the advice of others;
The many-colored thoughts of various men,

         Crossing or contradicting as in life,
         The poet casts again through his own prism,
         Not caring if he now displease the many,
         That he may please them some day as much more.
         But I will not deny that here and there
         Thy work may need the file, and soon will send thee
         A copy fairly writ. But this thou gav'st me
         I cannot part with till I have enjoyed it
         In company with my sisters. If thou bring'st it
         More perfect back, we shall have a new delight,
         And we can give thee, too, our friendly judgment.

Tasso.   Excuse my asking thee to send the copy
         As soon as may be; in my work my mind
         Is now absorbed, for now it must be all
         It e'er shall be.

Alph.   And I respect thy earnestness;
         Yet I could wish thou wouldst, for some brief space,
         Enjoy the world in freedom; dissipate
         These thronging thoughts; sweeten by exercise
         The fevered blood. Then would thy senses
         Tuned to new harmony, do for thee all
         Which thou, by zeal, dost vainly seek to compass.

Tasso.   My prince, it seems so; yet I am then best
         When I at will can give me to my task.
         The labor which I love can work my cure,
         For this luxurious ease befits me not.
         Repose of body brings not that of mind;
         And I, alas! feel that I was not destined
         On the soft gladsome element of day
         To sail unto the sea of future times.

Alph.   All that thou seest and feel'st still leads thee back
To the deep, far recesses of thy soul.
Of all the pits that fate has hung for us,
Those in our hearts are deepest—most alluring
Their flower-wreathed brinks. O, heed my voice!
Be not so closely wedded to thyself;
The poet gains thereby, but the *man* loses.

Tasso.   Vainly thou speak'st; vainly I strive; I find
Still day and night alternate in my bosom.
When I muse not, nor paint poetic visions,
Life ceases in my soul. Can the poor silkworm
Pause in his task because he works his death,
And from his life's last forces eager he bestows,
Then rests within the shroud his substance shaped.
O, may I only hope to share yet further
His destiny! In new and sun-bright realms
To unfold my wings into a higher being.

Alph.   Tasso, who givest to so many hearts
Redoubled joy in life, wilt thou ne'er learn
To know that being's worth whose better part
Thou dost possess tenfold beyond the measure
Allotted to thy brethren of this world?
Farewell; the speedier thou makest return,
The warmer shall thy welcome be. Farewell!

SCENE III

TASSO, *alone.*

Tasso.   Yes, yet be firm, my heart. 'Tis the first time,

And hard the practice of dissimulation.
Antonio's mind sounds in his words and voice.
If I give heed, I shall be sure to hear
That echo on each side—Be firm, be firm!
'Tis but a moment longer; and who late
In life begins to feign, has the advantage
Of his past reputation for sincerity.
O, I shall end with masterly composure!
(*After a pause.*) Too rashly that was said. She comes
she comes—
The gentle princess comes. Ah, what a feeling!
She comes—suspicion and chagrin dissolve
To sorrow at the painful, lovely vision.

Scene IV

Princess. Tasso.

Prin.   I hear we are to leave thee; that thou dost not
Go with us to Ferrara on thy way.
I trust thy absence will not be a long one.
To Rome thou goest?

Tasso.   I seek that city first;
And if my friends receive me as I hope,
Shall there remain to give the final polish
To my Jerusalem. There are assembled
So many master spirits, and, besides,
In that imperial and hallowed city
Each stone has a language, every street a story;
And these dumb teachers, in their solemn majesty,
Will find an attentive pupil in your poet.

And if I cannot there perfect my work,
Nowhere can it be done. Alas! I feel
As if I ne'er could bring aught to perfection,
Or reap success from any enterprise.
That I may alter, but cannot perfect,
I feel—I feel it sadly—the great art,
Which to strong souls brings added strengthening
And sweet refreshment, will to mine be ruin.
But I will strive. From Rome I go to Naples.

Prin.   Why wilt thou venture? The stern prohibition—
Equal against thy father and thyself—
Has never been revoked.

Tasso.   I go disguised.
In the poor garb of shepherd or of pilgrim,
I easily shall thread the crowded streets
Of Naples unobserved. I seek the shore;
Then find a boat, manned by good, honest peasants,
Returning from the market to Sorrentium,
Where dwells my sister, who with me formed once
The painful joy of our lost parents. I speak not
While in the skiff, nor yet at disembarking;
I softly climb the path, and at the gate
I ask, "Where dwells Cornelia?" and a woman,
Spinning before her door, shows me her house.
The children flock to look upon the stranger,
With the dishevelled locks and gloomy looks.
At last I reach the threshold—open stands
The door—I enter.

Prin.   Tasso, look up; wake up and know thy danger!
If thou art conscious, tell me! Is it noble

To think, to speak, thus selfishly, regardless
How thou dost wound and sicken friendly hearts?
How has my brother favored thee! his sisters
Have treasured thee; thou carest not, feel'st it not.
One moment's passion blots out all remembrance
Of love and favors past. Wilt thou, then, go,
Leaving such pain and care behind? (*Tasso turns away.*)
        'Tis pleasant
To speed the parting guest with some kind token,
Recalling hours which we have passed together,
Were't but a piece of armor or a mantle.
But richest gifts to thee are useless, who
Dost wilful cast them all away, preferring
The long black robe, the scallop shell and staff.
Thou choosest to be poor, and yet wilt rob us
Of what without us thou canst not enjoy.

Tasso.   Thou dost not, then, wholly repel me from thee.
O, heavenly words! most sweet, most dear assurance!
Direct, protect, receive me as thy servant.
Leave me in Belriguardo, or transfer me
To Consandoli, as thou wilt. The prince
Has many stately castles and fair gardens,
Which you but seldom honor with your presence
Even for a day. From them choose the most distant,
Which you, perhaps, for years may never visit;
There send me. I will be your faithful warder;
There will I prune the trees, cover the citrons
With boards and tiles in autumn, and preserve them
'Neath matted reeds. Fair flowers shall dress the beds,
No weed shall grow in avenue or alley;
And mine be also charge over the palace,

To open windows at the proper times,
To guard the pictures against damp and mould,
To sweep the stuccoed walls with a light broom,
To keep the marble pavement white and pure.
No stone, no tile, shall be displaced, nor grass
Find leave to grow in any cleft or chink.

Prin.   I know not how to act. I find no comfort
For thee or us. O, would but some good angel
Show me some wholesome herb, some healing beverage,
That would have power to pacify thy senses,
And make us happy in thy cure: all words
Are idle, for the truest touch thee not;
And I must leave thee; but my heart stays with thee.

Tasso.   My God! she pities me, she does indeed;
And could I then mistake that noble heart,
Maintain my mean suspicions in her presence?
But now I know her and myself again.
Speak on those words of tenderness and soothing;
Give me thy counsel; say, what shall I do?

Prin.   We ask but little from thee; yet that little
Has ever been too much: that thou would'st trust us,
And to thyself be true! Couldst thou do this
Thou wouldst be happy, and we be happy in thee.
We must be gloomy when we see thee so;
Impatient when so oft we see thee need
The help we cannot give; when thou refusest
To seize the hand stretched out to thee in love.

Tasso.   Thou art the same who came to meet me first!
Angel of pity and of love, forgive

That my eye, clouded by the mists of earth,
Mistook thee for a moment. *Now* I know thee,
And open all my soul to adoration,
My heart to tenderness beyond all words.
Ah, what a feeling! what a strange confusion!
Is't madness which draws me thus towards thee?
Or is't an elevated sense of truth,
In its most lovely, earth-born form? I know not.
It is the feeling which alone can *make* me
Most blest if I may venture to indulge it,
Most miserable if I must repress it.
And I have striven with this passion—striven
With my profoundest self—have torn in pieces
The heart which beat with such devotion for thee.

Prin.   If thou wouldst have me listen longer, Tasso,
Avoid expressions which I must not hear.

Tasso.   And can the goblet's rim restrain the wine
Which foams above it? Every word of thine
Kindles my soul with fires unfelt before;
With each word beam thine eyes more clear and soft;
My soul dilates, each sorrow flies, I'm free,—
Free as a god,—and this I own to thee.
The power that fills me now thy lips poured on me,
And I am wholly thine. Of all my being
No atom call I mine, apart from thee.
Ah, I am blinded with excess of light!
My senses waver with excess of bliss!
I must approach. My heart throbs wildly towards thee;
I am all thine—receive me to thyself! (*Clasping her in his arms.*)

Prin.   (*Breaking from him.*) Away! (*Hastens out.*)

Leon. (*Who has been some time approaching.*) What, what has
       happened, Tasso? [*Follows the* Princess.

Tasso. (*Attempting to follow.*) My God!

Alph. (*Who has been approaching with Antonio.*) He raves! Beware
       that he escape not. [*Goes out.*

Scene V

Tasso. Antonio.

Anto. Had thy suspicion groundwork? Wert thou ever
       Girt round by foes? Were their chief now beside thee,
       How would he triumph! Poor unfortunate!
       I scarcely now what 'twas I saw. A thing
       So monstrous, so entirely unexpected,
       Must make the mind stand still a while in fault
       Of something to compare this deed withal.

Tasso. Perform thine office, for I understand it.
       (*After a long pause.*) Thou art well worthy of the prince's
           confidence.
       My staff is broken; thou art free to torture me;
       Pull in thy hook; make thy prey feel its sharpness;
       Thou art a precious work-tool for a tyrant,
       Whether as jailer or as torturer;
       Each part thou playest as if born for it.
       (*Towards the scenes.*) Go tyrant! now, dissimulation over,
       Thy slave in chains, 'tis thy fit hour for triumph.
       I know what griefs thou has prepared for me;
       Yet go; thy presence rouses my abhorrence,

Unfeeling despot, go—and be detested!
(*After a pause.*) Yes; now I am an outcast mendicant,
upon the very spot where I was crowned
A victim for the altar. They lured from me
My poem—all my wealth—with their smooth words.
My all is in their hands which could secure me
Another home, or shelter me from hunger.
Thus 'tis that they would have me rest, and thou
Art the deviser of this fell conspiracy.
My poem now will never be perfected;
My fame can never be further diffused;
My enemies may freely spy my faults,
And I be first despised, and then forgotten.
Therefore, should I accustom me to idleness,
Beware lest I o'ertask my mind. What friendship!
What tender care! I long have felt this plot
Spinning and weaving round me; now 'tis finished,
And braves the light of day in all its ugliness.
And thou, too, siren, who with honeyed words
Enticed me to my ruin, now I know thee.
But why so late? Thus we deceive ourselves,
And venerate the wicked, as they us.
Men know each other not, except, perhaps,
The galley slaves to one bench chained together,
When none can gain by loss of a companion,
And all as villains are received at once.
But we must courtly flatter other men,
Hoping they will return our compliments.
How she, who was to me a shrinéd saint,
Has dropped her mask! I see her as she is:
Coquettish, full of little arts—Armida,
Deprived of all her charms. Yes, thou art she;

The tale I framed was a presentiment.
And then her crafty little emissary!
How mean, how paltry looks she now before me!
This is the snare to which her soft steps guided.
I know you all. That is some satisfaction;
And though these moments rob me of all else,
I should not murmur, since they bring me truth.

Anto.   Tasso, I listen with astonishment,
Well as I know how lightly thy rash spirit
Flies from the one extreme to the other.
Bethink thyself! Repress this frantic passion.
Thou dost blaspheme; thou usest such expressions
As, though thy friends may pardon them, from feeling
How wretched is thy state of mind, thou never,
When calmer, wilt forgive unto thyself.

Tasso.   Tune not thy tongue to gentleness; talk not
Thus reasonably to a wretch who now
Can find no comfort save in self-oblivion.
I feel myself crushed to my inmost marrow;
And must I live to feel it? Now despair
Seizes upon me with relentless grasp,
And 'mid the fiery tortures which consume me,
These blasphemies are as low groans of pain.
I must away: if thou look'st kindly on me:
Go, show it now, and hasten to my departure.

Anto.   In such distracted state I cannot leave thee;
I will be patient, whatso'er thou sayest.

Tasso.   I am thy prisoner, then. Well, be it so;
I will not make resistance—am content.

       Here will I sit, and memory will torture me,
       Recalling all that I have willful lost:
       Now they depart. O God! I see the dust
       Raised by their chariot wheels, and I must stay.
       They leave me, and in anger. O, might I
       But kiss her hand once more, ask her forgiveness,
       Hear from her sweet mouth, "Go in peace, my friend!"
       O, might I bid farewell! I must, I must!
       I could plead with her. No; I am an exile—
       Banished, despised. I never more shall hear
       Her heavenly voice—never more meet her eye.

Anto.   Be thou reminded by the voice of one
       Who cannot hear thy voice without emotion;
       Thy case is not so desperate. Be a man;
       Collect thyself, and all may yet be well.

Tasso.   And am I, then, so wretched as I seem?
       Is all, then, lost? Could this one shock suffice
       To crumble my life's tenement to dust?
       Remains no talent, now, which might support
       Or pleasure me? Are all their fires extinguished
       Which warmed my breast but now? Have I a nothing,
       Absolute nullity, so soon become?
       Yes, it is really so; I am now nothing!
       She has forsaken me, and I myself.

Anto.   Perhaps to find thyself again, a better,
       Wiser, and happier man.

Tasso.   Thou sayest well.
       Have I forgot so many instances
       Which history offers us of noble men,

Whose sorrows and whose fortitude might rouse
My soul to emulation? No; 'tis vain.
There's a last refuge, nature's providence
Supplies to miserable men like me—
Tears, sobs of pain, when the o'erladen heart
Can bear no more. I have, besides, the gift
To make my sighs and groans melodious,
To express my anguish in the deepest, saddest,
Most piercing notes. How many grieve in silence!
The gods have gifted me to tell my sufferings.

        (ANTONIO *goes to him, and takes his hand.*)

O noble man! *Thou* standest firm and still;
I am indeed but as the storm-tossed wave;
Yet do not thou condemn a soul less steadfast,
Since he who piled the rocks on their foundations,
Ne'er to be moved save by his awful voice,
Gave to the wave its eternal motion;
He sends his storms, the obedient billows waver,
Rise, fall, clash, or combine, as the winds will.
Yet these same waves, in fairer moments, mirrored
The glorious sun. The pure, cold stars have smiled
At their existence doubled on the surface
Of the proud element, which rose to meet them.
Now vanished is my sun, and gone my peace.
I know myself no longer in this turmoil;
No longer shame I to avow my weakness.
The rudder breaks; the trembling skiff gives way,
And rocks beneath my feet. With both my arms
I clasp thee. Stir not. Here is all my hope.
The mariner thus clings to that rude rock
Which wrecked his friends, his fortune and his home.

Index

Index

Index

Index

Index

Index

About Our Contributors

JUDITH STRONG ALBERT received her Ph.D. from Saint Louis University in 1978. She was awarded two stipends by Radcliffe College to study Margaret Fuller and Annie Ware Winsor Allen (1865-1955). She has lectured in the Women's Studies and History Departments of the University of California at Berkeley and San Francisco State University. In addition to a dozen articles published on the contributions of nineteenth century educators to twentieth century thought, she has written a chapter on nineteenth century women teachers for *Women in Western Tradition* (1989). At present, she is completing *Circle of Influence: Minerva's Women, 1843-1912*, her book about the women who attended Fuller's Boston Conversations.

RENATE DELPHENDAHL received her Ph.D. from the University of Zürich, Switzerland and is professor of German at the University of Maine. She was the recipient of two fellowships from the National Endowment for the Humanities to study "Literature and Alienation," and "The Origins of Romantic Literary Theory." In 1985, she served as a visiting professor at the University of Ulm, Germany. Among her publications are a book on Grillparzer entitled *Lüge und Wahrheit in Wort und Bild*, and articles on works by Goethe, Novalis, Hesse, and Bachmann. She has published numerous book reviews that appeared in *Cauda Pavonis*, *The German Quarterly*, *The Journal of Evolutionary Psychology*, *Modern Austrian Literature*, and *Monatshefte*.

MARGARET A. LUKENS has taught literature at the University of Colorado at Boulder and Swarthmore College, and is now an assistant professor of English at the University of Maine. Refusing to specialize more than the minimum necessary for professional survival, she writes about and teaches Native American literature, African American literature, popular novels by early American women writers, and captivity narratives, among other things. Besides her work on Margaret Fuller's journalism, her recent research includes work on mixed-blood identity in Mourning Dove's *Cogewea, the Half-Blood*; she is currently editing a volume of theoretical and pedagogical approaches to the works of Leslie Silko.

JOAN VON MEHREN is a graduate of Vassar College, and did graduate work at the Sorbonne and the University of Buffalo. Although she makes her home in Cambridge, Massachusetts, she has lived in Japan, Canada, Italy, Germany, France, England, and India. She speaks French, Italian and German fluently. Her *Minerva and the Muse: A Life of Margaret Fuller*, being published by the University of Massachusetts Press, will appear in 1994.

MARIE MITCHELL OLESEN URBANSKI is a Professor of American Literature at the University of Maine. Her book *Margaret Fuller's Woman in the Nineteenth Century: A Literary Study of Form and Content, of Sources and Influence*, was published in 1980. Essays on Fuller appeared in *Feminist Theorists* (1983), edited by Dale Spender and in *Nineteenth-Century Women Writers of the English Speaking World*

(1986), edited by Rhoda Nathan. Some of her other publications concern Joyce Carol Oates, Susan Sontag, Louisa May Alcott and James Fenimore Cooper. She edited the *Thoreau Journal Quarterly* for four years.

Printed by University of Maine Printing Services

Designed by Michael Fournier